A PRIVILEGED BOYHOOD

A PRIVILEGED BOYHOOD

Alexander McRobbie

Richard Stenlake Publishing

© Copyright 1996 Alexander McRobbie
First published in the United Kingdom, 1996
by Richard Stenlake Publishing,
Ochiltree Sawmill, The Lade, Ochiltree, Ayrshire, KA18 2NX
Telephone 01290 423114

ISBN 1 872074 61 8

Published by
Richard Stenlake Publishing

Printed by
HarperCollins
Glasgow

A PRIVILEGED BOYHOOD

Contents

FOREWORD

This series of stories deals with the kind of life I led until I was twenty one, and covers the era from 1926 until 1947, one of the most turbulent periods in Britain's history.

Glasgow's insalubrious tenements have long been demolished, and are now only a memory in the minds of a generation that is now over sixty. The way of life I describe is gone forever, and few would want to undergo the often painful experience of recollecting their slum past. It is a task I have avoided until quite late in life. The passage of time didn't lend enchantment to my view of growing up in Glasgow, but it did bring tolerance—and the ability to laugh at experiences which were once painful. I kept recalling that brilliant record in which the Monty Python team try to outdo one another in describing their impoverished childhood. After hearing that sketch, no raconteur could begin a monologue by declaring, 'When I was a child we were so poor that even the mice left our house for a better one!'

The Glasgow I describe is not a 'heather, haggis and kilts' depiction of 'Bonnie Scotland'. In the 1930s, over half of Scotland's population of five million lived in Glasgow and the nearby industrial areas. The tenement dwellers' lifestyle was more typical of Scotland than the romanticised image of a tartan-clad crofter tending his shaggy Highland cattle on heather covered moors.

I doubt if my long-dead father would have been pleased

with this account of my upbringing. He was very proud of Glasgow and its status as 'the second city of the empire'. He often told me that it was a privilege to be born and brought up in Scotland, especially in Glasgow. Here then is the story of my privileged boyhood.

ALEXANDER McROBBIE
Surfers Paradise, Australia.

THE NIGHT BEFORE PAY DAY

At age eleven, while attending Woodside Academy, I wore my school uniform with pride. I was the only boy from our area who went to a 'snob' school. My uniform was a grey jacket and short pants with the school crest on the jacket pocket. At boys' school outfitters, expensive blazers with the crest already attached could be purchased. But my mother bought a grey jacket at half the price then bought the cloth crest and sewed it on to the pocket. She had to buy a Billy Bunter type school cap, the school grey and maroon stockings, and a pair of black shoes for school wear. They were the first shoes I'd had.

At my primary school, most of the boys wore boots. As a student from a needy home I received two pairs of boots free each year from Glasgow Corporation Education Department. Pupils were not permitted to go barefoot to school, or attend in sandshoes. As soon as they were received, the sturdy black boots were studded to make them last longer.

I never objected to wearing the boots because they had no obvious marking that showed they were 'Corporation issue', but I also received two jackets and two pairs of short pants free each year, and I violently objected to going to school wearing Corporation clothes, although many boys wore them without concern. The free clothing was made in only one colour, a mottled tweed, so its origin could not be disguised.

By skilful use of her treadle Singer sewing machine, my mother made me pants out of cheap grey flannel. Instead of a jacket, I always wore a jersey to primary school, so I wasn't obviously from a 'welfare' family. The Corporation clothes were worn outside school hours when I had to do anything that involved getting my clothes dirty.

At Woodside Academy I got out of school at four o'clock then had a half hour's walk to our two roomed tenement house in Grove Street. In winter it was already dark when school ended. The street lights had been lit by the gaslighters, called the 'leeries'. They were men who used long poles with a flame on top which were pushed up into the gaslights to turn the gas on then light the jet. Winter nights were usually cold and bleak, often with rain and sleet that made the ground slippery. After school was over I usually stayed on and took part in some of the recreational or other activities. But on Thursdays I went straight home, knowing I would be needed. I ran most of the two miles, schoolbag on my back, knees blue with cold, nose red and chilled, teeth chattering.

I let myself in to the house by slipping one hand through the letterbox and tugging up the key on its long string, then opening the door. The key was then popped back through the letterbox. That was how the family got in. When we went to bed at night, the door was locked from the inside and the key left in the lock, but during the day, access to the house was easy. Many homes in which there were a number of children coming and going had the same system. In better areas of the city, people often left their door key under the mat. In our part of Glasgow there were no doormats outside the house. A mat would have been stolen immediately.

Although we lived in a tough neighbourhood, burglaries were rare. My mother put it down to the fact that we had nothing in the house worth stealing. My father used to say that any burglar who broke into our house would 'take one look round then probably leave sixpence on the table to help the poor buggers.' My father also voiced the opinion that only an insane burglar would ply his trade around Grove Street when almost any other part of Glasgow, except the Gorbals, offered better pickings.

At 91 Grove Street, in the Cowcaddens district of Glasgow, Thursday was the worst night of the week because it was the day before my father was paid. On Thursdays the last of my mother's housekeeping money ran out. She was totally insolvent until Friday when my father came home with his net weekly wage of one pound nineteen shillings and sixpence.

By Thursday, everything pawnable had been pawned. Our credit at the local shops was frozen until something was paid off accounts that were often six weeks behind. Every source my mother could borrow a shilling from had been tapped until on Thursdays her purse was empty. Often she didn't even have a penny for the gas meter, much less money to buy food for two adults and five children.

When I let myself into the lobby on Thursdays, I knew that things were grim if there was no yellow gaslight streaming from under the kitchen/living-room door. That meant there was no gas for lighting or cooking. Bracing myself, I went into the kitchen and was pleased if the coal fire was alight. At least the room would be warm.

My mother, sister Jean and brothers Bill and David, were huddled close to the fire, my mother sitting in the room's one easy chair, with baby Gordon in her lap. She had a book in one hand and by the firelight she was reading the kids a story.

I unhitched the schoolbag from my shoulders then moved closer to the fire and held out my hands to its warmth. I said I was glad there was a fire. My mother said there was just enough coal to last the night and maybe tomorrow for breakfast. 'The worse thing is, I've nothing for the tea,' she sighed. 'Not even a penny for the gas.' My normally optimistic mother had a hopeless look in her eyes. I told her not to worry, I'd scrounge something before tea time.

The alarm clock on the mantelpiece above the fireplace showed it was after four thirty. My father got home at six thirty, and he expected his tea to be on the table within ten minutes. If it wasn't ready, there could be a bitter argument after he accused my mother of being a bad financial manager.

I picked up my schoolbag, then went through the lobby into the front room. By the light from the street lamp outside I changed out of my school uniform and into my despised Corporation clothes. There was dirty work to be done, for I was going 'midden-raking'. This involved scavenging among the communal middens, a group of large square garbage bins which were located in shed-like structures in the back yards of every tenement block. Beside the middens were the communal wash-houses where the women did the family wash.

The middens were regularly visited by semi-professional midden-rakers who lived by collecting anything valuable to fill the hessian sacks they carried. But the professionals only worked in daylight so they could inspect the contents of each bin as they rummaged through it. We rarely saw a midden-raker. Nobody in our neighbourhood ever threw away anything of value, not even a jam jar. The best pickings were found in wealthier areas where people were so rich they could afford to throw out empty bottles rather than take them back for the deposit refund.

Like the professionals, I went to one of the better areas of the city, running all the way. And so my midden-raking began. My target was jam jars. One pound jars carried a ha'penny refund, two pound jars brought a penny. Empty soft drink bottles, complete with rubber stoppers, also brought a penny refund. A great prize was a Lucozade bottle which brought thruppence. I found these quite often because I had located a midden which was used by a wealthy invalid who consumed several bottles of Lucozade a week.

Early in each scavenging round, I picked up a large paper

carrier bag with string handles. Into this I placed my booty. It was difficult working in the dark, although there was often a light at the midden entrance. Much of the garbage was foul-smelling and bottles and jars could be mixed up with all kinds of muck. Often I had to work by feel and became expert at locating a single jam jar in the middle of a paper package of potato peelings, rancid meat offcuts or congealed porridge. There was no plastic in those days, old newspapers were the standard wrapping material.

Midden-raking in the dark had its hazards. The bins contained many empty tin cans. In those days the only can openers were the kind that ripped open the top of a can, leaving the lid attached, and grabbing the serrated edges of one could result in a nasty cut. Broken glass was also a hazard to probing fingers. I often received painful cuts and lacerations. It was a wonder I never contracted tetanus.

It was chilly as well as stinking work. My knees were blue with cold and my fingers almost numb from getting them wet amongst the rubbish. But I was always successful and within an hour I had collected enough refundable glassware to give me at least sixpence once I returned them to a shop. Sometimes, if I found a Lucozade bottle, my bag would be worth ninepence.

Converting my booty into cash had one problem. Shops would only accept jars if they were clean, with no traces of sticky jam inside or outside the glass. I couldn't take them home and wash them with hot water from the kettle, as I was often a mile from home when my scavenging ended and had a deadline to meet, for it could be six o'clock by then. So I had to find a communal tap and wash the jars in cold water, using my chilblained fingers to remove all traces of the jam. That was really cold work in winter.

A further, minor problem was finding shops which would accept the jars and bottles and pay the refund. Many shopkeepers objected to paying out cash unless a purchase was made at the same time. Some would only allow credit on the jars and you had to take goods to the value of the returns. This was no use to me, I needed the flexibility of cash. But I always found a sympathetic grocery shop assistant who would cash in my returns. Middle-aged women were the best marks and I became expert at looking like a street urchin.

Finally, with up to ninepence in my hand, I sprinted back to our own neighbourhood. From the butcher, who we dealt with regularly, I asked for some bones for our dog. He knew we had no dog—we could barely keep ourselves—but he gave me a wrapped package of bones and often quite usable offcuts and scrag ends of meat. Sometimes the package would weigh three or four pounds, most of it bones, but food nevertheless. Being near closing time, he was often glad to get rid of the day's offcuts which were otherwise tossed into a bin to be thrown out.

Next stop was a corner shop which sold bread. Loaves were quite high, with a thick black crust on top and a white softer crust on the bottom. Unwrapped and unsliced, they sold for thruppence. At each end of a tray were three smaller loaves called 'end loaves'. They sold for tuppence ha'penny, but were good value because they were only marginally smaller than regular loaves.

The fruit and vegetable shop was next. Here you could buy what was called chipped fruit and vegetables. Most of it was stuff which had begun to rot in places, or had been squashed. For thruppence you could get up to seven pounds of vegetables, including that staple, potatoes. From the dairy shop I bought a bottle of skimmed milk for tuppence, with a penny being the bottle deposit. I'd now spent about sevenpence and had at least a penny left. In my carrier bag I had enough food to make a substantial meal for two adults and five kids.

After my shopping spree, I'd get home about six fifteen, toting my heavy bag. The first thing I did was put a penny in the gas meter so we could have light and, later, gas for cooking. I placed my shopping on the kitchen table and my mother and siblings crowded round to see what I'd brought.

The first thing my mother did was cut four slices off the loaf. They were for my father's lunchtime 'piece' to take to work next morning. Within minutes she'd started her Scottish peasant woman's culinary magic. Meat and bones began simmering in a big iron pot—the basis for potato soup. The vegetables were peeled and the 'bad bits' cut off. By the time my father got home a substantial meal was being prepared and there were savoury smells in the kitchen.

When told he'd have to wait half an hour before dinner was ready, my father would complain about my mother's bad management. She'd tell him he was lucky he was going to have *anything* to eat. 'If it wasn't for your big son there would be nothing on the table tonight,' she'd tell him. I was indeed the big son. Even at eleven I was taller than my father, who was only five feet. By age fourteen I towered over him by more than a foot. I think he vaguely resented my height, which seemed unnatural because my mother was as short as he was.

In 1937, Britain was still in the grip of the Great Depression which began in 1929. Indeed at the end of 1940, after more than a year of war, there were still over half a million unemployed in the United Kingdom. It was 1941 before anyone who wanted to work could find a job. Pro rata to the population of the time, it was probably the worst depression in the world's history, but I found nothing abnormal about the era because I'd never known times to be any better. At our level, to survive took ingenuity, self-reliance and considerable native optimism, and my scrounging was proof of how it was possible for families almost on the breadline to live off the leavings of wealthier people.

I rarely received any praise from my father, but the gratitude in my mother's eyes made the filthy midden-raking expedition worthwhile. Such expeditions were almost routine every Thursday. It was something that had to be done, not only to feed the family, but to have gaslight later so I could do my homework.

A HUNTED LIFE

The Glasgow tenement dwellings were mostly built during the nineteenth century, to house the masses of men and women who migrated from the country to the cities, where work was to be found in the labour intensive factories and shipyards. When the earlier tenements were built, their living facilities compared favourably with the often dilapidated cottages which were home to the rural working classes. Tenements were built of solid blocks of stone so were well insulated against the cold, their roofs didn't leak, and above all, even the poorest tenement house had running water, a real 'modern convenience' for many farm workers who had previously hand-pumped their water or drawn it from a well.

Tenement houses also had that modern marvel—gas lighting. This replaced paraffin lamps and tallow candles. Bright gaslit streets meant social life could take place after dark. In country areas the poor often went to bed when darkness fell.

In the cities, the essential coal for heating was delivered by the coalman from his horse-drawn cart, carried into the house then tipped into the coal bunker. There was no need to cut peat or wood for the fire, or to stock up for winter. The coalmen plied the streets daily. To order a hundredweight bag of coal only required placing the coal merchant's cardboard sign in the window. He'd spot it and come to the house to take the order.

All tenements had proper lavatories, or water closets. Six

families often shared a lavatory, but human waste was disposed of by 'pulling the plug', instead of using a stinking earth closet. The streets were paved, making it easy to push a pram, or just take a stroll. To people who lived in primitive rural slums, the conveniences of the tenement lifestyle were many, with shops at almost every corner. The produce they sold was cheap compared with country towns where there was no competitive mass market like in Glasgow. And the amusements of the time were rarely more than five minutes walk away. For many years the popular music halls and vaudeville theatres thrived alongside the new cinemas which brought first silent films then the 'talkies'. But above all, living in such close proximity to other people meant that the slum dwellers seldom lacked company. In the country, a farm labourer could go for days and see only the same few people.

To country dwellers who moved into the cities, the tenements were paradise. This should be remembered when the landlords are criticised for having exploited the accommodation needs of the poor. They felt they were supplying a basic human need, at economical rents, and the modern dwellings they offered were rented as fast as they could be completed.

Unfortunately, the early tenements were constructed *too* well. Solid, and built to last, many stood for over a hundred years, receiving little or no modernising. They also became overcrowded to an extent that their builders didn't visualise, even though large families were the norm in the Victorian era. Two adults and five children was considered an average sized family then, and they could fit into a room and kitchen without too much discomfort—by the standards of the time. When the Great Depression forced many city workers on to the breadline, more and more people packed into one or two-roomed dwellings to spread the cost of the rent. Households of ten people were not uncommon, and often the parents, six children and one or two elderly relatives lived in two rooms. Such gross overcrowding was contrary to Glasgow City Corporation's bylaws. But how could anyone evict people into the streets? In the thirties, the population density in Glasgow's slums was the highest in Western Europe.

We were fairly lucky. Our one room and kitchen was home to only seven people. In some tenements up to a dozen people lived in a house the same size as ours. Even one-roomed tenement 'homes', known as 'single ends', saw up to ten people herded together in grossly unhygienic conditions. 1934 statistics record that 175,000 Glasgow 'houses' had no baths and 105,000 had no internal lavatories. Today's overcrowding in some third world communities is not dissimilar to what I experienced in my Glasgow boyhood.

Around Glasgow there were varying standards in tenement buildings. Some up-market places even had carpet in their entrance 'closes' and on the stairways. Others had grass and trees in their communal courtyards, always called the 'back court'. A room and kitchen in such places rented for up to fifteen shillings a week, while the rent for our tenement house was ten shillings. But our building was not the worst in Glasgow. In the Gorbals, some run-down tenement houses rented for 7/6 a week, or less.

Among the working classes, there were definite social sub-stratas. The 'upper' working class had a family income of about four pounds a week. They were the foremen class and similar. Once a family earned five pounds a week they moved to the lower middle class and occupied the better tenement buildings, or got out of them altogether.

My father's wage was two pounds a week, so economically, we were considered lower working class. However, we were of the 'respectable' lower classes. We dressed fairly neatly and were well turned out compared with some of our 'skid row' neighbours. As children we didn't play truant from school and we didn't steal, or when we did, we didn't get caught. We only stole from department stores, who we felt could afford it. Our family rarely got into fights and we weren't 'known to the police'.

Below us were the lowest of the low, families whose kids ran around in rags—real ragamuffins. The adults were always drunk, on the cheapest fortified wine, or methylated spirits, or worse, a deadly brew made from boot polish. Permanently on the dole, they were people who had lost all hope of ever getting out.

My parents never lost hope of one day breaking out of their slum existence. We were more fortunate than most of our neighbours because we had the safety valve of spending at least two months of every year in Ayr at my grandmother's place. In my case, what helped me survive, and even extract some pleasure from my impoverished childhood, was imagination.

I was about seven years old when I found I had the ability to withdraw into an imaginary world that was so real I could stay in it for hours. Being always hungry, my first fantasies involved retiring into a marvellous underground storehouse that was a kind of Aladdin's cave, crammed with every kind of foodstuff. Not exotic foods—as I had no experience of them. My storehouse was packed with cases of baked beans, tins of biscuits, tinned fruit, bully beef, bottles of lemonade, little triangles of Swiss cheese, jars of jam, bars of chocolate—all the things we rarely saw. Every night, in the cavity bed I shared with two of my brothers, I would slide below the bedclothes and enter my underground cave. I had to pull the clothes over my head because the street light outside the window made the room very bright. In pitch darkness my imagination ran riot as I decided what I was going to feast on that night.

In a strange way, my hunger was somewhat assuaged after I'd sampled the goodies from my storehouse. Eventually, the pangs of hunger eased and I would fall asleep under the bedclothes. I didn't really want to go to sleep. It was too

22

marvellous being the owner of such a wonderful store of edibles. Sometimes I would manage to stay awake for several hours before I finally dropped off.

By the time I was ten, my imaginary cave had expanded to include a section devoted to toys. I had few toys, but I had plenty of free catalogues which temptingly illustrated Hornby train sets and accessories, Dinky toys and Meccano sets. My favourite window shopping was viewing the Christmas toy displays in the big stores in Argyle Street. There was always an elaborate working model railway display to make my mouth water.

At Christmas I rarely received a toy. My presents were always new clothes, which I felt was unfair because I would eventually have to be given them anyway. One special Christmas present was a proper handkerchief, treasured because our hankies, or nose rags, were squares of cotton which my mother cut from old singlets.

I guess the lack of anything except home-made toys was one of the most irksome aspects of poverty. One book I borrowed from the public library was called *101 Things A Bright Boy Can Do*. The projects included making toys from wood, buttons and flattened tin cans, and I made things like pushalong cars, although there was no way I could make a Hornby train set.

Working from the catalogues, I created an imaginary railway layout in my secret cave. I expanded it every night until it was as elaborate as any in the department store windows. The amazing thing was that after I'd added a branch line, complete with signals and station etc., that expansion stayed locked in my imagination. The next night, everything I had imagined the night before was still in place. The train schedules I'd developed were committed to memory and I could start an operation and follow every train as it stopped and started, shunted or loaded freight, exactly on schedule. In some ways, it was better than the real thing because there was no financial limit to its expansion. There was never a night when I didn't slide under the bedclothes and retreat into my wonderful cave of imaginary treasures.

The reality that lay above the shabby bedclothes was unpleasant. We boys never wore pyjamas, but slept in a shirt, usually one that was too frayed to be worn outside the home. Sometimes we slept in the same shirt we would wear to school. My brother Bill slept beside me while infant David lay at our feet. In winter, three bodies certainly kept the bed warm under the quilt that served as sheet and blanket. Bill, unfortunately, was a bed wetter. It was a rare night when he didn't wet the bed. Often I didn't know he'd 'peed the bed' until morning, when I'd wake to find my shirt sticking to my back and the bottom blanket soaked. My mother put a rubber waterproof sheet under Bill's side of the bed, but he invariably rolled off it during the night and peed on me. When I woke to find myself soaked, there was no bathroom where I could wash. I had to sponge my body in front of the kitchen sink until the smell of urine had gone. It wasn't a pleasant start to a day. My father was disgusted at Bill's bed-wetting and would give him a belting for his 'crime'.

Basic hygiene was a problem. A weekly bath in the zinc hip bath was a treat, especially if I could get in before my sister and brothers. We all used the same water. An occasional kettle of hot water was added when the bath cooled. I'm sure my mother never used the hip bath. She simply couldn't have fitted into it. Now and then she would visit the Corporation bath house where a private bathroom with running hot water could be hired for thruppence.

I had a fetish about cleanliness and I hated our kitchen where there always seemed to be spilled sugar or sticky jam on the linoleum covered floor. It was forever untidy and by my standards, dirty. This wasn't surprising because the room was used by seven people for eating, washing, cooking, playing and for some of them, sleeping too. It was hopeless trying to clean the room while there were people in it. It became untidy as fast as it was tidied.

When I turned eleven, I persuaded my parents to leave me in charge of my sister and three brothers, including Gordon, then a baby, while they went out to the cinema. They rarely went out together because one had to stay home and 'mind the bairns'. But I assured them I was quite capable of looking after the kids, and the house too. If baby Gordon had teething pains I could give him a Steedman's Powder then smear jam on his dummy and put it in his mouth until he fell asleep. If his nappy needed changing I could do that too. If any of them needed to go to the toilet they could use the enamel chamber pot so none of us had to leave the house to go to the communal lavatory.

After the first trial night my folks were delighted to return home and find there had been no problems and all the kids were sound asleep. They were even more delighted at the surprise I'd prepared for them. After they'd left for the pictures at about seven, I got the kids to bed then started on a massive clean up of the kitchen. My parents got home at ten thirty, so I had about three hours to transform our squalid living-room, which measured only nine feet by twelve.

Working like a beaver, I washed and dried the teatime dishes, but didn't put them away as our only storage space in the kitchen, apart from the drawers in the dresser, was a big cupboard, called the 'press'. It held packets and tins of flour, salt, sugar, tea and oatmeal, crockery and cooking utensils. The shelves were usually lined with newspaper which quickly became stained and torn. During the day I'd purloined some sheets of white drawing paper from school. After I'd ripped out the old newspaper shelf lining, I replaced it with clean white paper, pinning it down with drawing pins, also 'lifted' from school.

25

I then washed every utensil before placing it in the cupboard, and put the grocery items into new brown paper bags which I'd snitched from a shop. Then I washed down the wooden cupboard door, and after that gave the dresser the same treatment. I emptied it then lined it with new paper before replacing the contents. I scrubbed the stained oilcloth that covered the dresser until it was as clean as it would ever be, doing the same with the oilcloth on the kitchen table. I scrubbed the wooden sink boards and polished the tap with Brasso, then I turned my attention to the fireplace and the brass fender. I used Brasso on the fender and Zebo Black Lead polish on the grate, oven door and cooking top until the fireplace gleamed. I even polished the coal scuttle!

Then I washed down the walls, which were covered with floral patterned wallpaper. There were always numerous jammy smears on the wallpaper, caused by kids' sticky fingers, and I used several kettles of hot water and a lot of Lifebuoy carbolic soap during the cleaning project. It ended when I got down on hands and knees and scrubbed every inch of the linoleum floor. When I'd finished, the room not only looked good, but smelled good too.

Towards ten thirty, my final touch was to prepare a cup of tea for my parents' return. When they got home, the kettle was 'singing' on the hob and the teapot already heated, waiting for boiling water to be added.

My mother was tremendously impressed when she came into her sparkling kitchen. So was my father. 'It's like a palace!' my mother exclaimed. This was a major exaggeration, but the kitchen had never looked so clean and tidy. From then on my parents usually had a weekly night at the pictures, confident of my ability as a baby-sitter. Almost every time they went out I would give the kitchen a thorough cleaning, but frustratingly, by the next night it would be as untidy as ever. I could understand why my mother had given up trying to keep the overcrowded room looking decent.

My mother's pride and joy was her window box, which sat on the sill of the kitchen window overlooking the back court. Window boxes were rare in our building, but I think having a miniature garden reminded my mother of her country upbringing. She got seeds and bulbs from her old home in Ayr and managed to grow flowers in spite of Glasgow's grimy, sooty atmosphere, caused by the smoke from hundreds of thousands of coal fires and industrial chimney stacks. She cultivated smallish flowers, like crocuses and anemones, but they made a colourful display which lightened the drabness of our home and took her mind off the constant struggle to make ends meet.

Finding ten shillings for our weekly rent was always a problem. We were usually up to a month behind with the rent payments and the spectre of eviction was very real. Our rent was collected weekly by the factor, the landlord's agent. He called every Monday morning about eight o'clock and covered the entire building, collecting the money then entering the payment in the tenant's rent book. On Mondays when my mother didn't have the rent money, my small brothers and sister were kept in bed in the kitchen and ordered to keep quiet on pain of a good belting. My mother would sit in the only easy chair and wait until she heard the door bell jangle. She would whisper, 'Go and see if it's the factor, Alex.'

I would tiptoe along the lobby then crouch down behind the letterbox slot and raise it by the merest fraction. I couldn't see upwards, but could see the caller's feet. By his polished brown shoes I knew it was the factor, so I'd tiptoe back to the kitchen and tell my mother it was indeed him.

'We'll have to keep very quiet and still until he goes,' she'd warn the kids.

Usually the factor took about an hour to cover all four floors of our building. On his way downstairs he'd tug on our doorbell again in case somebody had come home. When he finally left, my mother would heave a sigh of relief. We were safe for another week.

It was often a hunted lifestyle, but we became streetwise at an early age. As a boy, I knew our part of Glasgow backwards. I was a good runner and knew all the short cuts, which was handy if one was being pursued by bigger boys, or occasionally by the police. We became expert at 'hopping' tram cars and hanging on to the pole on the boarding platform until the conductor made his way towards us. Before he could thump us, we'd jump off, if possible when the tram slowed at a corner, or was held up by traffic. When we were making our way downtown, we'd hitch rides by indulging in the dangerous practice of hanging on to the back of a truck, then dropping off when the truck slowed, or when a policeman saw us and blew his whistle to alert the driver.

In our part of Glasgow the police always moved around in pairs. They often walked the beat with a savage-looking German Shepherd restrained by a shoulder harness. We feared the dog much more than the constables, who were no match for us when it came to a chase. They might have outrun us on the straight, but we ducked down lanes, dashed through back yards, squeezed between iron railings, climbed stone walls and if necessary dropped down into the sewers. We ran like lavatory rats and could even escape the police dogs, mainly through our ability to scale high walls, finding scanty hand and foot holds like skilled mountaineers. Once safely on top of a twelve foot high wall, some boys delighted in urinating down on to the snarling dog, which infuriated the panting 'polis' when they caught up with the bedraggled animal.

Walking the beat in our part of Glasgow was not a popular assignment. The police feared the notorious razor gangs and their bloody conflicts. In Glasgow, a gang battle was called a 'rammy', and smaller-scale 'rammies' were commonplace in our area. These often developed from a 'sherriking', a peculiar Glasgow ritual.

A sherriking began with a woman who had a serious grievance against her husband, or de facto. She might nurse her grievance for months until her resentment reached the stage when she felt she had no option but to have a public showdown with her man. Her intention was to 'shame' him. The venue for the showdown was usually the pub where her man drank with his cronies. Supported by women friends and relatives, the aggrieved wife would march there. Word quickly spread that there was going to be a sherriking and other women would join the march, many of them carrying babes in arms. The wife would carry her baby at her bosom, the theory being that even the lowest man wouldn't hit a woman who was carrying a baby.

Outside the pub, the wife would begin screeching a recital of her man's wrongdoings. The women would yell for Tommy McGinty to come out and face the music. Eventually, Tommy was forced to walk out on to the pavement to confront his screaming woman. His fellow drinkers, even his closest pals, urged him to be a man and go out and face the shrew's wrath.

The object of the sherriking was to provoke the man into striking his woman, and by heaping insults upon him she usually succeeded. The insult which finally provoked him to hit her often disparaged his sexual prowess and the size of his erect penis. No Glasgow man could stand for such an insult, and he would scream, 'Put that bairn down and I'll knock yer fucking teeth out, you whoor!'

Sometimes the woman would pass her baby to a relative, then arms akimbo, goad her man into hitting her. When he did strike her she would reel back, crying in agony and often spitting blood from a split lip. That signalled the start of the rammy, and the women would attack the husband. Some of his mates would come to his aid and begin sparring with the women. News would reach male relatives that their women were in a rammy, so they would rush to the scene to defend their females. Within ten minutes there could be up to a hundred people scuffling in the street. They would be surrounded by as many as two hundred onlookers, including children, who yelled encouragement or abuse at the combatants.

From crowded tenement windows high above the fighting, residents would yell out to the fighters, egging them on, or telling them to break it up. Sometimes tenants would drop water-filled paper bags down on the milling mob. People who were hit by a water bomb were lucky. Some residents dumped the contents of their chamber pot on to the fighters. Others would drop empty bottles on to the street, adding the hazard of broken glass to the battlefield.

A battle with fists and boots could go on for hours as each side called for reinforcements in the shape of friends or relatives. But such brawls were relatively minor compared with the all-out battles between the vicious razor gangs who were numerous in the city. Apart from their favourite weapon, the cut-throat razor, the gangs used axes, bayonets and knives. A razor gang on the rampage would sometimes burst into a cinema and terrorise the audience, but their main stamping grounds were the cheap dance halls in poor districts. Like American gangsters, the Glasgow gangs had their 'molls', many of whom encouraged their man to display his 'valour' by cutting up a member of another gang.

Before I was twelve I saw many gang fights, but stayed safely on the outskirts of the battle. The Glasgow police tended to follow my example. Armed only with batons, they had no stomach for a close quarter engagement with often drunken razor-wielding savages. When a gang battle flared, the usual police tactics were to seal off the street in which the bottle-throwing conflict was taking place. When the 'warriors' had maimed enough of one another, the police, accompanied by German Shepherds, would move in and drag the wounded men into Black Marias. The unwounded escaped by going to ground in nearby tenements. Many households would give refuge to a fleeing gang member, not because they approved of the gangs, but because they had a natural aversion to the police and sympathy for the underdog.

Violence permeated every aspect of slum life, even sport. In the 1930s the two best soccer teams in the First Division were Rangers and Celtic. Rangers were all Protestants and Celtic were mostly Catholics. Their supporters split into sectarian camps, so religious bigotry dominated any match between the two teams. When I was about eleven my father took me to Ibrox Park for a semi-final between the blue and the green. The supporters grouped themselves on a green side and blue side. It would have been unwise—indeed foolhardy—for a lone Rangers' supporter to have stood among a group of Celtic fans, or vice versa. After half time the teams were one-all. Then suddenly Celtic scored a goal. The Celtic supporters went into hysterics of joy while the Rangers' fans booed and yelled 'Foul!' From the Rangers' ranks a voice bellowed, 'Fuck the Pope!' There was a roar of rage from the Catholics who yelled back, 'And fuck King Billy!'

This resulted in a shower of empty beer bottles being hurled from the Rangers' ranks into the Catholics' area. Retaliation was immediate. Bottles flew from the Celtic supporters' lines back at the furious Protestants, and even onto the field, aimed at Rangers team members. Within minutes, angry fans surged onto the field as a strong phalanx of policemen formed a protective cordon round the players. Only a warning over the loudspeakers that the game would be abandoned if the pitch wasn't cleared restored order. The match continued and mercifully ended in a draw. Had there been a winner, the losing team's supporters would certainly have started a big rammy and the razors been unsheathed.

DAYS AT THE COAST

In one major way we were more fortunate than most of the families in our building. Much wealthier families than ours— even bank managers on a princely five pounds a week— couldn't afford long annual holidays by the seaside, yet the McRobbies spent two months every summer in Ayr.

June, July and part of August were the long school holidays, and Glaswegians who could afford it tripped off to the coast for at least a week in summer. Ayr was one of a string of seaside resorts dotted along the Clyde estuary. During the Glasgow Fair, Glaswegians descended upon Ayr en masse. There was a kind of love-hate relationship between the Glasgow visitors and the resort dwellers. The residents looked forward to the arrival of the visitors because they brought money into the town, but they hated their uncouth Glasgow ways, and called them 'Glasgow keelies', which roughly translates as hooligans.

At the height of the season, the visitors paid exorbitant sums, like five pounds a week, to rent one room in a private house in Ayr, or more if they stayed at one of the town's many boarding houses. The McRobbies' total weekly income was two pounds a week, so obviously a holiday would have been a rare event in our lives but for two factors. Ayr was my mother's home town and her mother, Jeannie Hewitt, lived there with my mother's three bachelor brothers at 55 Green Street. The dwelling was a mansion compared with Grove Street. It had a downstairs bedroom, a large front parlour, two upstairs bedrooms, a living room, a scullery and a bathroom with a lavatory. There was also quite a large garden.

Uncles Tom and David used the front parlour to sleep in at night. Apart from the double bed, it was furnished with a couch, two armchairs and an oak table on which stood that modern marvel, a radio. Grandma Hewitt had the ground floor bedroom as her private domain, while the smaller upstairs room was Uncle Alec's when he was home, although he spent most of his time away at sea. This left the large upstairs room for Jessie McRobbie and her brood.

When my father joined us for weekends, all seven of us slept in what was called 'the big room'. It had two recessed beds, one of which my parents slept in, usually with the smallest child. Brothers Bill, David and I took the other bed, in a head-to-toe arrangement. My sister Jean slept on the floor on a mattress.

During the summer holiday peak fortnight in August, my grandmother rented out the big upstairs room to a family of Glasgow holidaymakers, who paid five pounds a week for it. They used it only for sleeping, spending most of the daytime hours at the beach. The weekly rent for 55 Green Street was less than ten shillings. Grandma had been a tenant for nearly fifty years, and two weeks holiday letting in summer produced ten weeks rent, so my thrifty Grandma felt it was worth us having to crowd up a bit to permit the big room to be let.

While holidaymakers were staying, the McRobbies slept all over the house. My mother shared the little bedroom with Jean and my two smaller brothers, while Bill joined his two uncles in the front room. I slept in a cupboard under the stairs—in beside the gas meter and a mass of hanging overcoats.

When we went to Ayr each summer, we lived rent free, but it was assumed that upon our arrival, my mother would take over all the housekeeping and cooking for her mother and brothers as well as her offspring. Grandma had had a bad fall which led to her being confined to bed, so she was always pleased to see her daughter who took over the household chores from her brothers. My mother well and truly earned her keep during our rent free vacations in Ayr.

The other factor that made our annual holidays possible came about because my father was an employee of the London Midland & Scottish Railway. He drove an LMS horse and delivery cart, not a locomotive, but he received the same benefits as other railway employees. The major perk was free travel on the company's line, which served much of Western Scotland, including the Glasgow-Ayr route. He could have several free tickets a year for himself and his family. These privilege tickets, or passes, meant that the train trip to and from Glasgow cost us nothing.

Preparing for the trip to Ayr was a major operation for my mother.   We had two cheap fibre suitcases, and everything we needed for a two month vacation had to be packed into these. They were usually bound shut with rope because the locks had long given up the ghost—in fact they'd completely fallen off.

My mother and five children comprised the travelling party. One of the children was a babe in arms who was carried by Mrs McRobbie. My sister Jean carried a big bag which contained the baby's nappies, bottle and feeding necessities, and it was my task to lug the two suitcases, my brothers being too small to carry much except some miscellaneous parcels.

It would have been marvellous if we could all have piled into a taxi and been driven to the railway station. But nobody in our part of Glasgow ever took a taxi. In fact, I don't think I ever saw a taxi in Grove Street. It was not a place where taxi-users resided, or ever visited. Thinking back, the fare then would probably have been about two shillings for a three mile ride, but such expenditure would have been impossible. For two shillings my mother could produce three meals for the family.

Once our brood was assembled, with hair brushed, noses wiped and toting our burdens, we walked the fairly short distance to New City Road. Here we caught a tram for St Enoch Station. The fare was tuppence for my mother. The rest of us, being under fourteen, rode free.

Just boarding the tram was a major operation. My mother scrambled on first, the rest of the family following. She was a woman of ample proportions, and with her babe in her arms she needed two seats in which to settle herself. Jean and two small brothers occupied another seat for two while I struggled to stow the suitcases in the space under the double decker tram's stairs. During the tram ride I stood beside the suitcases to keep watch over them. In Glasgow it was not uncommon for unattended luggage to be stolen by a quick moving passenger. One way or another, the McRobbies certainly got value for their tuppenny tram fare.

We disembarked from the tram as close as possible to the station, but it was still a long walk burdened as we were. One thing we never had to worry about was time. My mother was the kind of woman who didn't believe she'd really caught a train unless she was on the platform at least half an hour before departure time. She used to say, 'We must get there in plenty of time. You never know, the train might leave early.' It was no use telling her that while trains might occasionally be late in departing, they never departed *before* the scheduled time. 'You never know,' she said darkly, 'you never know about trains.'

I remember once we arrived at the station about forty five minutes before our train's departure time. As we approached the platform where the Ayr train stood there was a warning toot from the steam locomotive, then suddenly the train pulled out. My mother nearly had hysterics. 'It's leaving us behind!' she cried, 'It's going away early!'

A kindly porter assured her that the departing train was being shunted out to make way for ours, which would shortly take its place. 'You're a wee bit early, missus,' the porter said. 'We haven't even got your train cleaned yet.'

My mother's other reason for arriving early was so that we could get a compartment to ourselves. This was absolutely essential because inevitably the baby would need its nappy changed during the journey. There were no disposable nappies, so the soiled one would be rolled up and tucked into the baby's bag. Other passengers in our compartment didn't enjoy the odoriferous changing process, so my mother was doing them a favour by dissuading them from riding in our company.

The Glasgow-Ayr wasn't a corridor train. Once in a compartment you stayed there until the train halted at a station. The Ayr train was usually very well patronised, and as it stopped at a number of famous golf course towns, such as Troon and Prestwick, many of the passengers wore plus fours and carried bulging golf bags. As departure time drew near and the train filled up the compartments became crowded.

My mother's technique to dissuade people from entering our compartment was to seat herself and drooling babe at one window seat, then place brothers Bill and David and sister Jean with their faces pressed to the other window and the door window. Jean usually had a runny nose, while David could be relied upon to dribble disturbingly as he pressed his, by this time grimy, face against his window. It was remarkable how many people made a dash for our compartment and started to wrench the door open then thought better of it when they saw who their travelling companions would be. When travelling *en famille*, the McRobbie clan rarely failed to have a compartment to itself.

The trip to Ayr took about an hour and a half, but the hard part of the journey began on our arrival at the station. The walk to the bus stop wasn't too far. Boarding the bus was no more difficult than boarding the tram had been, and I didn't have to stand guard over our suitcases—we were in Ayr, described by

36

Robert Burns as the town of 'honest men and bonnie lasses'. But the local SMT (Scottish Motor Transport) bus only took us to Ayr's Main Street, and it was a fair hike from there to Green Street. On my own, I could do it in twenty minutes, walking briskly. Moving at my mother's speed it took forty minutes, with frequent stops for a rest.

Even although I was a tall lad from age ten and very fit, the two suitcases were a heavy burden. I couldn't manage much more than about two hundred yards when I had to stop to relieve the strain on my arms. The solution was to send brother Bill on ahead to Green Street, to return with the 'bogie'—a barrow which was used mainly for collecting horse dung from the streets to use as garden manure.

When I was eleven, Bill was nearly seven and a very good runner. We'd only completed about half our walk to Green Street when Bill came panting towards us with the barrow. The suitcases, parcels, small brother David and baby Gordon were all packed into the bogie which I pushed or pulled to Green Street. I must say I was glad when Grandma Hewitt's cottage came into sight. We soon unpacked our belongings, which now smelt faintly of horse dung, and were ready to begin our holiday by the sea.

HOME DELIVERIES

I was in my teens before I realised that when some women
gave birth they had a doctor, or a trained midwife in attendance.
I'd learned from the movies that many women, at least in the
USA, went to hospital to have their offspring. But in our street
there were no such refinements.

In Glasgow, the childbirth mortality rate was the highest in
Britain. In 1932, Glasgow's infantile death rate was an incredible
11%, compared with 6.7% in the English cities of London and
Birmingham. In the tenement districts of Glasgow, the infantile
death rate was six times greater than in the better areas of the
city. Two out of seven children failed to survive in our family.

My mother was the preferred midwife in our tenement,
although she had no training that I knew of. By the time I was
eight she'd had four children. The first two were boys, one of
whom was stillborn, the other dying a few hours after birth. My
mother named them both Alex, and she often told me that I
was her first Alex to survive. She seemed to regard this as a
tribute to my tenacity, and to her own.

I asked her once what happened to my two dead brothers,
but she was evasive. In those days home births were
commonplace all over Scotland. Births were rarely registered
until days after the event; sometimes they weren't registered
for weeks, or even registered at all, as many young adults
discovered when they had need of their birth certificate.

It was extremely rare in our area for a stillborn child to be given a funeral, unless its parents were Catholics. Even the tiniest and most basic coffin cost money, and there were always some funeral expenses. As a result, a stillborn child was often wrapped in newspapers, placed in a shoe box and clandestinely buried in a corner of some municipal park. In cases where the mother was unmarried and the father had refused to 'stand by her', a baby that didn't survive was sometimes wrapped in newspapers then dropped in a communal midden some distance from the mother's place of residence. I was never able to discover how my two predecessors were disposed of, but I knew they hadn't had funerals. The money involved could be put to better use by the living.

Apart from her three Alexanders, my mother gave birth to Jean when I was two years old, and Bill when I was four. I have no memories of their births. When my next brother, David, was born in 1934, I was eight and I have an excellent recollection of his arrival. My youngest brother, Gordon, was born in 1937 and I remember his birth well too.

My mother gave birth to David and Gordon on the recessed double bed in the kitchen. No doctor or midwife delivered them. Instead, my mother was attended by a gaggle of women neighbours, all of whom had borne children themselves. My strongest memories of David's birth are being told by a neighbour, Mrs Lynch, to hurry and get some old newspapers. Lots of them.

Like most poor households, we didn't have many old newspapers around. We probably only bought two papers a week; one on Saturday for the racing form guides and one on Sunday for the racing and football pool results. Few newspapers were thrown into the midden in a clean condition; they were used to wrap something in, like potato peelings or rancid dripping. To locate a reasonably thick bundle of old papers involved me sprinting several blocks to a wealthier area. I knew all the 'middens' within a square mile of our home and was an accomplished garbage bin scavenger, or 'midgie raker' in the Glasgow parlance.

Within twenty minutes I was back with a heavy bundle of relatively clean newspapers which I pantingly presented to the assembled birth attendants. By this time my mother had gone into labour, but she didn't seem to be in any great pain. I was shooed from the kitchen and told to go and carry pails of hot water from neighbours' homes.

I had no idea why, but apparently plenty of old newspapers and lots of hot water were essentials during childbirth. There wasn't a dwelling in our building which had running hot water, so neighbours pitched in and boiled water on their coal fires or gas rings. It was my task to carry brimming pails or kettles from homes up to four storeys above our own.

After that, my next job was to take my young sister and brother into the front room and keep them quiet and amused until I was called for. Bill and Jean were too young to know what was going on. All I knew was that our mother was going to have a baby. At eight I still more or less believed that babies were brought by the stork, or found in a cabbage patch. But as a realist, I knew storks flying over the slums of Glasgow were unheard of, while cabbage patches were a rarity in our world of asphalt and concrete.

The thought that a baby was grown inside a woman's belly never occurred to me, nor did the manner in which babies were conceived. I knew nothing about the copulatory act. To ask too many questions about it, or about conception, was to be accused of having a dirty mind—by one's own parents!

In Glasgow, obviously pregnant women were a rarity, although there must have been many of them around; babies seemed to be born every week in our crowded tenement buildings. But maternity clothes were voluminous and in my mother's case she was always very fat, or 'stout' as she preferred to say. Pregnancy didn't make her look any different from usual.

During her pregnancy there were no obvious changes in her disposition. She still cooked for us all, washed our clothes and ran the house as usual. She attended no pre-natal clinics, if such existed, and as far as I know she never visited a doctor, not even to have her pregnancy confirmed. She *knew* when she was pregnant.

My mother never contemplated engaging a trained midwife for the birth—they cost money, although it wasn't a large amount. Registered midwives wore a navy blue uniform with a little nurse's cap, and almost all did their rounds by bicycle, with a wicker basket strapped on the front handlebars and rear carrier. I presumed these wicker baskets contained old newspapers and a billycan for boiling water!

When spotted in the street, midwives always seemed to be pedalling furiously, making frequent use of their bell to clear pedestrians from their path. I expect they were often in a hurry to reach a patient in labour. It was a far cry from dramatic movies in which harried police officers rushed a pregnant woman to hospital, sirens wailing on their squad car.

All midwives seemed to be called Miss, which I thought rather strange. Misses never had babies themselves; that only happened after a Miss became a Mrs, and then by some alchemy she began to produce babies. I always felt that midwives should have some personal experience of childbirth, like my mother had.

When brother David was finally born the news reached me in the front room by the sound of his cries. Shortly after I was called into the kitchen to see my mother in bed with her new infant who was already sucking on her ample breasts. That was one aspect of procreation that wasn't concealed from children. Seeing a baby being breast fed was considered a natural experience.

By the time my youngest brother, Gordon, was born, I was an obstetric veteran aged eleven. Both David and Gordon were born after I had arrived home from school. I think my mother timed it that way. The redoubtable Mrs Lynch was once again head midwife and as soon as she told me my mother was about to have a baby I said, 'Right! Newspapers and hot water!'

'Good lad,' she said, 'Away you go!'

I didn't even stop to change out of my Woodside Academy uniform. I was round the wealthy middens in a flash and back in no time with a bundle of *Daily Records*, *Scottish Daily Expresses* and even some copies of the upmarket *Scotsman* dumped by a wealthy household. Next I performed my hot water carrying duties until finally I was shooed into the front room to await the arrival of our new sibling and keep Jean, Bill and infant David amused.

Gordon's birth took some time. My mother was still in labour when our father got home from work at half past six. I don't think he was allowed in to see her. There was woman's work being done in the kitchen and it was no place for a man, not even the child's father. Finally Gordon's first cries were heard about seven thirty and there was a wail of relief from Jean, who cried, 'Now maybe we'll get our tea!'

It was indeed well past our tea time. I could have gone and bought us fish and chips, but my father didn't have enough money. My mother normally had an emergency cash hoard in her purse, usually about two shillings, but it would have been a bit infra dig to poke my nose into the delivery room and ask for Ma's purse. So we had to wait until some of the midwives took pity on us and cooked something in their kitchens for us.

Women in areas like ours didn't get the luxury of much rest after bearing a child. Next day, my mother was up and cooked the tea as usual. The extra mouth she had to feed was not a drain on the household finances. Baby Gordon dined well on her breasts.

Oddly, the only time my mother saw a doctor after giving birth was when she took her male children to be circumcised when they were about a month old. Most gentile mothers in our area didn't have their baby boys circumcised. I discovered this when having a pee up against a wall in the company of other boys, where it was quickly noticed that Alex had a 'bowler hat'. There was no opprobrium attached to this, but I felt a certain envy for boys with foreskins which snugly protected the tip of their dicks. When they peed, it was almost like watching a conjuring trick. They'd slide back the wrinkled foreskin then presto! There was a bright pink dicky-di-do ready to urinate.

When she wasn't having children herself, Jessie McRobbie was a popular midwife with women all around our building. I accompanied her to many of her deliveries, mostly in my role as scrounger of old newspapers and carrier of hot water. My mother never lost a baby, or struck any complications during a birth.

In many ways, the first few months of an infant's life could be hazardous, unless its mother had accommodating relatives. The concept of baby-sitters hadn't been developed, not that we could have afforded one anyway, and when a mother was forced to go out and didn't have a pram, she often left the baby alone in bed with some pillows on either side to prevent it rolling.

We could never afford a pram, or a stroller, or even a cot. A baby usually slept between its mother and father until it was old enough to be transferred to a bed which it shared with its siblings.

When my mother had to go out shopping, or to deliver the washing which she did at home for wealthier neighbours, she couldn't cope with carrying a baby too. So the infant was left at home. My mother often told me that when I was her only child, she left me on the big bed with our dog, Nellie, which laid itself along the front of the bed to prevent me rolling on to the floor.

In retrospect, I'm amazed that we could afford to keep a dog. Possibly it was because we were better off before my sister

43

and brothers arrived. I remember Nellie, who died when I was about six. She was a brown-eyed, black and white Border Collie bitch, very devoted and protective.

When I went to school at age five, it was to Grove Street Primary School which faced our tenement block, only a short walk across the road. Before school was due out at three o'clock, my mother would open the door and let Nellie out. The dog would race into Grove Street then pause while she looked each way for oncoming traffic, dashing across to the school when the road was clear. She waited outside the gates for me to emerge and greeted me with paws on my shoulders and lots of wet licks. Tail wagging, she led me home, where, if she was lucky, she got a well-gnawed marrow bone to have another chew at before it was put away for later.

After Nellie died we never had another dog while we lived in Glasgow. Apart from the cost of feeding it, a cramped tenement was no place to keep a dog, although many homes had a cat, which was able to survive on any kind of scraps. A cat also kept the mice down. Most Glasgow tenements were infested with mice, and by resetting a trap, it was often possible to catch three in a night.

My mother was absolutely terrified of mice and couldn't even set a trap, as her hands trembled so much at the thought of the little rodents. But by the age of seven, I was an expert mousetrap setter, using the absolute minimum of slightly scorched cheese as bait and setting the prongs of the trap so it was on a virtual hair trigger. In the mornings I had to dispose of the dead mouse before my mother would even set foot on the floor by her bed.

However, the woman who feared tiny mice had absolutely no qualms about the possible complications of childbirth. She talked quite knowledgeably about such things as a breach birth, and turning the baby around before it could be born. However, she must have been midwife in attendance at about two births

44

a month, so I guess she knew her way around a womb. In our buildings, quite a few girl babies were named Jessie in honour of their deliverer, who made no charge for her services.

SITTING THE QUALLIE

Unlike many children, I loved going to school. It meant an escape from a cramped existence in a house that always smelled of boiled cabbage, Lysol disinfectant (to control the bugs) and where the cheap furniture was usually covered with a film of coal dust from the bunker under the food cupboard.

At school, things were clean. Even the lavatories were much cleaner than the communal toilet we shared with five other families. More importantly, at school I had my first experience of people who actually seemed to care about their charges. At home, we were never a demonstrative family. From age five, I never dreamed of kissing my mother, nor can I remember her kissing me. Kissing was reserved for babies or very wee bairns. At five, and going to school, I was a 'big boy', especially as I was the oldest child. Big boys didn't cry, suck their thumbs, or expect to be kissed or praised for their small successes.

I have searched my memory, but cannot recall ever being hugged by my father, or ever wanting to hug him. Lest this should sound like self pity, I must stress that the avoidance of most expressions of affection was the norm in many Glasgow homes in our strata of society. I considered it quite normal, and never felt in any way deprived.

At primary school, all my affection was directed towards, and returned by, two of my teachers, and my one close school chum. A major reason I liked school was because I was always at the top of the class, or second from the top. My best friend,

46

and the only boy I had anything in common with, was also the only English boy in a school where all the other pupils were Scottish.

Lionel Watson lived in quite a good part of Glasgow. His English parents brought him to Scotland when he was two, but because of their influence, he didn't 'talk Scottish' like the rest of us, but always spoke with an English accent—'as if he had a plum in his mouth', my mother sniffed.

People who tried to 'talk posh' were scoffed at in our circle where everybody spoke in the unmelodious Glasgow vernacular. To speak English properly was regarded as putting on airs. However, in the classroom, most pupils tried to talk posh when speaking to the teacher. In the playground they reverted to the Glasgow patois.

I liked Lionel's English accent, but I never once invited him into my home, although it was just across the street from school. I was too ashamed of the place where I lived. But I often visited his home, which was a fair walk from school.

The Watson household was my first experience of a well-kept, tidy Glasgow home. It only had two rooms, like ours, but it was bigger, everything smelled nice, and the furniture was polished. The Watsons ate off a table which was covered with a cotton cloth instead of the tattered oil cloth which was a permanent fixture on our kitchen table. They had electric light as well as gas for cooking, and a gas fire. I'd never seen one and had assumed every house was heated by a coal fire with a coal bunker in one corner. The Watsons also had a bathroom with a bath and a wash basin, and hot running water. It was a mansion compared with Grove Street and I spent as much time as possible at Lionel's place.

Their family was very well off compared with the McRobbies. Lionel told me his father did something in the city. When he went to work he was always very well dressed, usually in a navy blue pin stripe suit. Lionel showed me his father's wardrobe and I was amazed to find that Mr Watson had four other suits apart from the one he wore. My father had one, called his 'good suit'—rather a misnomer because he didn't possess a second best one, or even a sports jacket. His good suit lasted a long time because every Monday morning it was pawned (for five shillings) then redeemed on pay day each Friday for six shillings—about twenty per cent interest for the week.

When Lionel and I were eight we went downtown to Argyle Street, and Lionel showed me his father at work. Impeccably dressed, the dapper Mr Watson spent all day standing outside a tailors' shop. When a male window-shopper showed any interest in the many suits displayed, Mr Watson would approach him and start chatting about the merits of the merchandise. He would tell the potential customer that he, Mr Watson, bought his clothes at this shop; that he knew the manager personally, and could organise a nice discount if the customer would like to come inside and try on a suit. Once in the shop, a sale was often made, usually on hire purchase (2/6d deposit and 2/6d a week).

Mr Watson worked for the store on commission, although the customer was kept in the dark about that. When I told my father how he earned his living, he scoffed, 'Bloody tout!' Nevertheless, Mr Watson earned about four pounds a week, twice my father's earnings.

Part of the bond between Lionel and me was because we alternated as top or second top of the class, which meant we always sat alongside one another. In those days, each oak and iron-framed desk seated two pupils. The top boy sat at the top right hand desk with the second top boy next to him. The rest of the boys sat in declining order of their scholastic merit, with the class dunce in the front row right under the teacher's eye. It was a co-educational school, but the girls were segregated and sat on the left hand side of the classroom, in the same hierarchical arrangement. There was an aisle about six feet wide separating the girls' side from the boys'. This ascended in a series of steps, leading to the five levels on which the desks were arranged, and let the teacher keep an eye on pupils at all levels.

It was down these steps that we descended fearfully when summonsed to the front to receive the leather strap, or 'tawse' as it was called in Scotland. Lionel and I rarely received the strap, which consisted of three or more whacks to the outstretched palm. Apart from being well-behaved, we were 'teacher's pets' because we grasped things immediately. In examinations, our good marks helped lift the class average.

One of our favourite teachers was Mr Douglas (I never knew his first name). He was in his early thirties and had a good, if quirky, sense of humour. There were no organised sports at primary school, but at lunchtime we played football in the playground, taking over a large area of the asphalt yard. The goalposts were chalked on brick walls at each end of the playground and the centre line marked on the ground. Nobody could afford a proper soccer ball, so we used a 'ball' consisting of a bundle of rags tightly bound with masses of string.

Mr Douglas, who told us he'd played football at Glasgow University, often spent his lunchtime refereeing or coaching us. Lionel and I were good players, myself at centre half and Lionel at centre forward. Mr Douglas thought we showed promise and spent a lot of time giving us tips. In Scotland football was never called soccer. It was just football, or 'the fitba'. I never heard the term soccer until I went overseas.

Our most favourite teacher was Miss Moyse, a red-haired woman in her early twenties. She was very attractive and I think Mr Douglas was keen on her. Miss Moyse was the only daughter in a very wealthy family who lived in a three storey mansion in the Great Western Road. Her father was an important executive in a Clydeside shipyard at a time when the yards were in their heyday. Later, through her father, she helped get a job for my father when he was unemployed.

Miss Moyse had a beautiful speaking voice, with only the faintest Scots burr. I intensely disliked the Scottish accent in females, especially the harsh Glasgow accent. I made an early resolve that when I married, it would be to an Englishwoman, one who spoke English properly. To this day I regard a woman's voice as the most important factor in her attractiveness.

The only thing that prevented me having a crush on Miss Moyse was her red hair. I did not like red-haired females. My mother had bright red hair but I'm sure this was not the reason. Anyway, I much preferred girls with dark hair, the blacker the better. Miss Moyse had a delectable figure and when she sat on her high stool at her desk her skirt rode up and we boys could see almost to the top of her silk-stockinged legs. None of us had reached puberty, so there was nothing sexually arousing about seeing up a woman's skirt. The thrill came from the knowledge that we were being sinful by even looking at our young teacher's gorgeous legs and suspenders.

I'm sure Miss Moyse could easily have taken a job at one of the city's fee-paying schools, but she seemed to genuinely like working at a Glasgow Corporation school in a slum area. She also went out of her way to encourage her brighter pupils. In 1938, when I was eleven, the Empire Exhibition was held in Glasgow and Miss Moyse took Lionel and myself to visit it. She paid for everything, including our meals and snacks, and led us round every exhibit, explaining things we didn't understand.

The Empire Exhibition was the last of the international trade fairs to be held before World War II began. It was staged at Bellahouston Park from May until October, and during that period it had 12,500,000 visitors from all over the world. The canny promoters ended by making a profit, something rarely achieved since by such fairs.

What we saw at the Exhibition was a graphic portrayal of the British Empire at the peak of its influence—'an empire on which the sun never sets'. To me, it was a mind-expanding experience to see a replica of the Victoria Falls in the Rhodesian pavilion; red-coated Royal Canadian Mounted Police on horseback outside the Canadian exhibit; rubber tree tapping in Malaya; sheep being shorn in the New Zealand pavilion, and real live kangaroos in the Australian exhibit. That day, I decided I was going overseas as soon as humanly possible. I never imagined that within nine years I would be an officer stationed in one of the last outposts of the empire, my duty to help preside over the end of the colonial era and hand Malaya over to its people.

The only other primary school I attended was in Ayr where I was a pupil for about six months. This followed our family's moving to the seaside so my mother could look after a bed-ridden Grandma Hewitt. After the stability of Grove Street, starting at a new school was quite traumatic. I had to get used to new teachers and make new friends, and in addition, the method of teaching at Ayr was very different from the techniques I was used to. In school at Ayr, I was well ahead of my classmates in subjects like reading and arithmetic. But when it came to handwriting I was almost illiterate compared with them. The problem was that in Glasgow, primary school pupils were first taught to write in block letters. Learning cursive writing began later. I could write as fast in block letters as anyone else could in 'running writing', but I was not allowed to use block letters in school work. I had to start from the beginning and learn how to write longhand. It was a painful process, practising nightly as part of my homework. In subjects like composition, for which I always got top marks, my essays lost points for bad writing; no allowance was made for me being a longhand illiterate.

Another major difference between the Ayr school and my Glasgow one was that there was no educational film afternoon there. In Glasgow every Friday afternoon we saw films in a darkened classroom, all documentaries of course, screened on a Bell and Howell 16mm projector. There were many nature and travel films among them, and often long documentaries from a genre then in its infancy. It was a marvellous and pleasurable way of learning and I assumed every school used film as a teaching aid. Years later I discovered that in the thirties, Scotland was ahead of the world in using educational films in the classroom.

However, high tech teaching methods didn't exist at my school in Ayr. The dominies used the traditional cramming technique based upon the three Rs—Reading, Riting and 'Rithmetic. My new teachers were fond of administering corporal punishment, not with a cane, but with the leather tawse, laid vigorously across the offending pupil's outstretched palm. On cold winter mornings we tried particularly hard to avoid getting it; three strokes of the strap on a cold palm is more painful than when the skin is warm.

In our school in Glasgow the strap was used fairly rarely, although the school catered for pupils from a very tough neighbourhood. We had a number of women teachers and getting the strap from them was a breeze, for none of them could lay it on very hard (although one wisely pretended to be in agony after a strapping by a female). There were women teachers in Ayr too, but they didn't carry a strap. Instead, a male teacher was called in from another classroom to properly chastise an erring pupil. This teacher was usually annoyed at having to leave his class, so he really laid into the culprit. I thought this system was grossly unfair. If a woman teacher decided you were to be punished then she should do her own dirty work. I longed for the gentle and caring Miss Moyse, who never strapped me once.

When we returned to Glasgow, much as I hated the prospect of resuming life in our tenement after the spaciousness of a house with a garden, I was very pleased to return to my old school. My chum, Lionel Watson, was still there, as was the wonderful Miss Moyse.

One benefit I got from my brief and mostly unhappy schooling in Ayr was the ability to write longhand. At Grove Street the class was just starting to learn it, and I was miles ahead of them which was one reason I was moved up a class.

I attended Grove Street Primary School until I was eleven, when I sat what was called the Qualifying Examination. Normally, pupils were twelve when they sat 'the Quallie', but I had been moved up a class because I had mastered everything at my age-level and was wasting my time. My chum Lionel didn't sit for the exam and sadly for me, he moved back to England.

The purpose of the Quallie was to separate pupils into two classifications. The top ten per cent went on to secondary schools where, if they wished, they could continue school until they were sixteen or seventeen when many went on to university. At secondary school pupils studied new subjects like French and Latin, German, science, botany and art. Scotland's professional people came from this group.

The other ninety per cent of primary school pupils went on to semi-technical schools where the emphasis was on woodworking, technical drawing, leatherwork—and for girls, domestic science, typing and dressmaking. They became Scotland's tradesmen, artisans, wives and mothers. Attendance at such schools ended at age fourteen. The class system was instilled into children at an early age.

When being allotted a secondary school, there were a few scholarships available for the pupils who came at the very top in the Qualifying Exam, to fee-paying schools where pupils could stay until they were eighteen. I won such a scholarship to Woodside Academy. It was a long way from Grove Street, in a better part of the city, but I enjoyed every foot of the walk. The Academy was a boys only school where the masters wore gowns and mortarboards, and when I started there, I truly thought I had arrived at the type of public school featured in my favourite reading, the boys' school weekly, the *Magnet*. Set in Greyfriars, the famous Billy Bunter was one of the pupils at this fictional English public school.

A few years later, we moved to Ayr to live permanently and I became a pupil at the Grammar School, one of the happiest periods in my scholastic life.

BEACH SAFARI

Our Glasgow neighbours envied the McRobbies for being able
to get away to the popular seaside resort of Ayr every summer,
where we spent the school holidays at my grandmother's place.
But our stay in Ayr was no holiday for my mother. In fact, she
worked harder there than she did in Glasgow, where she only
had my father and her five children to look after. 'Only' is used
relatively of course. Many people would consider a family with
five children to be a large one, but a brood of that size was
quite common among poorer people in Scotland. My mother
had seven brothers and a sister, and when they were born at
the end of the Victorian era, a family of nine children was not
unusual.

In the days before social security, children were regarded
as an insurance policy for their parents' old age. It was felt that
if a couple had many children, at least one or two of them would
look after the old folks in their declining years, provide a home
for them, and see them decently buried. Which is what usually
happened.

Three generations of one family living together was very
common. It was almost unheard of to stick grandma or grandpa
away in an institution for the aged or infirm. Even if the matriarch
or patriarch became quite senile and dotty, he or she was cared
for at home by at least one child until the very end. In my
Grandma's case, the caring was done by two of her bachelor
sons who lived with her.

During our long summer stay in Ayr, this caring role was taken on by my mother who not only looked after Grandma, but also her two brothers—as well as the five children. My uncles welcomed my mother's arrival, for it gave them a break. For example, they could both go out at nights whereas usually one had to stay at home because bedridden Grandma might need some kind of attention.

My uncles, and to a lesser extent Grandma, were never very enthusiastic about my mother bringing her brood of young children with her to Ayr. But it was part of the deal, because we couldn't be left in Glasgow where my father had to work six days a week. Small kids could certainly be a nuisance in what was normally an all-adult household. We broke things, messed up the house, trampled on flower beds, permanently occupied the single lavatory, pried into cupboards, and worst of all yelled and squabbled as active kids do. At weekends, 'getting rid of the kids for the day' had a high priority in my uncles' plans.

It became my duty, as the eldest son, to take my sister and brothers to the seashore every Saturday and Sunday, and on many weekdays as well. Being holiday time, there was no school, which usually got rid of us for most of the day.

When I was ten, my sister Jean was eight, and at that age many girls would have been delighted to take charge of one or two of their younger brothers. But when Jean was a baby, my mother had dropped her at the top of the narrow and steep stairway in Grandma's house. Jean had rolled all the way down the stairs, striking her head as she went. When she was taken to the doctor he said that she hadn't sustained any injury from her fall, although as she got older it became obvious that Jean's development had been impaired. She was quite unfit to look after her small brothers, unless she was supervised herself.

As her only daughter, Jean's condition was a great tragedy for my mother. In our social strata, a daughter usually became her mother's household help from an early age, learning to cook, sew and do all the other domestic things that were regarded as a woman's lot. Jean's unreliability was the reason I assumed, and was expected to assume, many of the family duties that would normally have fallen upon the eldest daughter. As a result, I was landed with endless household and family chores. The worst one was having to constantly look after most of my siblings.

The brother nearest to me in age, Bill, was about four years younger than me. He was named after my father and was very like him in many ways. I think that Bill was my father's favourite child. I had no desire to take his place, or to grow up to be like my father. I was a 'mother's boy' in the sense that I empathised with my mother's problems and did everything I could to lighten her burden.

As a child, my brother Bill lived a relatively carefree life, taking little or no responsibility for his younger siblings, or for helping around the house. He usually woke very early, found something to eat, then vanished for the day with a gang of boys of his own age. When he was pressed into service to look after one of his small brothers he made a muck of it and was soon banished from the house for the day.

To relieve her conscience about expecting me to perform the family duties of both eldest son and daughter, my mother often told me, 'I can't rely on Jean, or on Bill. You're the only one I can depend on.' No words could be better calculated to inspire a boy with a well developed sense of responsibility. 'You've got an old head on your shoulders,' my mother and grandmother often said.

Having to cope with these responsibilities meant that I became grown up before my time, but I never lamented over a childhood that was less than carefree and distinctly short on play. On the contrary, I *wanted* to become grown-up as early as possible and enjoy the benefits and privileges of adulthood.

My mother was conscious that my early boyhood years

involved me taking on more than my fair share of the family responsibilities. Until I was twelve, being granted a 'day off', to spend it as I wanted to with boys of my own age was a rarity. I treasured those days when, free of responsibility for my younger brothers and sister, I could go off with my friends on the dozens of active pursuits that absorbed boys of that age. These ranged from bird-nesting and rock climbing to fishing from a rowboat or trapping rabbits, not expeditions on which one could safely take children under five. It took all my time to look after myself and avoid injury during some of our more adventurous and hazardous types of play.

When I was charged with taking the kids to the seashore for the day, it was expected that I wouldn't bring them home until at least four in the afternoon, and preferably closer to teatime at six o'clock, after which they could be put to bed. As our departure time was around nine am, I was expected to keep them away from the house for at least eight hours. To help me, my uncles contributed a certain amount of cash to buy various goodies and special treats as a bribe to keep the kids amused all day

The basic food for our lunch was jam sandwiches prepared by my mother, which wasn't very exciting. Some apples from the tree in our garden were also included, but these weren't regarded as a treat, as they were green and bitter—other more exotic fruit was almost unheard of in our household, either in Glasgow or Ayr. At that time, my youngest sibling, Gordon, was 'on the bottle' and was fed milk from a banana-shaped bottle with a teat on one end and a valve on the other. Gordon's bottle was filled, then wrapped in his spare nappies. We also took his dummy and some sugar and water to dip the dummy into.

To purchase the essential goodies that made the day away worthwhile, I usually received tuppence from my mother—a halfpenny each to spend on Jean, David, Gordon and myself. My uncles were a better source of funds and I applied a mild form of blackmail to squeeze as much as I could from them. Uncle David was usually good for threepence, as was Uncle Tom, and if I promised I'd keep the kids away until after five pm, I could often extract another penny from each of them. With a treasury of tenpence at my disposal, I was quite flush.

Preparing for our safari took some time. An essential vehicle was the baby's carriage, a kind of leatherette-covered pram which could convert into a pusher in which the baby sat up, secured by leather straps. It was a cheap conveyance, but fairly spacious. In with baby Gordon went his nappies and bottle; the sandwiches; the bathing costumes; towels; buckets and spades, and a spare pair of knickers for Jean, who had a habit of forgetting to slide her pants down when she did a wee.

After thankful farewells from the adults, I pushed the well-laden pram to our first stop, one of the neighbourhood shops. I bought a large bottle of Tizer for threepence (with a penny refund on the bottle later), and a selection of sweets, mostly of the boiled, long-lasting type. I kept threepence back for buying ice creams when we got to the shore.

I made these purchases at a local shop because at the shore, where there was only one kiosk, prices were much higher than in the town. A threepenny bottle of Tizer cost sixpence at the kiosk—and they wouldn't give a refund on the bottle. At the kiosk, sweets were also dearer. Their ice creams were over-priced too, but we couldn't carry ice cream on a summer day, so were forced to buy it from the robbers at the beach.

The kiosk's prices were what we locals called 'visitor prices'. Overcharging at seaside resorts was common throughout Britain. The beach front operators only opened for about six months of the year and claimed they needed to rake in the money during summer so they could survive during the winter months. Locals tried to buy the absolute minimum from these seaside vendors.

The destination of our family safari was the Newton Shore.

Ayr had two shores, the Newton and the Town Shore, and the latter had a proper esplanade with various types of amusements including a putting green facing the beach. It also had a stretch of powdery sand which made it one of the finest beaches in the British Isles. There was hardly any rock on the Town Shore, or any shingle or pebbles.

The Newton Shore was the opposite: almost all rocks which were contained within a long series of saw-toothed timber breakwaters. There were only occasional patches of shingle 'beach' from which to bathe. Facing the beach was a sprawling fertiliser works called Danny Wyllie's. Between the factory and the shore there was some overgrown ground bisected by streams which carried milky overflow from the fertiliser works down to the sea.

For children, this was a much more interesting beach than the Town Shore. The receding tide left many rockpools where we could catch all sorts of small marine life, like sardines and starfish. Whelks and mussels clung to the rocks, and whelks were a ready-made delicacy which we prised out with a pin then ate, still wriggling as they slid down our gullets.

Few holiday visitors went to the Newton Shore. There were no deck chairs for hire, or any beach on which to place them. Also, the sea at the Newton Shore was home to masses of crabs, some quite large. When one of these sank its claws into a bather's toe, it could cause a painful injury.

The Town and Newton Shores were a fair distance from Green Street, and to get there took more than an hour's walk when pushing a pram and shepherding two kids. The road to the Newton Shore was unmade for part of the route and it was hard work pushing over drifting sand and stony ground. Additionally, the route involved negotiating a very steep hill that formed a bridge over the railway lines. Consequently, it was quite a slog reaching the shore, but worth the effort. And apart from that, the time it took to get there and return home filled a good part of the day.

We usually set up camp on the shore where one of the smelly, milky streams from the fertiliser works disgorged into the sea, staining the rocks white. The main project I organised was damming the stream with stones and shingle. This kept four-year-old David occupied. On one of the rare occasions when Bill was in charge of the kids, he made David drink some of the poisonous effluent from the stream. David became violently ill and had to remain in bed for some time after being treated by the doctor.

When I organised damming a stream, Jean would help, for a while anyway. But her interest was short-lived and she had a habit of wandering away. On our safaris, we were always losing Jean, and searching for her occupied much of my time. I usually found her with some other party of beachgoers, to whom she had attached herself. She always had the appearance of a waif, and would often cadge some lunch or sweeties from generous holidaymakers.

My other responsibilities included making sure none of the siblings became sunburned, which could be very painful and led to recriminations from my mother when I brought them home. Also, when we went into the water, I had to ensure that they didn't drown; while my uncles were pleased to get rid of us for the day, I don't think they wanted to lose any of us permanently.

Other chores involved feeding the baby and changing his nappy. Cleaning the soiled garment then rinsing it in the sea was the worst part of the process, but baby Gordon and infant David were really very good and gave me little trouble so long as I could maintain a supply of edibles for them. Jean was the problem, particularly on the long trek home.

Walking to the shore in the morning was a breeze when everyone was fresh, but when it came to going home, my charges were usually worn out from the day's activities, and very irritable. Gordon, of course, had an armchair ride in his pram. David just wasn't capable of walking all the way home, so he sat on the foot-rest of the pram with his legs thrust over the axles. Jean, who was ten, couldn't keep up with the not very rapid pace I set as I pushed the well-laden pram. She lagged behind and I was constantly having to stop and wait for her to catch up. Inevitably she'd sit down in the middle of the road, crying, and refuse to walk any further. She was a fairly hefty girl for her age and if she'd got into the pram she would have filled it to capacity. Finally I was forced to readjust the load. David sat in the pram with Gordon in his lap. Jean then sat on the footrest with her legs shoved through to the rear axle. Our beach paraphernalia was hung in bags from the handlebar or thrust into any available space beside the infants. And so the family outing proceeded.

Pushing the pram up the big hill was simply beyond my strength, so Jean was prised from her place on the step and forced to walk beside me. At the top of the hill she resumed her position on the footrest, and that was how we usually returned home after our day at the shore. However, it was no use complaining to my mother that I was worn out after my day's excursion, as it hadn't been a picnic for her either; she'd taken the opportunity, while there were no kids underfoot, to do the family washing.

At Green Street, there were no mod cons of any kind. No electricity, hot water service or washing machine. The scullery was dominated by what was called the boiler, which was a huge zinc-lined vat inside a brick and cement structure. The vat probably held about forty gallons of water. Under it there was a fireplace in which a coal fire was lit on washdays. After a considerable time, this brought the water to boiling point. The vat was filled by running a garden hose from the tap in the scullery sink, but when the washing was finished, the dirty water had to be bucketed out and poured down the sink. Sometimes, during dry spells, it was carried out into the garden, bucket by bucket, to be poured on to the vegetable patch.

My mother was forced to do the washing twice a week. There were four adults and five children in the household, and additionally my father brought his week's dirty clothes with him when he came down from Glasgow for the weekends. So she faced a formidable pile of clothes, sheets, pillowslips, towels and other items on wash-day. My uncles sent their dress shirts to Ayr Steam Laundry, but their working clothes went into the family wash along with everything else.

My mother boiled up the 'clean' clothes first, such as pillowslips, tea towels, and tablecloths. The cleaning agent was Sunlight Soap, which she bought in long bars for sixpence. This was grated into flakes, using the kitchen grater, then tossed into the boiling water. The 'whites' were washed first, then, before being hooked out of the water with a short wooden pole, a little calico bag of Reckitt's Blue was swirled around to 'make the whites whiter'.

After rinsing the clothes in cold water in the scullery sink they were put through the hand-turned wringer to squeeze the excess water from them. Then they were piled into the cane clothes basket and carted outside to be hung on the clothes lines. During rainy weather, which was frequent, drying the clothes was difficult. Several pine clothes horses were brought out and the washing hung on them, usually in the kitchen-living room where there was always a fire burning in the fireplace.

After the whites were washed, other items were boiled in increasing order of dirtiness. The water was never changed— just topped up occasionally with fresh soap flakes to maintain the suds. The final batch included socks, underpants and similar, although my mother pre-washed such items by scrubbing them on a large zinc scrubbing board with a scrubbing brush rubbed in soap.

By the time I returned from the shore with the brood, the

water in the vat had cooled until it was merely warm. My mother would declare, 'We can't waste all that good hot water!' So the kids would be lifted into the vat to have a bath. Jean, as a girl, went in by herself, then David went in next, sometimes with my father, who took the opportunity of having a hot bath too. I opted out of the communal bath by stating that I'd had a good wash while swimming at the beach.

After the washing had dried and been brought in, my mother sorted it. Although she culled it thoroughly, she was still left with a massive pile of items to be ironed. She ironed almost every day, using a flat iron heated by placing it in front of the bars of the fire until it reached the correct temperature, and ironing on the kitchen table which was covered with a blanket. When I was quite young she taught me how to do the more straightforward ironing and I became adept at this task, although I confess it's a chore, like nappy-changing, which I have avoided ever since.

On returning from a hard day looking after the kids at the shore, any resentment I felt disappeared when I saw how my mother had spent her day, literally slaving in a boiler room. Taking the brood to the shore was infinitely preferable to helping to do the family washing.

PLEASURES OF THE FLESH

In Glasgow in the 1930s, sex played a larger part in the lives of the working classes than it did in those of more affluent people. Sex was a major pleasure for the poor because it cost nothing— unless a female accidentally fell pregnant, when a price was certain to be involved. If a married woman became pregnant the couple faced the cost of raising an unplanned child. If the pregnancy was out of wedlock and the man refused to acknowledge fatherhood and marry the girl, then he faced having to pay child maintenance, which was 7/6 a week. After being advised of a girl's pregnancy, many young men said dolefully, 'Looks like I'm going to be up for 7/6 a week.' But except when a prostitute was involved, sex itself cost nothing.

In our part of Glasgow most prostitutes charged 2/6, or half a crown, for a 'short time'. Some unfortunate older women made their bodies available for even less than this. One grim story told how a visiting English seaman had sex with a Glasgow harlot. When he'd finished, not being aware of the going rate, he pressed two half crowns into her hand. In the dark, she felt the coins and thought they were pennies. 'Aw, Mister,' she wheedled, 'couldn't you make it thruppence?' But even when they charged rock bottom rates, few prostitutes worked our area because hardly any men could afford to pay 2/6 for such a transitory pleasure—plus the cost of a condom.

However, with non-commercial sex, even the cost of a condom could be avoided by practising coitus interruptus, the

65

birth control method favoured by poor Catholic couples, of whom there were many in our neighbourhood. Alternatively, an investment could be made in a heavy-duty condom, which was made of thick rubber and could be reused. These cost more than disposable condoms, but could withstand months of hard wear.

Condoms were always called French letters, and around our area used 'Frenchies' were a common sight, lying on the ground in the street and on the grass in parks. We received absolutely no sex education at home, and got none at school either. Indeed, almost any mention of sex in the house was regarded as disgusting and could result in a severe belting from my old man. We quickly learned not to talk about anything to do with sex.

It wasn't until I reached puberty at thirteen that I understood what a French letter was used for. I was familiar with them by sight from about age six because there was an attractive nineteen-year-old girl, Betty Ewald, who lived with her parents and three younger brothers in a house one storey above us. Betty had a procession of ardent boyfriends, but like most courting couples from the slums, finding the privacy in which to make love was virtually impossible.

Betty's home was identical to ours. Her brothers slept together in the cavity bed in the front room, and she had an iron-framed single bed in the same room. Her parents slept in the cavity bed in the kitchen-living room. Consequently, there was no place at home where Betty and her suitor could be alone together. Her boyfriends were similarly disadvantaged, and that traditional place for serious necking, the motor car, was an impossible dream for a girl from the slums who rarely met a man who owned a car. Generally, the most private venues for kissing and cuddling were the back seats of the stalls in the local cinema, known as the 'passion pit'. A fair degree of tolerance was displayed by the cinema usherettes, who kept an eye on canoodling couples. While a great deal of feverish activity went on underneath an overcoat spread across the couples' laps, 'going all the way' was not acceptable, and to attempt to do so brought the offending couple into the full glare of an usherette's flashlight.

Dark places in municipal parks were a favourite venue for courting couples. There they could go all the way—if the numerous Peeping Toms didn't bother them. But in winter, or when it was raining, the park was an uncomfortable place. Lying on cold, wet grass was no picnic, even for the passionate.

The warmest and most secluded place for intimacy was on the landings of 'closes'. Most lovemaking, from mutual masturbation to copulation, took place standing up. Intercourse in this fashion was known as having a 'knee trembler'. In winter, the landings were reasonably warm, and at least the couple were out of the biting wind and sleet.

The landing outside our front door was lit by a gas lamp, but this lamp was within reach of a tallish man, and late at night, after the movies had finished, Betty and her boyfriend would park themselves underneath it. Standing facing one another, Betty's back pressed against the wall, they indulged in what I later realised was sexual intercourse. After about eleven Betty's boyfriend would reach up and turn out the single stairway lamp so the couple could canoodle in darkness. This was a bit of a bind for the residents of the three houses on the ground floor level who had to go up the stairs to use the communal lavatory. When I slipped out of the house to use the toilet late at night, I often knew that Betty and her boyfriend were at it, but as they had their clothes on, it just looked as if he was pushing her against the wall. She made little moaning sounds, but he didn't appear to be hurting her. I could barely see them in the dark as I fumbled my way upstairs—we couldn't afford the batteries for a handy thing like a flashlight.

But the next morning there was usually proof that the couple had enjoyed a knee trembler. Betty's boyfriends discarded the used French Letter by tossing it down the stairs which led to the basement dwellings. I was about seven when I found my first one. Overcome with curiosity, I picked it up and took it home to ask my mother what it was.

She, of course, was horrified. In fact she became so overwrought that the shock brought on her palpitations—an ailment she suffered from frequently. She snatched the well-filled French letter from my hand and tossed it into the fire where it sizzled for a few seconds before disappearing.

I remember her crying, 'That's that Betty Ewald! She's a disgusting whoor!' My mother didn't like Betty because she wore lipstick and mascara. She herself only ever wore a light dusting of face powder, and maybe a dab of Californian Poppy perfume sometimes. To her, further cosmetics were acceptable on film stars, but a nice Scottish girl didn't paint her face like a whoor.

During my primary school years, my lack of interest in anything to do with sex was total. I had often seen my little sister naked when she was having a bath, but found nothing interesting about the female genitalia. Indeed all she seemed to have was a dimple where I had a dick. My knowledge of physiology was nil. Like many small boys I firmly believed that girls 'peed out of their bum', deduced from watching them squat when they urinated out of doors. In fact, the only part of a girl's body that interested me was her bottom, not her hairless vagina or her flat chest, and seeing a girl's bare bum was mildly exciting only because looking at it was 'dirty'. Girls rarely displayed their bare bottoms to boys, but one or two young ladies in our neighbourhood could be persuaded to let us have a look under their skirts. Some girls charged a fee for exposing themselves, although often this was only some sweeties. But one girl, wee Rachel Morrison from a basement tenement house, let any number of boys have a good look at her for a halfpenny.

A school friend, Charlie Butler, who was about two years

68

older than me, paid Rachel's fee which entitled him and two others boys, including me, to have a look at the mercenary nymphet's genital area. It was then that I had the first sexual experience that I can remember—a painful one!

While Rachel was exposing herself she demanded that we boys take out our penises and let her see what we had. Charlie needed no urging, nor did the other boys. However, at age seven, I was embarrassed at the idea of displaying my insignificant organ to a girl. But I took it out anyway.

Rachel fondled each penis in turn and the boys may have got an erection, I can't remember, but I do remember how she asked me to put my penis in her mouth. Urged on by Charlie and co, I complied, whereupon she bit hard into my little organ, causing blood to spurt from it—and causing me considerable pain. Crying with agony and dripping blood, I rushed upstairs into our house and showed my injured manhood to my mother. Horrified, she had an immediate attack of the palpitations. The doctor was called—one of the few times I can recall one visiting our house—and I was given an injection. He cleaned and bandaged my lacerated organ, leaving the tip free so that I could pee, and instructed my mother that the bandage was to be removed twice a day so that I could sit in a bath of Condes Crystals for half an hour. I remember every detail of such a painful experience.

My penis remained sore for many days and it was some weeks before the wound healed and I could pass water without pain. There was a major altercation between Rachel's mother and mine, who called Rachel a 'dirty little slut'. Rachel's mother responded by saying that I was a 'filthy little boy'. I was warned never to go near Rachel again and was happy to comply. Such a painful childhood experience might deter a male from ever again accepting any offer of oral sex from a female, but I must say that this incident had no lasting negative effect on me.

The second sexual experience I can remember also took

place when I was about seven. Quite close to our house was a little lane used by vehicles which delivered goods to several businesses whose rear entrances were in the lane. One was a wholesale bakery which supplied many retail outlets around Glasgow.

During the day, the bakery workers, who were all male, came out into the lane to have a smoke. Smoking was not permitted inside for fear that a cigarette butt might get into the baking and lead to a complaint. Such incidents were not unheard of. My mother once found a dead mouse in one of the bread rolls we bought for breakfast. To make it worse, when halving the roll, she actually sliced through the tiny corpse. The experience made her genuinely ill and put her off that type of roll for life. My father demanded compensation from the bakery, eventually settling for six free rolls a day for a year. Had we been able to afford a solicitor, my mother could probably have received some financial settlement for the undoubted shock and anguish she experienced. But the bakery in the lane near our house wasn't the one which made the roll with the mouse in it.

When the workers came out for a smoke they left the bakehouse doors open and small boys like myself, always hungry, could see inside and savour the sight of tray after tray of cakes, buns, rolls and loaves. The tempting odour used to make my mouth water. I quickly became chummy with the bakery men and they would occasionally give me a free cream bun. A big red-headed man called Rory was especially nice to me. One day he invited me into the bakery and showed me its marvels. He let me kneel up on a bench-like seat so I could watch him work at the flour-covered table where he was rolling dough. He asked if I'd like a meringue and I slavered at the prospect, only rarely getting to taste such treats. He produced a creamy meringue and placed it in front of me as I knelt on the bench, then told me to pull my jersey and shirt up so I wouldn't get flour on them as I leaned against the table. He said I mustn't go home showing signs that I'd been in the bakery, nor must I tell my parents I'd been allowed in. Rory said he would get into trouble for letting me in and giving me free cakes.

Child molesters have the ability to attune themselves to a child's mind, and what he said sounded quite sensible. I felt grateful to him for taking a risk to give me such a treat.

He gave me a second meringue and while I leaned against the table gobbling it, with my shirt and jersey rucked under my armpits, he went behind me, then said he'd pull my trousers down so they wouldn't get flour on them. He slid my short pants down to my knees then positioned himself behind my bare bottom and pressed hard against it.

I found absolutely nothing unusual about this. Four other bakers were present at the time and they went on with their work as if nothing was happening. Occasionally, one of them would place another meringue before me while Rory pressed against my rear. He made no attempt to penetrate me; had he done so I would have been painfully aware of it. Now I realise that he had taken out his penis and was rubbing it against the crease of my buttocks. I know too that he ejaculated because, before he pulled my pants up, he wiped my bottom with a cloth, telling me that I'd got some cream on my bum. This brought guffaws from his co-workers although at the time I had no idea why they laughed.

I visited Rory regularly and the procedure was always the same. He never attempted to bugger me or fondle my genitals; he got his pleasure purely from frottage. However, after about three months of kneeling over the table with my pants down— and consuming delicious cakes while Rory stood behind me and gripped my buttocks as he rode against me—disaster struck.

One day I went to the bakery as usual after school and waited until the men came out for a smoke. But this time Rory

71

wasn't among them. When I enquired where he was his co-workers told me that he'd left the bakery. They gave me no reason for his departure, and when I asked if I could come inside and have my usual free cake the men told me to go away and not come back. I was quite shattered at the sudden end to my gourmet treats.

Weeks later, some of my school friends began talking about the man in the bakery down the lane who had been arrested for interfering with small boys. Apparently I wasn't the only lad who Rory had played around with, but one of the other boys must have told his parents what Rory did. At about the same time my mother warned me never to go near the bakery down the lane. She wouldn't tell me why, and I never told her that I had already been a regular visitor there. Although only seven, I sensed that it would be wise to say nothing.

The only other sexual episode that I remember from my pre-puberty days was one I came close to becoming involved in. The 'Furniture Van Orgy', as the newspapers labelled it, was the talk of our part of Glasgow for many months. It was a scandal that rocked ten families, all of whom had a pre-teenage son or daughter who participated in sexual acts organised by a man the police described as an 'evil sexual deviant'. I could easily have been one of the participants, but for the fact that at age eleven, my interest in sex was negligible. Additionally, I was never a fully-fledged member of one of the gangs of boys in our neighbourhood.

Membership of a gang was almost mandatory in our part of Glasgow. As a loner, a boy was vulnerable to being beaten up or having his possessions stolen by older, bigger and tougher lads. But if you were a gang member and you were picked on, your pals would take retribution by giving the offender a 'good kicking' on your behalf. To do harm to, or insult a gang member meant you had offended the entire gang. The gangs were very territorial. There was the Grove Street Gang, the Scotia Street

72

Gang and the Balmain Street Gang, all within a few blocks of each other in our neighbourhood. But one gang member could walk through another gang's territory without danger. If you were known to belong to a gang then other 'gangsters' usually left you alone. Any attack could lead to an all out gang war.

Gang members were mostly boys under fourteen, too young to go to work. After a lad started work he usually dropped out of his schoolboy gang and acquired other interests. But, as a working lad got older, he could join one of the senior gangs, which included Glasgow's infamous razor gangs, whose favoured weapon was the cut-throat razor. Juvenile gangs used their fists and booted feet as their main weapons. But belts with a heavy buckle, or sticks, were also employed sometimes.

Girls were never admitted to boys' gangs, nor were there any girls' gangs that I can recall. But sisters of gang members were often used to keep a lookout for the police when a gang battle was imminent, or were placed as decoys when the gang went on a shoplifting expedition. Girls were also used for sexual purposes, as was the case in the Furniture Van Orgy.

The orgy was organised by a man in his forties called Sammy McPherson, who drove a furniture van for a removals company. He was allowed to take his van home every night and it was a familiar sight parked outside his Balmain Street tenement.

Most of the orgies took place on Sundays inside Sammy's van, and I had friends, all older than me by a year or more, who participated in them. They were lads who had reached puberty, and unlike me, knew that their penis was not merely a waterpipe, but a potential source of considerable pleasure too. One of my friends, Charlie Butler, was a 'regular' and told me what took place inside the locked van. He urged me to join in the proceedings, telling me that Sammy gave all the boys and girls threepence for participating—and for keeping their mouths shut. The money was tempting, and had I reached puberty I would probably have joined in. But at the time I was more interested in spending my Sundays reading.

Nevertheless, I was curious about what took place inside the furniture van. I liked Sammy McPherson, as did everybody else, kids and adults alike. He was a very obliging man and often carted bulky items free for neighbourhood families when they were 'doing a flit'. A moonlight flit was what you did when you moved out of your abode late at night when the factor was unlikely to observe your departure.

Sammy was also active in the local Sunday School and was involved in all kinds of children's activities, such as supervising sporting events in a nearby park. He had no children and it was said that he was a widower. In retrospect, Sammy had the essential stock-in-trade of a child molester—the ability to make children like him. Even quite young children rarely put their trust in someone they dislike, but Sammy had no such problems, especially with the additional allure of his van. For both boys and girls it was a treat to be allowed to sit behind the wheel, moving the gear stick and pretending to drive. Sammy had no need to entice children into his van; they queued up to climb aboard, and there was often a boy behind the wheel while a girl sat alongside on Sammy's knee.

Charlie Butler told me that on Sundays five boys and five girls usually got inside via the driver's door. Inside there were stacks of blankets and old mattresses used for packing furniture; light was supplied from a battery-powered lantern. Sammy, the generous host, supplied the lads and lasses with bottles of fizz, cream buns and sweeties. In due course he suggested that they all stripped off their clothes, because it was hot inside the closed van, the only ventilation coming from a roof fan which only worked when the van was moving.

When the boys and girls were naked, Sammy persuaded the girls to suck the boys' penises and to fondle one another's genitals. Oral and manual sex seemed to be as far as things went, as Sammy didn't want any of the girls to become pregnant.

74

I asked Charlie Butler what Sammy did while the boys and girls indulged in sex play. Charlie said that he just sat back and 'tossed himself off' while he watched. At eleven, I didn't know what masturbation was, but was familiar with the expression 'tossing off'.

Sammy's downfall came through his generosity. His payment of threepence was a large sum for kids who rarely even received a penny a week for pocket money. Inevitably the children's affluence was noticed by some parents and eventually an irate father blew the gaff. The police were brought in and immediately launched an investigation, and after a few weeks five boys and five girls were charged and appeared before the Juvenile Court. Everyone in the neighbourhood followed the case with avid interest. We all knew the families involved and the furniture van orgy was the staple of women's gossip sessions for weeks.

When we received news of the verdict there was an outcry: each of the boys was sentenced to twelve strokes of the birch, while the girls got 2/6 as witnesses' expenses. Charlie Butler told me that his twelve blows on the bare bottom from a springy birch rod had been administered with great force by a hefty jailer. Although each lad's father was permitted to watch his son's chastisement and see that no blood was drawn, Charlie still had red birch marks three months later. The boys' parents were indignant at the girls getting off so lightly, and indeed for being portrayed as victims. Some parents claimed that their son had been led astray by an older and more sexually experienced girl. The girls' parents took the opposite view of course: their virgin daughters had been forced into the orgy by the unprincipled boys. Opinion in the neighbourhood became irretrievably split over the issue. People who had been friends for life never talked to one another again, and I was forbidden to play with any of the boys or girls who had been involved in the scandal.

My only involvement in the case was when I was interviewed by two police constables during the initial investigation. At the time, dozens of kids were interviewed. Mine took place in the presence of my mother, while my father was at work, and was conducted by two burly policemen, accompanied by a large German Shepherd dog. I was much more afraid of the dog than I was of the 'polis', one of whom laboriously wrote in his notebook throughout the interview. I told them what I knew, which was that I had been invited to come to Sammy's van one Sunday, but I couldn't remember who had invited me. In Glasgow, I quickly learnt not to tell the police anything about my friends.

My mother staunchly defended her eldest son's innocence. She told the policemen that I was a good boy from a respectable family, and that my father was an ex-serviceman from the Great War. The two policemen were probably glad to escape from my mother's vehement protestations.

So what happened to Sammy McPherson? He simply vanished. He left the furniture van outside his tenement and was never heard of again. The police drove the van away and kept it as evidence at the court case, much to the chagrin of Sammy's employer, who wanted to put it back to work.

THE GASMAN COMETH

At Grove Street there was no electricity. Gas was used for lighting and to heat the two rings on which most meals were cooked. Food was also cooked and kept warm in the ovens on both sides of the coal fire, which burned through summer and winter alike. A big smoke-blackened cast iron cooking pot hung from a steel hook or 'swee', which swivelled from one side to place the pot over the fire. Apart from cooking soup and porridge, the pot was used for heating water to fill the zinc hip bath, brought out once a week on Fridays for the family bath night. The house only had one tap, over the kitchen sink. There was no running hot water.

The sole source of illumination in the kitchen-living room came from a single gas mantle above the fireplace, which had to be replaced about once a month. But the most important piece of equipment in the room was the gas meter, which stood on a high shelf near the door. It was a penny-in-the-slot meter, with a series of little dials which measured consumption on the front. A penny supplied about five hours of gas lighting, but when the rings were lit too, the penny was used up much faster. In wealthier parts of Glasgow, there were shilling-in-the-slot gas meters, but in poor areas penny meters were standard.

About once a month the gas man called. Everybody made sure there was someone at home to greet him, as after he had emptied the meter, he counted out a rebate which was given to the householder. This rebate, about fifteen per cent, was for paying cash for gas used, rather than paying on receipt of an account.

There was often as much as ten shillings in our meter, all in pennies, which meant a cash rebate of 1/6. With that sum my mother could buy six large loaves of bread. But sadly, the McRobbies rarely received the full rebate, or indeed any money at all. Our household had a stock of Australian, New Zealand and Irish pennies, the same size as British pennies and as readily accepted by the meter. These foreign pennies had been given to us by our sea-faring Uncle Alec, who returned from long voyages with some copper coins he couldn't change into sterling. When money was particularly tight the foreign pennies went into the meter. We knew we'd get them all back. As the gas man counted the money into shilling piles he always flicked the foreign pennies into a pile of their own. He never missed one.

When he'd calculated our rebate, he paid it first in the foreign coinage, then added maybe three British pennies to make up the total. So although our refund never came to much, we still had the foreign coins to use in the meter again.

We often tried to pass off the foreign pennies in the shops, usually by placing one between two British ones, hoping the shopkeeper wouldn't notice. But like the gas man, Glasgow shopkeepers had an unerring ability to detect a non-British coin. By courtesy of Uncle Alec, we had some Australian sixpences which we tried to spend too, without success. Then my father discovered that Aussie sixpences worked in cigarette slot machines which gave a packet of ten Capstan for sixpence. So that got rid of them!

In the poorer parts of Glasgow, many attempts were made to bilk the gas meters. The container that held the coins was a strong metal box secured by a brass padlock which the gas man unlocked. Even if a key could be obtained to open the padlock and allow access to the pennies, such a theft would have been pointless because the meter readings would reveal the discrepancy and the householder would be charged with stealing from the Corporation's gas department. This could lead to six months hard labour in the city's notorious Barlinnie Jail.

The cleverest gas thief I heard of developed an 'everlasting' penny, an ordinary coin in which he drilled a tiny hole to feed a length of fishing line through. After the penny was inserted in the slot and the knob turned to activate the gas supply, the man was able to withdraw the coin by pulling gently on the fishing line. On meter-reading day the gas man found a difference between the amount of gas consumed and the amount of money in the box, but he put this down to a meter fault.

The ruse continued for some time until the meter thief became too greedy and began selling pennies on strings for sixpence each. That was his downfall, for which he got twelve months, not for bilking the gas department, but for defacing His Majesty's currency.

GRANDMA HEWITT

In 1935, when I was nine, the McRobbies had a six month sojourn in Ayr at my grandmother's house. This followed a bad fall suffered by Grandma Hewitt after she collapsed during a dizzy spell. She cut her head badly on the metal fender in front of the fireplace, and lay unconscious for several hours until the first of my uncles came home from work and found her lying in a pool of blood.

The doctor was called but Grandma rallied enough to strongly resist being taken to hospital. She'd never been in a hospital in her life, although she'd had seven sons and two daughters, and didn't intend to make her first trip then.

Apart from suffering a severe head wound, Grandma Hewitt had also damaged her hip, and she never walked again after the accident. The hip could possibly have been fixed had she gone to hospital, but she had a real fear that if she succumbed to this she would never come out alive. Her fear of hospitals was shared by many people of her age who had been born in the latter half of the nineteenth century, and she was convinced that a hospital was a place you went to die in. If you took to bed in your own home, however, and were looked after by your own kin, then you could live for a long time. And in her case she was right. Grandma Hewitt survived for seven years after her fall.

After Grandma's accident my mother was summoned to come to Ayr at once. The summons came by telegram. There was no phone at Green Street and, of course, none at our house in Glasgow either. In fact, we didn't know anyone in our neighbourhood who had a telephone. I was home from school having my lunch when the telegram boy rapped on our door knocker. I accepted the buff coloured envelope and took it in to my mother. She turned white when she saw what I was holding. During the Great War of 1914-18 the only telegrams received by most working class households were from the War Office, advising that a son, brother or husband had been killed in action. To my mother, a telegram always meant bad news.

After she got the telegram from my Uncle Tom telling her that Grandma was seriously ill, my mother made plans to leave for Ayr the next morning. She had no choice but to take all her children with her. My father had to work six days a week, so there was no way he could look after the brood. My mother was the elder of two daughters, but her sister, Jean, had married a Canadian soldier during the war and was now living in Nova Scotia. It was the inescapable duty of a daughter to look after a sick mother, or father, no matter how much it disrupted her life and that of her family.

The family's two suitcases were quickly packed and I was sent across the street to the school to tell the headmaster that Jean and Bill McRobbie, and myself, would be leaving for Ayr next morning due to a family emergency. When my father came home from work at six thirty, he was told the bad news. To him the worst aspect was that he would probably have to fend for himself for a week or so. In the event, he had to live a bachelor existence for over six months while my mother stayed in Ayr.

The next morning my father, who worked for the railway company, left early for work to arrange a free train pass to Ayr for my mother and us kids. Via a combination of Shanks' pony and tram we got to the station where the free pass was waiting for us, and on arrival in Ayr we were met at the station by Uncle Tom. In view of the gravity of the situation, and the likelihood that grandma might die at any time, Uncle Tom splurged out on a taxi to take us and the luggage to Green Street. It was the first time I'd been in a taxi, or any kind of motor car, and I think it was a first for my mother too.

Grandma improved rapidly after her daughter arrived and the old lady could stop fretting about who was going to look after her sons. The McRobbies settled in the big upstairs room, just like we did every summer holiday time, although this visit was even less of a holiday than usual. After it became apparent that my mother's stay in Ayr might last for months, the three school-aged kids had to continue their education, so we were enrolled at a primary school within walking distance of Green Street.

Grandma needed almost constant attention. She had to be fed and at first this was by means of an invalid's feeding cup with a little spout inserted between her lips. Her 'meal' often consisted of Bengers Invalid Food, or Horlicks and milk, accompanied by lemon and barley water three times a day. While Roses bottled lemon and barley water was freely available, it was regarded as being inferior to the real thing, and I quickly learned how to make the brew myself. This involved boiling barley in a saucepan of water for about fifteen minutes then straining the liquid off into a muslin-covered jug. Half a lemon was squeezed into the jug and when the mixture cooled, there was about a pint of lemon and barley water The remaining barley mash was eaten by us kids as a cereal, sprinkled with sugar and mixed with milk. In our household nothing was wasted.

What with looking after her two brothers and four kids, plus waiting hand and foot on grandma, my mother was a very tired woman when she got to bed at nights. Grandma woke very early in the morning, at about five am. This was well before my two uncles had to rise for work, and to give my mother a break I volunteered to attend to Grandma's needs each morning. This included giving her the bedpan, which involved hoisting her hips off the bed and sliding the pan under her bottom.

At first, Grandma was hesitant about letting her eldest grandson perform this service, for she was a very proud old lady. But eventually she had to accept my bedpan services, because the alternative was to wake my mother and have her come downstairs to do it. Grandma appreciated that her daughter needed all the sleep she could get. Even with the extra time in bed, she would still have to be up at seven thirty to prepare breakfast for my two uncles.

So after five am, I emptied the bedpan and cleaned it. Grandma then insisted that I spray her room with Jeyes Lavender Essence, which I pumped from a hand operated atomiser. In the meantime I'd put the barley and water on the gas ring—grandma liked it made fresh each morning and preferred to drink it warm. With kindling and newspapers, I also started the coal fire in the kitchen-living room. Apart from having warmth for my own comfort, my mother would need the fire going to toast bread and cook the porridge for breakfast.

After I'd given Grandma her drink in the feeding cup, I prepared the rest of her breakfast. This consisted of a soft-boiled egg mixed into very small squares of soft bread which I had to spoon into her mouth. The finale was a cup of tea, served in the feeding cup.

I usually had grandma's breakfast completed by five-thirty when I brought her a wet face cloth so she could wash her hands and face, and dab herself with eau de cologne. I ate some barley cereal, made toast and jam for myself and had a cup of tea. Then I brought the big cast iron kettle to the boil and stood it on the hob. A large blackened cast iron saucepan was also brought to the boil then set aside. My mother would later cook porridge for seven people in this pan.

The next hour and a half was the most enjoyable part of the day for me. Until it was time to wake my mother up, I had the kitchen to myself and I occupied the time by reading books, most of which were borrowed from the local free library. I had tickets that let me take out three books at a time, and on Saturdays alone I needed three titles to keep me going during Sunday as I devoured them so fast.

On weekdays my mother looked after Grandma until I got home, but she eagerly awaited my arrival back from school because I would then read aloud to her until tea time. Grandma wasn't capable of holding a magazine or book to read it, and apart from that her eyesight was poor, even with glasses. Her literary tastes favoured the twopenny weekly women's papers, and these mainly contained love stories, although some had murder stories too. Most of these seemed to be about women who poisoned their husbands, or wives who were killed by their husbands then buried at the bottom of the garden. Periodicals of the time included the *Red Letter, Secrets, Peg's Paper* and the *Peoples' Friend*. This last was one of grandma's favourites and I had to read every page of it, including the regular sections like 'Readers' Letters', the doctor's page and 'Advice to the Lovelorn'.

At nine to ten years old, some of the stuff I read aloud went way over my head, but it certainly made me familiar with long words, even if I didn't understand their meaning. From the doctor's page I learned that many women were troubled with haemorrhoids, which I eventually discovered meant piles. Acne was another problem for many younger female readers. Older women were bothered by hot flushes, while constipation seemed to afflict all ages. For a ten year old boy, I became quite knowledgeable about female ailments!

In later years, during my journalistic career, my early experience paid off when I became editor of two Australian women's magazines, *Woman's World* and *Woman's Day* and worked briefly for the British *Woman's Own*.

Grandma's other favourite reading was novels of the love

story type. Three of the best-selling authors of the time were Ethel M. Dell, Annie S. Swan and Ruby M. Ayres, and I think I read every one of their novels to her, borrowed from the library on Grandma's ticket. Her eyes lit up when I came home with a new novel. She couldn't wait until I could sit beside her bed and read it to her.

As well as reading to Grandma after I got home from school, I also had to do another session after tea. This usually began about seven thirty and sometimes I'd have to keep it up until she dropped off to sleep a couple of hours later, when thankfully I could tiptoe from her room. Reading aloud was quite tiring work, partly because for dialogue I altered my voice to suit each character. If it was a woman speaking I pitched my voice high (a fairly easy feat for a boy of ten). When speaking a man's part I made my voice as deep as possible, and if it was a foreigner, I adopted an appropriate accent.

Grandma thought I was a great reader, even better than my mother, who was glad to relinquish the chore to me. At nights, after I'd read for nearly two hours, I'd check if Grandma was still awake and listening. When I read to her she tended to have her eyes closed, so she could visualise what I was describing better. To see if she was still awake I'd skip a large chunk of the text and if she didn't notice the jump I knew she had dozed off. But if she was awake she'd immediately realise what I'd done and protest 'That disnae sound right, Alex. You must have missed a bit.' She was a very attentive listener.

After about six months of us being in Ayr, my father had enough of his bachelor existence and we returned to Glasgow. To replace my mother's services, my two uncles engaged the services of a young woman called Peggy to look after Grandma and act as housekeeper. But every summer, during the school holidays, we still went to Ayr and stayed at Grandma's. I was warmly welcomed because Peggy rarely read to Grandma. Her working hours ended at teatime when she went home to her own place, and although nobody knew it at the time, Peggy was involved in an affair with my Uncle David.

Some years later, after the war began in 1939, the McRobbies privately evacuated themselves from Glasgow, as the government urged women and children to do in case the Germans bombed big cities. As Scotland's major industrial centre, Glasgow was a likely target for the Nazi bombers. My father stayed on: railway workers were considered to be in an essential occupation, but he visited us most weekends when he brought his washing to Ayr for my mother to do.

When we became more or less permanent residents of Ayr Grandma was still bedridden, but she was able to get up and dressed and sit by the front room window for a few hours a day. She could chat to passers-by through the open window and see something of the life of the street, instead of being confined to a back room. But Grandma often said she would like to get out into the town again, and see what changes had taken place during her years in bed. Her two sons offered to get a wheelchair for her but she scoffed at the idea—she didn't want to be seen to be so helpless by people she knew. Before her fall she had been a very active woman. But my uncles persisted, and finally brought home a hired wheelchair for her to at least sit in and get the feel of. After a few weeks Grandma decided that she would try 'a wee outing', just to the end of the street, so she could see the harbour. She dressed carefully in her best hat with a dark veil which she could lower over her face if she wanted to be incognito. She preferred my mother, rather than one of my uncles, to push the wheelchair on her first outing, and thought they could call in at the family grocer's shop to buy a few things.

My mother got me to come with them so I could do some of the pushing if she 'got puffed'. I was thirteen at the time, but already six feet tall with lots of stamina. Pushing the wheelchair was a breeze anyway because Grandma was small and frail, and on that first outing I did most of the work. It took all my stout mother's energy to amble along beside us, much less push a wheelchair.

After that first outing, Grandma gained confidence in my pushing skills. For her next trip I went solo, and these excursions soon became almost daily until she got too ill to leave her bed. Gradually I extended the outings and pushed Grandma all around Ayr. She was keen to see Main Street because her family had run a grocery shop in the town centre and she wanted to see if the shop was still there. Wheeling Grandma around town, I soon learned how well known and how respected she was. On every outing she was greeted by people who knew her, and I had to stand by while she chatted with this one and that. Even Ayr's Lord Provost (the Mayor) was pleased to see her and chat with her.

Our most ambitious outing was a virtual day trip to Burns' Cottage, at Alloway, about five miles from where we lived. Like many residents of Ayr Grandma had never bothered to visit Burns' Cottage, although it was an internationally-known tourist attraction. But she wanted to see it before she died.

Equipment for such a long trip included Grandma's bedpan, tucked in beside her in the chair and covered with a cloth and shawl. As it was summer we also took a bottle of Tizer for me, and some lemon and barley water for Grandma. We also carried Grandma's 'bottle', a red coloured medicine which she had to take three times a day. Thus prepared, we set off one Sunday morning at a fairly smart pace, although as we got to Ayr's outskirts I had to stop frequently so Grandma could look at some new building or other that she hadn't seen before. By myself, walking briskly, I could have covered the distance in about two hours, but there were a few hills to be climbed, and with the wheelchair it took us nearly three hours.

When we got to Burns' Cottage there were many other visitors there. I pushed Grandma into the grounds so she could have a good look at the great poet-philosopher's humble abode, and it was then I discovered that to actually go into the cottage cost sixpence. Grandma debated this expense for all of two minutes before deciding that we didn't need to go inside. It was enough for her to be able to say she'd seen the place. So we had lunch at a tea-room and Grandma bought a postcard of Burns' Cottage to send to her other daughter, my Aunt Jean, in Canada.

After two cups of tea, and the lemon and barley water she had consumed during our trip, it was potty time for Grandma. I enlisted the sympathy—and aid—of an elderly waitress at the tearoom who wheeled her out to an unoccupied room where she could use the bedpan. Then we began the trek home.

We hadn't gone far before we were hit by a heavy summer shower. This didn't bother Grandma because the wheelchair had a large hood, rather like a pram hood, which I raised to keep the rain off her. There was also a waterproof lap cover which snapped on to the outside of the chair-arms and covered her legs, so she was fairly snug and dry. Walking behind the chair, I was quickly soaked to the skin. Even if I'd had an umbrella it would have been useless because I needed both hands free for pushing, and as there was no sign of the rain letting up I decided to run the rest of the way, which is what I would have done had I been alone. I warned Grandma that we were going to move faster than usual, but told her not to worry, because the chair had a good brake.

I broke into a fast trot and found that the faster I went the easier it was to move the chair along. My main sport was long distance running—so I had considerable stamina and maintaining a run for an hour or more was no problem.

Once we reached the High Street it became more tricky to keep up the pace because there were pedestrians to be avoided and intersections to negotiate. But we fairly bowled along and I didn't need to use the brake once. When we got home and

Grandma was lifted from the wheelchair, I expected that she might be somewhat shaken after her thrilling ride. In places the chair had almost gone on to two wheels when I cornered at speed. But no, her face was glowing like a young girl's.

'Well!' she told my mother, 'I've never come down the High Street so fast in all my life! It was like being in a Hansom cab except we were on the pavement!'

Grandma was of a generation that remembered horse-drawn vehicles like Hansom cabs. She mistrusted motor cars. I think her first ride in an automobile was when the hearse carried her to the cemetery.

After her trip to Alloway she assured my mother, 'Aye, Jessie, your boy is a very good driver.' For a reward she gave me the sixpence she'd saved by not going into Burns' Cottage.

AT THE PICTURES

For the poor, the main sources of entertainment—apart from sport—were the cinema, the vaudeville theatre, listening to the gramophone, parlour games—and playing cards. After card playing and games like Tiddlywinks, the next cheapest entertainment was the wireless. However, buying and maintaining a radio cost money—especially if it was a battery-operated set. We had no electricity in our Glasgow home and there was none in my grandmother's home in Ayr either.

It was 1938 before our household at Grove Street acquired a wireless. Unfortunately, we didn't keep the first set for long—the weekly payments plus the cost of batteries and charging the accumulator were too much for the budget and the radio was repossessed after we'd had it for only ten weeks.

I remember that first radio very well. It was a Cosser push-button model—the very latest, made of gleaming black bakelite, retailing at two pounds ten shillings. My father bought it on 2/6 deposit with weekly payments of 2/6 for fifteen weeks. This meant that with interest, he would end by paying four pounds for the set. At the time, bank interest rates were about three percent.

Because we had no electricity, a battery-operated set was our only option. The main Exide dry battery cost 7/6 and couldn't be recharged. It lasted for about six weeks if the set was switched on reasonably often, but because of its novelty value, we had it on almost constantly. The set also needed a glass-cased accumulator which had to be charged every week at a garage, costing twopence.

After we'd 'owned' the set for eight weeks we were already two weeks behind with the payments, having spent the instalment money on a new battery. By week ten, my father admitted defeat and returned the set to the store. But he still wanted a radio in the house because he'd enjoyed the convenience of listening to race broadcasts and knowing immediately if the horses he'd wagered on had won or lost. A deal was hammered out with the radio store. No credit was allowed for the deposit and payments already made on the Cosser. Instead we became the possessors of a second hand Ekko radio, made of wood with a fibre-covered speaker. It was very difficult to tune and used to oscillate badly, so needed constant retuning, but the price was five shillings—a shilling down and a shilling a week for six weeks. We managed to keep the Ekko.

Popular radio programmes included one hosted by Ben Lyons and Bebe Daniels. Another great weekly favourite was a show featuring Arthur Askey and Richard Murdoch. In those days the BBC was the main source of radio programmes. A commercial channel, Radio Luxembourg, broadcast from Europe, but our wireless couldn't pick it up, mainly because we couldn't put up an outdoor aerial.

The reason we couldn't have an aerial wire hanging from our kitchen window was because we couldn't afford the compulsory ten shillings annual licence fee. Licence inspectors often cruised the streets looking for signs of an outdoor aerial, a sure indication that there was a radio in the house, and they would then call round and demand to see the licence. However, they had no power to force their way into a home so their chances of catching a family like ours were slim. When our radio was playing and there was an unfamiliar knock on the front door, the radio was instantly switched off. A child, usually me as the oldest, crept to the front door then eased up the letterbox and peered out to see who the caller was. Licence inspectors, school inspectors and rent collectors were well aware of this technique.

The man would kneel down and put his face close to the letterbox then say affably, 'Is your mother or father in, sonnie?'

'No,' I'd say, 'They're away at the pictures.'

'Oh, I suppose you've been listening to the wireless then?'

'No. We haven't got a wireless.'

'I'm sure you have, wee boy. We heard a wireless playing before it was switched off.'

'That wasn't the wireless. Mister. It was the gramophone.'

I had been well-schooled in dealing with unwelcome callers!

However, lack of an outdoor aerial confined our radio listening to the BBC's programmes relayed from Glasgow, most of which was stodgy stuff, at least as far as young people were concerned. Programming was heavy with classical music, talks and 'uplifting' material. When dance music was broadcast it was aimed at listeners who actually danced to it. Many people did this and based a social night in around music from the BBC. Leading bands of the time included the orchestras of Henry Hall, Jack Hylton, Geraldo, Victor Sylvester, Carol Gibbons and Joe Loss.

When World War II began, radio shows became much brighter, at least on the BBC's Light Programme. One wartime comedy show that captured a huge radio audience was called 'ITMA', short for 'It's That Man Again'. The man was Tommy Handley. Female crooners were featured in most comedy shows and one of note was Vera Lynn, the Forces' sweetheart. This was a triumph of publicity hype. When I joined the army I found that Vera Lynn was not especially popular, in fact parodying her somewhat mournful singing style was a staple in any army concert show! The real Forces' sweetheart was an attractive blonde singer, Anne Shelton. She sang livelier songs, and was much sexier looking than Vera Lynn.

After America entered the war and US servicemen and women began to arrive in Britain, the Americans set up the US Forces Network. They had a powerful transmitter which let the station be picked up anywhere in the UK, and the advent of this station was a boon to younger people. All the latest discs from leading American recording artistes, such as Bing Crosby, the Inkspots, the Andrews Sisters and the Mills Brothers, were aired on the AFN long before the BBC managed to get a copy. Teenagers adored the station with its professional American DJs and slick radio theatre shows of a kind never previously heard in Britain.

My parents and uncles did not like the American programmes. They detested crooners, even poor old Bing Crosby. When I had the set tuned to the AFN I would be commanded to 'switch that muck off!' My uncles preferred 'real' singers like Peter Dawson, most of whose work they had on gramophone records.

Before the wireless became available, the wind-up gramophone was the centre of entertainment in our home in Ayr. Our set was a large cabinet model with a big horn speaker as featured in HMV's trademark with the little dog listening to it. The phonograph was a His Master's Voice model, which my uncles had built into a very handsome walnut cabinet with two doors in front and shelves on which records were stacked. Later they got rid of the horn and replaced it with a more modern speaker fitted under the turntable.

Winding the gramophone's spring motor was a chore that nobody liked doing, but it was essential. The machine could get through a ten inch record after one full winding, but to play a full twelve inch disk it needed re-winding part way through. Most of my uncles' collection were twelve inches, the standard size for most classical music. Pop music by artistes such as

Gracie Fields and George Formby was issued on ten inch records.

My parents and uncles liked Gilbert and Sullivan and light operettas such as *The Merry Widow*. Their favourite vocalists included Richard Tauber and Peter Dawson. Favourite songs were 'The Road to Mandalay', 'Soldiers of the King', 'Old Man River' and 'The Flea', which used to keep them in stitches. While performing winding duties at our regular record recitals, I became very familiar with the voices of Caruso, Gallicurci, Paul Robeson and other famous singers of the time. Apart from winding the machine, my other duties included replacing the little steel needle after each playing, and carefully dusting the record's surfaces with a special felt brush before placing them on the turntable.

Nights spent listening to records were a major form of entertainment in homes all over Scotland. It was an egalitarian recreation. Rich and poor had much the same type of gramophone and bought the same records. While the music played my mother did her knitting, or some of the pile of sewing she always had to do. My father studied a race form guide in between commenting on each record. While the records were being changed, my uncles read books from Boots Library, mostly detective or adventure stories by 'Sapper', John Buchan, Freeman Willis Croft or Rafael Sabatini (*Captain Blood*). The Bulldog Drummond books were highly regarded too.

In Ayr, such musical evenings were generally quite peaceful occasions. My three younger brothers and sisters had been put to bed so there was none of the squabbling that seemed to go on eternally among small kids. The only dissension arose when I tried to play some of my pop records. Deanna Durbin was acceptable because she was a 'real soprano', but when I played anything by the Inkspots or the Mills Brothers the adults kept up a barrage of criticism. Swing records by Benny Goodman brought commands to 'play something decent!' and tunes by the young Frank Sinatra were dismissed as 'utter tripe!' In retrospect I have some sympathy for my elders. Different tastes in pop music accurately reflect the generation gap in any era. I remember my reaction to my children's devotion to the Beatles when they first issued records. I thought the Liverpool lads were awful, but eventually I changed my opinion and voluntarily purchased some Beatles albums.

After I began working I could afford to buy records—and a portable wind up gramophone to play them on. Then I played what I wanted to hear in the bedroom I shared with my siblings. They had little interest in swing or Sinatra, so I bought a few records like 'Dumbo' and nursery rhyme songs to persuade them to keep quiet while I listened to my collection.

During my boyhood in Glasgow, vaudeville was extremely popular and there were many vaudeville theatres in the city. They charged higher admission prices than the cinemas. The remotest back seats in the galleries, or 'the Gods', were cheapest, but at sixpence, were still too expensive for me. However, cheaper admission prices could be got by waiting until the show had started. If there were empty seats, often the case on weeknights, the management would let people in for half price. This meant missing perhaps the first two acts, but it brought the price down to cinema level. That was how my parents, and occasionally myself, managed to see some famous vaudeville artistes.

The 'kings' of the vaudeville circuit were undoubtedly the comedians. Oddly, English comics went down very well in Glasgow. English artistes who trod the boards in the 1930s included Tommy Trinder, Naunton and Wayne, Flanagan and Allen and the ribald Max Miller, billed as 'the Cheeky Chappie'. One of Miller's gags was to stride on stage then begin peeling a banana. He would intone as he stripped it, 'One skin, two skin, three skin...' There was a long meaningful pause before he leered, 'Five skin'. This brought the house down, but being unfamiliar with the term foreskin, I embarrassed my mother by loudly asking her why everyone was laughing.

Surprisingly, Scottish comedians didn't go down well in Glasgow. The exception was Wull (Will) Fyfe, a red nosed comic adored by Glasgow audiences. Most of his act consisted of him trying to sing his most famous song 'I Belong To Glasgow' while attempting at the same time to light a clay pipe. The fact that he was (supposedly) staggering drunk made it difficult for the match to connect with the pipe bowl. Most of the time he burned his fingers, and by the end of the act the stage was littered with dead matches. I committed his routine to memory and in later years performed it at various venues when I was forced to get up and contribute to the entertainment. Usually I only sang 'I Belong To Glasgow' when I was very drunk. I never felt that I belonged to Glasgow in any way.

Wull Fyfe was different from other Scottish comedians because he never wore anything traditionally Scottish. It was almost mandatory for a Scots comedian to at least wear a tartan Tam O'Shanter on his head, but Wull Fyfe wore the same cloth cap—the 'skippet bonnet'—that Glasgow working men wore. He never appeared in a kilt, or carried a cromach (the knobbly Scottish walking stick) and was never very popular in England because he didn't *look* Scottish. His accent was pure Glasgow which made him difficult to be understood outside the city. In later years, another Glasgow comedian, Billy Connolly, had the same problem.

A Scots comedian who was much better known outside Scotland than Wull Fyfe was Sir Harry Lauder, famous around the world wherever there were people of Scots descent. Lauder was very popular in England because he dressed to look like most people's idea of a typical Scotsman. He wore the Tam 'O Shanter, the kilt, the tartan stockings, the brogues and a sprig of heather in his lapel, and carried the knobbly walking stick that became his trademark. As a result he was not liked by the

Scottish working classes, who regarded him as a caricature. But he was a shrewd showman and when performing outside Scotland, he gave audiences what they wanted.

I never saw any stage plays in Glasgow or Ayr—the cheapest seats were more expensive than any of those in the vaudeville theatres. The first play I saw was when I was seventeen and in the army in Inverness. It was a performance of *Brighton Rock*, starring Googie Withers and John McCallum. Because I was in uniform I got in for half price, and after seeing it I was inspired to write and produce a show which was staged before an audience from my training battalion. I had no desire to appear on stage, but writing, producing and the mechanics of stage management fascinated me. During my military service I produced several shows.

The only other types of home recreation I can recall from my boyhood are table games like Ludo, Snakes and Ladders, Blow Football, and various card games. When Monopoly swept the market in the 1930s, a set cost twelve and sixpence, far beyond my family's budget. Apart from that, my parents never showed any interest in trying to become Monopoly millionaires. However, when we moved to Ayr, a friend who lived across the street had a Monopoly set and I used to play the game with him constantly. I couldn't afford to buy a set for myself, so I borrowed his board and accessories and made my own. Using crayons and coloured pencils I created the board, then with red, green and light blue inks I made the money, after laboriously printing the denominations by hand. I cut houses and hotels from strips of shaped wood then dyed them red and green by leaving them to soak in ink. Finally, I printed the Chance and Community Chest cards on pieces of coloured card. I ended with a Monopoly set that cost no more than a shilling, but it worked very well and on rainy days I often played it with my sister and eldest brother.

The greatest form of entertainment during the Depression

was the movies—not just in Glasgow, but all over the world, wherever people wanted to escape from the grim reality of their lives. In Glasgow, the pictures played an important part in keeping people sane.

When I began going to the movies in 1935, talking pictures had only been invented for six years. Our cheapest neighbourhood cinema was the grandiosely named 'Electric Picture Palace', a small run-down cinema in Maryhill Road which we kids called 'The Wee Elecky', or more commonly, 'The Bug Hut' because its cloth seats were undoubtedly home to lice and other vermin. It was not unusual to come out of the Saturday matinee itching and scratching.

The Bug Hut only charged kids under fourteen a penny to see the Saturday matinees, although the films were always B Grade features which had been previously shown at the first run cinemas, usually a murder story and a 'cowboy picture'. Our favourite cowboys were Buck Jones, Tom Mix, Ken Maynard and John Wayne. Bill Boyd (Hopalong Cassidy) wasn't as popular and Roy Rogers, The Singing Cowboy, wasn't rated at all. He was too clean and his gear too flashy, and we thought he was a bit of a sissy.

We preferred Westerns in which there was negligible 'love interest'—the heroine was a nuisance who held up the action. On the other hand we accepted the need for a heroine to be rescued by the far more important hero. However, when the hero and heroine engaged in 'mushy' talk, we yelled and shouted and threw empty ice cream tubs and other missiles at the screen.

A major crowd-puller at the Saturday matinees were the serials, which ran in episodes of about twenty five minutes for at least twelve weeks at a time. It was a tragedy to be unable to raise a penny to see the Saturday matinee. Anyone who did miss an episode of the serial would quickly find a friend who had seen it and demand to be told 'how he got out of it.' This

98

referred to the cliff-hanging ending of each episode in which it appeared that the hero had absolutely no chance of escaping from a gruesome death—and all because the stupid heroine had got him into danger.

Occasionally I scraped up enough money to see a first run movie. A nearby cinema, the Cambridge, in New City Road, let juveniles under fourteen in for twopence. It was here I saw some of the first Ginger Rogers and Fred Astaire films, and although they featured some kissing and cuddling they weren't mushy love stories, which I had no interest in whatsoever.

Ginger Rogers was the first actress I had a crush on. I accepted the fact that because of our substantial age difference there was little chance of my going to Hollywood and marrying her. But I fantasised that maybe I could become her chauffeur (after I learned to drive), or perhaps her bodyguard and save her from various perils, like the serial heroes did.

The next, and only actress I had a major crush on, was someone closer to my own age. I fell madly in love with Deanna Durbin after I saw her in *Three Smart Girls*. Later I saw every movie she appeared in, many of them four or five times over. I bought all of her records and in my teens kept a large scrap book stuffed with photos and cuttings about her. When I was fourteen I wrote my first and only fan letter. I did this clandestinely, because my love for Deanna was something I kept a close secret. I was fairly sure that I would have been laughed at if I'd revealed my devotion to this lovely girl.

As the return address on my fan letter to Universal, I used c/o the Slipway where I had started work. Within a few weeks I received a reply in the form of a postcard, with an autographed photo of Deanna on one side and a signed, pseudo-handwritten message from her on the other. As one of my duties was to collect the Slipway mail from the post office, nobody saw Deanna's reply. It would have been intensely embarrassing if anybody in the office had learned about my crush, and there would certainly have been ribald comments from the males which I would have found very offensive. My love for this young lady was entirely pure, and she *never* featured in my frequent masturbatory fantasies. That would have been defilement. It was OK to toss off looking at photos of Betty Grable or Rita Hayworth, but not Deanna. I could not sully her image with lustful thoughts or actions. She was the kind of girl one 'respected', not played around with. I remember when I was seventeen, during an army camp show, a soldier-comedian reciting a ditty that went:

'I had a funny dream last night
It really was a laugh.
I dreamt I was a cake of soap,
In Deanna Durbin's bath.'

I was so furious that I almost leapt up on to the stage and punched him. To defile my beloved was disgusting! Incidentally, that soldier-comedian was one of the 'Stars in Battledress' troupe who later won fame as a singer and comedian, but I never forgave him for publicly degrading my dear Deanna.

During World War II, Deanna Durbin had a much more important fan than me. He was Britain's Prime Minister, Winston Churchill. As soon as her latest film was ready for release he had a copy especially flown in from the USA and screened in his private projection theatre in the war room deep under London. Like many people, he found that Deanna's light-hearted movies provided a welcome escape from reality.

The kind of films I avoided were those in the 'love on the dole' genre. Movies about slum life, British or American, had zero appeal to me. Even today, I avoid 'kitchen sink' dramas. I saw more than enough of that lifestyle in Glasgow.

From thirteen I ceased to regard films as purely a source of entertainment and became interested in the mechanics of making them, in particular the writing of scripts. In 1940 I began reading *Picturegoer*, a weekly magazine covering the movies and movie stars. I was an avid filmgoer but was never very interested in pure 'fan' magazines such as the American *Silver Screen* and similar, which I sensed were phoney. But *Picturegoer* took a relatively intelligent view of the film industry and covered the contribution of individuals other than the stars. I was saddened when it ceased publication during the war because of paper rationing.

During my teens I bought several quite expensive books on film-making, mostly about the documentary film. From studying such books I was able to sell several documentary scripts to the Malaya Film Unit. At the time I was twenty years old and in the army, stationed in Malaya. But I never seriously pursued a film career although I did make one half hour documentary intended for TV when it began in Australia in 1956. From meeting many movie technical people I got the impression it was basically an unhappy industry—with too much idle time between films.

Sundays were black days as cinemas were not allowed to open on the Sabbath. Fortunately, the local film society had a special permit to use a cinema on Sundays to screen films for members only, and I quickly joined it. The films shown were never first releases but tended to be silent classics such as *The Battleship Potemkin*, *Metropolis* and similar. There were also the inevitable Charlie Chaplin silents, although I never liked the 'Little Tramp' much.

Today there has been a revival of interest in the 1930s movies featuring Laurel and Hardy and The Three Stooges. There have been many learned appreciations of their genius and popularity, but in truth, they were not all that popular when they were first screened and were B grade second features. In the case of the Stooges, shorts were used to fill out a double feature programme. The audience tolerated their slapstick while waiting for the big picture in the programme's second half. As a youth, I much preferred wise-cracking comics like Abbot and Costello, Olsen and Johnson, Jack Benny and Bob Hope.

My Sunday film visits broadened my knowledge of the cinema's history, and were also the bright spot in the unbearably boring Scottish Sabbath.

UNDER THE DOCTOR

The only time I can remember a doctor visiting our house in Glasgow was after I'd had my penis bitten by Rachel Morrison when I was seven. In our area doctors rarely made house calls, except to confirm that someone was dead and complete the death certificate. Most people were familiar with the signs of death, and the doctor's pronouncement was merely a legal formality. In our overcrowded and unhygienic environment, illness and disease were commonplace and funerals frequent.

A major reason that seeing the doctor was a rare occurrence was the cost. Doctors charged seven shillings and sixpence for a consultation at their surgery, and more for a home visit. However, like most working class families, we were members of a doctor's 'panel', so only paid 2/6 per consultation. The doctor recovered part of the difference from the compulsory health insurance fund which my father subscribed to through deductions from his weekly wage.

Mr McRobbie had frequent periods of unemployment when he went on the dole, drawing his unemployment money from the Labour Bureau (the 'Buroo'). A fringe benefit of being on the dole was that when visiting a doctor, we didn't have to pay anything, although we had a very low priority in being attended to at the surgery. The receptionist, who ruled the waiting room, sent people in to the doctor according to their financial status. Full fee-paying patients received priority. Panel patients were next, patients from a family on unemployment insurance went last, but we still weren't the lowest on the medical totem pole. The doctor received a small payment for treating us, but old age pensioners were not entitled to free medical treatment from a private doctor, although they could receive free treatment and hospitalisation at the outpatients' departments of the public hospitals. To the credit of their profession, most doctors treated pensioners free of charge, although the old folk often had to wait a very long time before they got into the doctor's office.

People who were too sick to go to work, or to attend school needed a note, or line, from a doctor to prove they were really ill. In the case of people who had a job, a doctor's line did not necessarily entitle them to sick pay. It merely let them keep their job because they were genuinely unable to turn up for work. Salary earners were often paid while off sick, but wage earners rarely got anything. Sick schoolchildren needed a doctor's line or else an inspector from the education department visited the pupil's home to check what was keeping him or her away from school.

For people like us, hospitalisation was free at the city's public hospitals. However, a lot of treatment, including minor surgery, was carried out at the outpatients' departments. On several occasions I accompanied my mother to the Western Infirmary and I remember the vast, drab, overcrowded waiting area with its rows of bench-like seats. As patients were seen, we slid along the benches until eventually we moved up to the top of our row and received the call to come and see a doctor.

Waiting one's turn took a long time, and to sit there for a whole morning was not unusual. There was no reading matter. The only thing of interest was studying the other patients and trying to guess what ailed them, although in many cases their illness was obvious, and I saw some stomach-churning sights.

One of our visits to the Western was to take my younger sister, Jean, to have her tonsils and adenoids removed. She could only be 'done' on a weekday so I was kept from school for the day to accompany her, along with my mother. We travelled to the infirmary by tram, and I carried a large shopping bag which contained the things Jean would need after her operation. After waiting for only a couple of hours, six year old Jean was taken from us by a nurse and whisked behind the scenes. We were told to move to another part of the building where we could collect her later.

We had been waiting at the collection point for about half an hour when a double door swung open and an orderly handed Jean, unconscious and smelling of chloroform, to my mother. A thick piece of blood-stained gauze was thrust into her mouth and she was snoring alarmingly. My mother carried her to the tram stop and we clambered aboard, at which point Jean started coming round. She began bringing up blood, so my mother laid her across her knee, face down, and I held one of the old towelling nappies from the bag under her face to catch the blood and vomit. This didn't go down too well with the other passengers, or the tram conductor, who all gave us a wide berth, so much so that the conductor didn't even ask my mother for her fare.

None of this fazed me, because I'd previously had my tonsils removed in the same manner at the same infirmary. On that occasion a woman neighbour had accompanied my mother to perform some of the nursing chores. The most enduring memory I have of this operation is receiving frequent saucers of ice cream while recuperating at home. Ice cream was quite a luxury so I pretended that my throat was more painful than it really was to prolong the treats. Fluids and ice cream were the only things a patient was supposed to have after a tonsils operation then. Today, methods have turned full circle. When one of my granddaughters had her tonsils out she wasn't allowed to leave hospital until she could swallow a piece of toast!

Hospitals and doctors didn't play a big part in our lives. Most ailments were treated at home by a variety of traditional 'cures'. In the tenements, where many people shared a communal lavatory, disease spread very rapidly. The smelly uncovered communal middens were a breeding ground for disease, and lack of a bathroom meant that people rarely washed all of their body. What are often called 'the usual childhood ailments' were quickly passed from one child to another. Before I was ten, I had had mumps, chickenpox, measles, whooping cough, diphtheria and scarlet fever. I don't know if there were inoculations against such diseases. All I ever received was a smallpox vaccination soon after birth.

The biggest killer in Glasgow was tuberculosis, or consumption. It was a disease that was greatly feared because it was considered incurable, although people who could afford expensive sanatorium treatment often survived for years.

Consumption was believed to run in families and we were warned to keep away from children who had 'consumption in the family'. When we moved to Ayr, we briefly employed a cleaning woman called Wee Aggie, who had TB. When she finished her labours she was always given a cup of tea. To make sure nobody else ever drank from Aggie's cup, my mother painted a black spot on the bottom of it. It was always washed separately from the other dishes and placed in its special place on a shelf.

Heavily influenced by *Treasure Island* (the 1934 Wallace Beery film, not the book), my brothers and I referred to Aggie's cup as having the 'Black Spot', the pirate's mark of imminent death. As a rather macabre juvenile joke we once crayoned a black spot on the bottom of a cup from the same set as Aggie's. We gave this cup to our sister Jean with her tea in it, then sombrely pointed out that it was Aggie's. My mother didn't think much of our sense of humour, and it took her some time to convince poor Jean that she wasn't going to die of TB.

In Glasgow, apart from disease-caused illnesses, a major

cause of hospitalisation arose through chronic alcoholism. A sardonic joke of the time said that the fastest way out of Glasgow was to drink six half pints of beer and six whisky chasers. Many couldn't afford the cost of such instant oblivion, and drinking methylated spirits was common among the poor. A slightly more upmarket drink, favoured by women, was 'Red Biddy', a generic term for cheap red wine or port, obtainable for about sixpence a bottle.

Staggering drunks on the street were an everyday sight in our part of Glasgow. When they were incapable of staggering they collapsed unconscious in the gutters. From there they were either picked up by an ambulance and taken to hospital to dry out or, occasionally, picked up by the police, taken to the station and charged with public drunkenness. The police didn't like carrying drunks in their smart Wolseley squad cars. Drunks vomited, urinated, and expectorated, so they travelled to the police station in a Black Maria instead.

Ambulances were often seen in our part of Glasgow for another reason: to collect victims of domestic violence; usually women who had been battered by their man. Fights between couples were often horrendous, frequently involving other occupants of a tenement building too, and a domestic beating often developed into a full scale brawl when the woman had male relatives to whom she could appeal to take retribution. I'm sure sheer frustration, especially in the case of the unemployed, contributed towards so many men taking it out on their wives, and sometimes their children too. It was a rare week when there wasn't a rammy in some part of our building.

Growing up where I did, I encountered more than my fair share of life-threatening hazards, malnutrition being one of them. Although as a boy I was never actually starving, I was constantly hungry. I would devour anything I could lay my hands on, day or night, and usually went to bed hungry and woke up even hungrier. My pre-pubescent fantasies all centred upon food. Not exotic food or a craving for sweet things which many children have, but ordinary everyday staples such as bread and jam, or a glass of milk. The only milk in our household was cheap skimmed stuff reserved for putting on our morning porridge. Only babies were fed whole milk.

One of my greatest pleasures was to stand outside a big baker's shop in New City Road, especially on cold winter nights. The bakers worked behind plate glass so people could watch them rolling dough, filling pies, baking loaves and making cakes and buns. There were exhaust fans at the top of the plate glass windows and the delicious odour of baking wafted out into the freezing street. I slavered at the mouth as I visualised eating some of the goodies I could see, and I spent a lot of time outside that baker's shop, or just going into grocery stores and walking around, savouring the tantalising smell of bacon, hams, cheeses and biscuits.

Our meals at home were very basic, made with the cheapest ingredients. For breakfast there was porridge and skimmed milk, followed by a slice or two of bread fried in hot dripping or lard, and a cup of tea. Lunch was bread spread with jam, but never with margarine *and* jam; that was considered to be 'a greedy feed'. Dinner was very often some kind of soup, mostly potato with a stock made from bones got free from the butcher. Sometimes barley was added, or lentils, to make it into a broth. The soup was served with slices of bread and margarine, and for sweet there was occasionally bread pudding, which we could sprinkle with sugar.

On Sundays we sometimes had eggs, but served as French Toast to make them go further. We also got meat for dinner, usually sausage-meat, made into patties and fried. Our other main source of animal protein was liver and tripe—offals were the cheapest items obtainable from a butchers—apart from the free soup bones.

For occasional between-meal snacks, we had biscuits, but

108

always broken ones. These could be bought at the grocers for a penny a large bag, weighing probably two pounds and containing an assortment which had pieces missing through being shaken up in the large tin boxes from which they were sold loose. The first thing that I ever stole from a Woolworth's counter in Glasgow was a handful of broken biscuits. Almost everything I pinched was for my stomach, and was consumed before I got home.

Fruit was almost totally absent from our Glasgow diet. The only time we regularly got any was after the annual Sunday School soiree, when we were given a bag containing some buns and an orange as we left the hall. More exotic fruit, such as bananas, was an impossible luxury.

We never ate fish—except as part of a fish and chip meal bought on the night my father was paid. My mother didn't cook dinner that night because she usually had no money to buy provisions until my father brought his pay home. I would then be dispatched to get the fish and chips plus bread, margarine and some other staples. I loved fish and chip night—the food seemed very exotic compared with our normal meals.

We never ate chicken or any kind of fowl, although on Sundays we would occasionally have rabbit, procured by my father through a friend who shot them on an estate outside Glasgow. They were often full of little lead pellets which we had to carefully avoid swallowing in case we got lead poisoning.

Our diet, consisting mainly of starches, sugar and fats, would probably horrify a modern nutritionist. Yet amazingly, we were all fairly healthy. Hungry, but healthy. None of us ever brushed our teeth—in fact I didn't own a toothbrush until we moved to Ayr when I could afford to buy one. The first time I had my teeth inspected by a dentist was when I joined the army at seventeen. I needed only two fillings and had no further dental treatment until I arrived in Australia after the war.

I suppose that in Glasgow in the 1930s, only the fit survived.

My mother firmly believed that the longer you could keep away from the doctor's, the more likely it was that you would stay healthy. She also believed that drinking plenty of water contributed to good health. So in Glasgow I drank lots of water. It was free and helped alleviate hunger pangs, but it wasn't very tasty.

SOLITARY PURSUITS

During my boyhood, the ability to escape into an alternative imaginary world made life more bearable. People can cope with all kinds of deprivation by imagining they are living in a better time and place, but in my teens I had experienced no better times. Instead, I escaped into a world of fiction, much of it pure fantasy.

From about age eight, I was a voracious reader. Apart from school books, the earliest 'literature' I can recall reading were the weekly comic papers, *Chips*, *Larks* and *Comic Cuts*. Later the *Dandy* and *Beano* began to appear, but by then I had graduated to more serious stuff, which didn't rely on illustrated panels to tell a story.

Scottish boys' favourite reading included weeklies such as the *Adventure, Rover, Hotspur, Wizard* and *Skipper*. They sold for twopence and were published on different days of the week from Monday until Saturday. But it was a rare event for me to have that much to spend on a comic, much less the money to buy five. Nevertheless, by holding back tuppence from message-running errands I did for neighbours, I usually managed to buy the *Adventure*, which I think came out every Monday. I read it from cover to cover in less than two hours, then printed my name on it, and passed it on to a friend who also read it then handed it on. By Tuesday, it had gone round four friends.

Another member of the group bought the *Rover*, reading it and passing it on until everyone had seen it. Using this cooperative system I had read all five of the papers and got my copy of the *Adventure* back by the end of the week. This could then be cashed in at a second hand magazine and book store for a halfpenny, the store reselling it for a penny. If you were prepared to wait until a week after its publication date, you could buy any weekly for half its published price. Much the same system was used by young women who wanted to read all the weekly women's papers, but could only afford one. The readership of these magazines, both boys' and girls', was considerably greater than their circulation figures.

These weekly magazines were often the only literature read for recreation by working class children. Novels were aimed at a more affluent strata of society; families with an income of four or more pounds a week. The average working man only earned two pounds, so hard cover novels, at two shillings and sixpence or more, were beyond the budget of poorer families. In 1935, when the sixpenny Penguin paperbacks were launched, poorer people were able to buy and own books for the first time.

Public libraries were the key sources of hard cover fiction, but were often slow in acquiring copies of popular works. Many libraries would not stock what the librarian, or the local authority, considered to be 'trash'. This included many of the most popular juvenile authors, as well as writers of women's romances and even detective stories. For a time the public library in Ayr would not stock Agatha Christies. However, there were many private circulating libraries which could be joined for a fee of about 2/6. This sum was to cover the cost of a book if the borrower failed to returned it, and books could be taken out for about a week at a cost of tuppence. Boots the Chemist had a circulating library at most of its hundreds of branches, and were usually very quick to acquire popular new titles. After I began earning money, I became a member of Boots' library as well as the local municipal library, which cost nothing to join and charged nothing for borrowing.

One reason for the popularity of boys' magazines in the 1930s was the absence of television. Even a radio set was uncommon in many working class homes: it was 1938 before we could afford one, and reading was the cheapest alternative leisure activity.

The boys' magazines were particularly popular because they offered escapist reading. Very few of the stories were set in Britain, except those of the detective and school adventure type. Their locations were mostly faraway places, including, of course, the Wild West, which we boys firmly believed still existed, complete with gun-toting cowboys. Australia, Canada, and South Africa were also frequently featured, and that exotic hotbed of action and adventure, the Khyber Pass, became very familiar to us.

However, in direct contrast to these action weeklies, my other favourite reading was the boys' school weekly, the *Magnet*. As an avid youthful *Magnet* reader, the only impression of it that remains with me is one of basically light-hearted tales of privileged boys enjoying life at an English public school. I was prepared to believe that schools like Greyfriars really existed, although to me they were places of pure fantasy. I knew I had no hope of ever attending such a 'snob' school, but it was pleasant to imagine what it would be like if I could have become a pupil there. I regarded public school stories in much the same way as I regarded the imaginative works of Jules Verne. I enjoyed them, but never felt that Captain Nemo really existed.

I was one of the few boys in my circle to read the *Magnet*, or a similar paper called the *Gem*. I doubt if either magazine was ever as popular in Scotland as they were in England, but I liked public school stories and there were several such tales in book form available from the public library. There was a series featuring a schoolboy called Teddy Lester, written by John Finimore, and set in the period before the Great War of 1914-18.

They seemed highly evocative of that era, and my mother confirmed many of the background facts in these stories, which were set in the time of her girlhood.

From about age ten I began reading the 'William' books by the remarkable Richmal Crompton. I was amazed when I learned that Ms Crompton was quite an elderly woman, and bedridden. Yet her stories were about one of the most active boys in fiction. I liked the William books not only because of William's escapades, but because he lived a middle class lifestyle. He moved among families with maids who served afternoon tea in the parlour. He had access to a biscuit barrel on the sideboard and could help himself when he felt like a snack. In our house anything placed in a biscuit barrel would have vanished into hungry mouths within seconds.

Boy Scout stories, or any books about Scouting—starting with Baden Powell's *Scouting for Boys*—were great favourites of mine too. I desperately wanted to become a Scout, but there was no troop in our part of Glasgow. Scouting was regarded as being for middle class lads, not the sons of working men.

At the time, Scouting placed a strong emphasis on 'bush' pursuits, especially hiking, camping, fieldcraft and tracking. There were no venues for such activities in our part of town. Instead, in working class areas, the most popular youth organisation was the Boys Brigade. Unlike the Scouts, members of the BB didn't have to buy an expensive uniform. All that was required was a hat, rather like a hotel page boy's cap, and an armband. The Boys Brigade had a religious/military basis, and parade ground style drill was carried out in parks and in the streets. But I never joined. I got enough religious instruction at Sunday School and the Band of Hope, essentially a temperance organisation. Before I was thirteen I think I had signed the pledge about six times in front of different preachers. When a lad did this he received a bottle of soft drink and a bag of buns as a reward.

At eleven, my favourite books were the Biggles series by Capt. W E John. I liked his first half dozen books best, starting with *Biggles of the Camel Squadron*, and *The Camels Are Coming*. The early stories were read as much by adults as boys. Although they were set during the Great War, they didn't glorify fighting. Instead, they had a 'futility of war' tone. During World War II, the Biggles books became particularly popular and were churned out rapidly to meet demand. They became formula adventure stories with an aviation background, aimed purely at boys. Like many fictional heroes, Biggles, Algy, Ginger and co. became ageless stereotypes.

My boyhood reading taste was mainly confined to light fiction; there was plenty of kitchen sink realism in my daily life, and I didn't need to read about it too. But I did read John Steinbeck's *Grapes of Wrath*, which made me realise that there were people worse off than us. In a lighter vein, P G Wodehouse was a favourite and I read everything he wrote. Another humorous writer of the time was Joan Butler, who I'm sure was really a man. His/her novels were more risqué than most readily available books. I also enjoyed detective stories by Edgar Wallace and Agatha Christie, as well as Leslie Charteris' early Saint stories.

I read some heavier stuff too, ranging from Jules Verne to J B Priestly. Prizes for coming top in English, of which I won several, were always books—mostly classics. Once I won a copy of *Les Miserables* and I still have it, but have never opened it. I rarely read the classics in my free time as I often had to study them at school.

One of my schooltime successes arose from my knowledge of the works of Dickens. In Glasgow there was an annual Dickens contest for junior and senior schoolchildren. There was a preliminary judging process at each school, based on pupils' essay writing skills. The two pupils who came top went on to represent their school at the Dickens Contest, and I was selected as our school's junior representative.

The set book for the contest was *David Copperfield*, and I was expected to read it through several times in preparation for the contest. After a month of swotting up on David C, my fellow competitors and I were given the day off school to sit the test. There were several hundred pupils from all over the Scottish Lowlands and we assembled in the vast examination room of Glasgow University. Our set paper consisted of several roneoed pages covering every aspect of the novel.

The exam lasted for over four hours, with a break half way through. Some weeks later I was advised I had come second in the Junior section—quite a triumph. No schoolboy from Grove Street had ever won anything of note, and I even got my name in the papers. My prize was the complete works of Charles Dickens, which looked somewhat out of place in our tenement kitchen where there were never usually any books on display. But my glittering trophy suffered the same fate as anything of value I tried to preserve in a household with four small children prone to playing with my possessions. Eventually many of Dickens' works were scrawled all over with crayon and generally trashed. The books were printed on a softish paper and some pages vanished when the family visited our communal lavatory. Standard toilet paper usually consisted of cut up squares of newspaper threaded with string and hung in the lavatory. As for *David Copperfield*, in spite of the thorough cramming I undertook, I can't remember the name of a single character today, apart from David.

One book that I avoided in my youth appeared about 1935 and was widely read by Glaswegians, amongst whom it became a classic. *No Mean City* was a harrowing tale of Glasgow slum life. Its authors, A McArthur and H Kingsley Long were journalists on a Glasgow paper and their story of the city's notorious razor gangs caused an uproar. Residents of the city's better areas were incensed by the grim picture the book painted of

Glasgow—a city then proudly labelled the second city of the Empire. But we knew that the squalid lifestyle *No Mean City* portrayed was grimly accurate. I forced myself to read it when I was about eleven. I read it again in my twenties, and it is still read today by people who marvel that anyone could have lived in such circumstances in a major British city. As a boy, reading *No Mean City* was very painful. I preferred my reading to be much less factual—and set anyplace except in grimy Glasgow.

I was generally an indiscriminate reader, and apart from boys' papers and adventure stories, I read every general magazine I could lay my hands on. The more expensive periodicals could be got at public libraries, and I became a regular reader of titles such as *Punch, Time & Tide*, the *Illustrated London News* and *Country Life*. The greatest appeal of *Country Life* was the section listing prestige properties for sale. I avidly read every word of estate agents' descriptions boasting 'twenty four room Georgian manor house set in three hundred acres of rolling Perthshire country. Separate servants' and chauffeurs' quarters above five car garage. Excellent fly fishing in river watering estate. Some rough shooting'. As a member of a family of seven who existed in one room and kitchen in a tenement, I found it fascinating to read about people in Scotland who lived in such homes—the Laird of the Manor probably even wore a kilt. In Glasgow at that time any civilian who wore a kilt was laughed at. Traditional dress was for daft Highlanders.

As well as getting my weekly stately homes fix through the prestige magazines, I also read many daily papers. We couldn't afford to take a daily paper on a regular basis, but I usually managed to scrounge one from outside the newsagent's. The thirties were the heyday of newspaper promotional contests, which often involved cutting and saving coupons. Multiple entries were permissible, but a coupon was needed for each one. Avid contest enterers would often buy several copies of the same paper, then rip out the coupon page, throwing away the rest of the paper outside the newsagents. That was how I managed to acquire at least one free paper every day.

For my age, and our social strata, I was well versed in current affairs. I avidly followed the rise of the Nazis in Germany, Italy's invasion of Abyssinia and the Spanish Civil War. My mother often used me as a reference source when an argument developed with her friends, concerning a date or some other fact.

In June 1939, when I was twelve, a major news story concerned the British submarine, *Thetis* which sank in Liverpool Bay on its trials. The crew were trapped and the drama continued for several days while divers tried to rescue them. Four sailors did survive by using the Davis Submarine Escape Apparatus, but the other ninety-nine perished. I became a walking encyclopaedia on submarines and escape methods. I memorised details of newspaper drawings and technical reports, and I can still recall every aspect of the *Thetis* tragedy. When it was finally raised, the *Thetis* was re-named the *Thunderbolt* and saw service with the Royal Navy until it was lost with all hands off Sicily in 1943. I often wondered how the crew reacted to serving in the death ship which had received so much gruesome publicity.

In Ayr I often read until late at night. Candles and candlesticks were in common use at the time and much of my reading was done clandestinely by candlelight after I was supposed to be asleep. I shielded the candle so its light wouldn't show under the door of the room where I slept, as my father wasn't above tiptoeing upstairs to try and catch me reading when I should have been asleep. But I had keen hearing, and when I heard a step on the creaking staircase I instantly doused the candle. By wetting my fingers and pressing the wick I avoided any tell-tale wisps of smoke, then thrust my book under the bedclothes and feigned sleep.

Like many children who read constantly, I began writing,

aiming, of course, to have my work published—and to earn money from it. In common with many aspiring writers, my first paid work was for items published in the children's pages of the daily newspapers. Contributions were often invited on a defined topic such as 'How I Spent My Holiday', and the usual prizes for winning articles were postal orders for a few shillings. I was eleven when I had my first item published in the Scottish *Daily Express*. I watched for the postman every day until the magic envelope addressed to Master A McRobbie arrived. It contained a postal order for two and sixpence, more money than I'd ever had to call my own, although as I'd expected, this was seized by my mother and instantly cashed. Two and six was deemed far too much money for a boy of my age to have, and by the end of the day it had been spent on essentials like food. I was allowed to keep tuppence.

I had several successes in the children's pages until by thirteen I was aiming at more adult publications. *Titbits* and *Answers* magazines ran many minor writing contests which paid up to a guinea for the best entries, and I was ecstatic when I won half a guinea for a hundred word snippet in *Titbits*. This ten and sixpence was given to my mother, and I was allowed to keep sixpence. Years later, in 1954, when I was working in London on *Womans Own*, the *Titbits* office was just along the corridor from where I worked. I told the editor that his paper had printed my first adult literary effort, and a friendship developed after which I gave him several contributions on a freelance basis. He accepted most of them and paid me the very satisfactory rate of five guineas for them.

By the time I was fourteen I had fairly regular acceptances from various magazines. I was working in an office by then, and had access to a typewriter which I quickly learned to use. Typing my contributions seemed to improve my success rate. I always used the office address when sending contributions, and as one of my duties was to collect the office mail from the post office twice a day, I could extract my personal letters before anyone else saw them. The prize money also came to the office, and I never told anyone in the family about my secret income as I knew my mother would have expected at least half of my occasional guineas. It was frustrating not to be able to reveal my literary successes and bask in the praise all new writers love to receive. But my mother was taking most of my weekly salary, so I felt no guilt about keeping these extra earnings. To avoid the chance of anyone seeing my byline in a magazine, I wrote under a pen-name.

By the time I reached twenty-one I was a full time journalist. Since then I have edited many different newspapers and magazines and earned my living mainly from some kind of writing.

FEAST AND FAMINE

After fornicating and gambling, prime pleasures of the poor were eating, drinking and smoking. Eating was a necessity, but the other four pastimes were held to be vices and were considered to be especially ruinous to the poor by the churches.

Our Glasgow diet was tasteless and monotonous. We only managed to get just enough food to keep body and soul together, with quite mundane foodstuffs considered luxuries in our household. For example, we couldn't afford to buy butter, although it was relatively cheap. In the days of Imperial Preference, produce from the British Empire sold in Scotland at very low prices, and New Zealand butter was the cheapest type, selling for even less than British butter. New Zealand lamb was another bargain, as was Australian tinned fruit, MacIntosh apples from Canada, British West African cocoa, and bananas and sugar from the British West Indies.

Instead of using butter, we spread our bread with tuppence-a-half-pound margarine. My mother, who had been brought up in rural Ayrshire where locally produced butter was cheap, didn't like margarine and as a very special treat would sometimes send me to get two ounces of butter. This was the smallest amount you could purchase. The grocer cut it from a large yellow block, using two wooden pats to shape it into a flat circle.

In the thirties, many foodstuffs were sold from bulk sources. Cheeses came in large blocks, and link sausages hung from hooks in long festoons from which the required quantity was cut off as requested. Bacon was sliced to order, and a loaf of bread could be cut in the same way; sugar was scooped from big hessian sacks, and tea was commonly measured from tea chests—although pre-packed tea was also available. Almost everything had to be weighed and packed. This was very labour intensive and it could take a long time to serve a customer. Most grocers' shops provided two or more high-backed chairs for women or elderly customers. Department stores did the same. Most traders also offered free home delivery as a matter of course, but the McRobbies couldn't wait long enough to have their shopping delivered. When we bought food it was needed immediately for the next meal; we had no well-filled larder to fall back on.

My mother hoarded her two ounce pat of butter and made it last for several days. It was for her exclusive use. Not even my father got any. When she used it she spread it thinly on a slice of bread then ate it plain, savouring its taste. But we never begrudged Mother her treat. Where food was involved, it was the only time she gave herself priority over her children and husband. When dishing up a meal she always served herself last, and sometimes she placed very little on her plate compared with what we got.

Although we were surrounded by an abundance of cheap produce from the greatest empire the world had ever known, we couldn't afford to buy more than bare subsistence amounts. Ironically, when World War II began we finally had enough money to buy more or less as much food as we wanted, although within a short time most foodstuffs were rationed— tea, for example, being limited to two ounces per week per adult. However, in spite of rationing, we ate better than we ever had before when we moved to Ayr at the beginning of the war. Locally caught fish was plentiful, and although eggs were rationed we kept hens so usually had plenty. At my grandmother's house my uncles tended a large vegetable garden. They grew potatoes, carrots, turnips, cabbage, cauliflower, broad beans, peas, and that essential of our desserts—rhubarb.

To us children, sweets or puddings were the best part of a meal. These included semolina, jelly, curds and whey—and stewed rhubarb. The rhubarb was doled out until it almost filled a plate then, if we were lucky, some custard was poured over it too. To me, this made it bearable. On Sundays, we usually got that much-anticipated treat—ice cream, to go on top of our rhubarb.

In those days a family bought its ice cream by taking a suitable sized jug to the shop. There it was filled with anything from three to sixpence worth of ice cream, to which the shopkeeper added a liberal splash of raspberry flavouring. As we had no refrigeration or icebox in our home, the ice cream was purchased at the end of the main course. In Ayr, the cheapest and best place to buy it was an Italian-run shop in Main Street and, jug in hand, I would be despatched to fetch it. I ran all the way to the shop, and especially fast coming back in summer, because the ice cream melted very quickly. I never objected to performing this chore because as the ice cream melted the liquid sank to the bottom of the jug, and I'd stop once or twice on the way back to drink off what had melted. This left the surface untouched, which fooled my mother, who always inspected the jug to check if I'd stuck a finger into it and scooped some out.

The habit of thrift was ingrained in my mother, and although we lived quite high on the hog in Ayr we still bought everything as cheaply as possible. One local baker opened at eight o'clock on Monday mornings instead of the usual time of nine. During this hour he sold everything that hadn't been bought by the close of business on Saturday afternoon. As the shop didn't open on Sundays, the goods were getting stale by Monday morning and were unsaleable at the regular price. This Monday morning sale was never advertised, but before eight o'clock there was always a long queue of women waiting to get in. Everything was very cheap. Delicacies like meringues, which normally cost threepence, went for a halfpenny. All kinds of cakes, scones and buns were sold for a fraction of the normal price, and although the goods were known as 'hard baps', they were quite edible. Queueing up and buying as many hard baps as I could get for a shilling was my regular Monday morning chore.

In spite of rationing, many working class Scots were better fed during the war years than they had been in peacetime. Most large factories or industrial complexes introduced subsidised canteens for their workers, and at Ayr Slipway, where I started work at fourteen, a three course lunch could be had for threepence. Many towns opened what were called British Restaurants—government subsidised canteens where nutritious meals were sold at close to cost. This was intended to maintain the population's health so that the war effort could continue with gusto.

While people ate reasonably well in spite of rationing, they fared much worse when it came to drinking. One of the ironies of wartime was that Scotch whisky became scarcer in Scotland than it was almost anywhere else in the world; even English pubs and spirit merchants seemed to be better supplied than their Scottish equivalents. This scarcity of Scotch arose because most whisky was exported to the U.S.A. as part payment for essential goods and war materials. The huge Johnnie Walker distillery at Kilmarnock was only a few miles from Ayr, but that didn't make it any easier for local people to get Scotch. Instead, some shockingly immature whiskies, with names like Old McSporran, were hastily produced to satisfy domestic demand, but even this firewater quickly sold out. However, we were better off for whisky than most households, mainly due to my quasi-black market activities, and I kept my uncles and father fairly well supplied with good proprietary brands which I procured from contacts at work.

At the time, whisky was endowed with medicinal properties in Scotland. When babies were teething and in pain, they were often given a toddy to soothe them. After my grandmother suffered the fall which confined her to bed for the last seven years of her life, her doctor prescribed a 'wee dram' to be taken once a day after her evening meal. Grandma, a God-fearing Presbyterian woman, had never touched alcohol in her life. Reputedly non-alcoholic ginger wine was her strongest tipple and she only took that at New Year.

Because whisky was very hard to procure, the doctor actually wrote out a prescription to our licensed grocer stating that Mrs Hewitt was entitled to one bottle of Scotch a week for medicinal purposes. Grandma drank the whisky only because it had been prescribed. At first she didn't like it and took it with hot water and sugar, like babies did, but she quickly weaned herself on to drinking it neat until her after-dinner dram became the high spot of her day.

My father's favourite brand of Scotch was Haig's, because the firm was owned by the family of Field Marshall the Earl Haig, who had been his commander-in-chief in France during the Great War. Although Haig was later revealed to be a military blunderer and architect of the unnecessary slaughter of untold British troops, my father's loyalty to his old C-in-C never wavered.

During our years in Glasgow, a bottle of whisky was a rarity in our home, but when my father did procure one it was always Haig's. At 12/6 he couldn't afford to buy it. He claimed he never actually stole a bottle, and that the whisky was 'a gift' he received in the course of his work as a horse and cart driver. One of his regular delivery jobs was carting cases of Scotch from John Haig's depot to the docks where they were loaded onto ships for export. At the time, whisky was packed in well-made wooden cases of a dozen bottles, with each bottle placed in its own slot and covered with a stitched straw jacket.

At the docks, the quantity of cases on my father's cart was carefully checked before they were signed over to the dockers, who then suggested that he go and have a cup of tea while they unloaded the whisky. When he retired to a watchman's hut for tea, the dockers piled the cases into a sling suspended from a big crane. As the slingful of cases was raised high above the ground, the crane driver 'accidentally' jolted his load against part of the ship so that the corner of one case was 'sprung' and a single bottle of whisky slid out, falling into the sure hands of a waiting worker. When the load was stacked in the ship's hold the pressure closed the case and the shortage went undiscovered until the consignment reached its destination.

My father was well aware of how the pilfering was done because it happened with every load of Haig's. When his cart had been unloaded he would find a bottle of whisky wrapped in newspaper in the harness box under his driver's seat. He said he got it for 'looking the other way', and as far as he was concerned he had delivered his load intact. Once signed over, it was no longer his responsibility, and the bottle of whisky in his cart was a 'pleasant surprise'.

Whenever my father had some money he drank heavily. He rarely drank at home, preferring the pub around the corner, and sticking mainly to beer which was cheaper than spirits. The pub was a dreadful place. At closing time drunks staggered into the street and, almost to a man, urinated against the wall of our building. The pub didn't have a lavatory, and although passing women berated the men for behaving like 'dirty beasts', that didn't deter them. They often turned from the wall to wave their penises at the women, inviting them to 'give it a squeeze'. Few women in our neighbourhood were shocked when a man exposed himself to them. They were used to the sight of drunken men and small boys peeing in the street.

As was common in working class parts of the city, women

126

were not admitted to the Grove Street 'Public House'. Even if they had been, only a real slag would have ventured into such a den of iniquity, where the floor was covered in sawdust to make it easier to sweep out if a patron vomited. I had read about the civilised English pubs where pork pies were served, people played darts and there was community singing. In Glasgow pubs, notices sternly forbade singing. As for food, all that was available were salted herrings, which were free, but which made thirsty patrons drink more beer.

Glasgow pubs opened from eleven until three when by law they had to close, re-opening from five until ten. Outside these hours, and especially on Sundays when the pubs were shut all day, people who wanted to drink did so at illegal 'shebeens', or sly grog houses. These really were disreputable places, often only one room in a tenement house. The beer and spirits were watered and the prices were high, but the shebeens were the only places where a working man could drink and find some conviviality outside legal licensing hours.

My father was a bad drunk, and his homecoming after a night on the booze was dreaded by my mother and I. Sometimes he went straight to the pub on his way home from work, especially on Friday nights when he had his pay packet, and if he wasn't home by six thirty my mother would know he'd dropped in for a drink. His pay was always desperately needed to buy food for the night's meal, and she would be terrified that he might spend too much money while out with his boozy mates. I was usually despatched to stick my head round the pub door and ask a helpful drinker if he could find Mr McRobbie because his wife wanted him to come home. Children weren't allowed to go into pubs, but could push the swing door open and try to attract someone's attention.

If my father wasn't too far gone, he usually came home reluctantly. On some occasions he would come to the pub door and give me a pound note, half of his pay, to take to my mother.

She dreaded this because it meant there was a good chance that he'd drink the remainder of his wages and not stagger home until after ten.

Between drinking and smoking, my father accounted for a good part of his pay. He was a heavy smoker—going through forty a day of his favourite brand, Capstan, when he could afford it. They cost a shilling for twenty, and when he had no cigarettes he was like 'a bear with a sore head' (my mother's description). She never smoked, nor did most of the women of her generation. It wasn't considered ladylike. In Scotland, only 'tarts' smoked, although it was accepted that film actresses could get away with it without losing status.

My father had started smoking at fourteen when he was a boy soldier in the regular army. He told me that when he was in the trenches in France a cigarette was often a soldier's only comfort. Certainly he seemed to suffer agonies when he didn't have any cigarettes. Although he preferred Capstan, when money was short he reluctantly bought Woodbines, which only cost fourpence for ten, or tuppence for a paper packet of five. To cater for the lowest income group there were vending machines in Glasgow from which you could buy two Woodbines and two matches—for a penny.

Like my father, I began smoking at fourteen when I started my first job, and continued for fifty two years, before finally giving up with the aid of nicotine patches. Along with most boys my age I started smoking because it was supposedly a sign of adulthood. There was no anti-smoking campaign in those days. On the contrary, that powerful influence, the movies, constantly encouraged people to smoke. When I was only ten or eleven, my friends and I often 'smoked' cinnamon sticks. We all wanted to look like our favourite cowboy hero, who usually had a cigarette hanging from his lips while he nonchalantly plugged the baddie in a smoke-filled saloon.

A WEE FLUTTER

A disproportionate amount of my father's weekly wage was spent on having 'a wee flutter'. Gambling played a big part in the lives of the Glasgow poor, and wasn't indulged in purely as recreation, although it filled many hours of the punters' time. The main function of betting was to maintain the *hope* of one day striking it rich and winning enough money to get out and start a better life. Most people were morosely resigned to the fact that their income from working was never likely to earn them enough money to provide anything more than the bare necessities, and their ultimate aim was to leave enough money for a decent burial. The spectre of a pauper's grave haunted many of the elderly and impoverished who had no relatives, or whose kin were too poor to pay the cost of a funeral.

In our house the Goddess of Luck was wooed through the football pools and horse-racing. From their two pounds a week income, my parents probably spent about ten shillings on the pools and horses. This pushed the family budget below the breadline, but the hope of a big win kept my optimistic mother going, and gave her the strength to face another week of struggling to make ends meet.

The churches and the well-to-do railed against the sin of gambling, criticising working class people who spent up to half of their meagre income on the pools and horses. Indeed, most gamblers would have been much better off had they not wagered so much, or anything at all, but in their dreary lives gambling was an important source of hope and conversation.

Discussing the chances of various football teams and racehorses took up hours of time in the lives of my parents and our neighbours. Quite heated arguments often developed as the merits of teams and jockeys were analysed. My father and mother were quite different in their style of betting. He carefully studied the form—of teams, horses and jockeys—then wagered accordingly. She bet on horses whose names she liked, or who were riding under an auspicious number which she read from her teacup. When selecting football teams, she literally used a darning needle to pierce the back of the coupon before inking in the squares the pin went through.

Wednesday night was pools night, and it followed an almost religious ritual. After the evening meal the kitchen table was cleared then covered with my father's football reference material, which included old newspaper cuttings, placings in the soccer league 'ladder', newspaper forecasts, and various statistical tables which he kept in exercise books. He would start work at about seven o'clock and at eleven was often still deciding how to mark his coupon. His wager of 3/6 was despatched in the form of a postal order. The entry had to be mailed and be postmarked by first post next day, but by this stage in the week our family finances were seriously depleted. Reserving 3/6 for the postal order, plus the penny ha'penny stamp wasn't easy. Sometimes, to get money for the postage, I would be despatched to one of the small 'open all hours' shops where we could make purchases on tick. There were about four such shops where we maintained a precarious credit rating. From one of these I would buy two bottles of skimmed milk at twopence each, with a penny refund on each bottle. I took the milk home and my mother emptied it into a jug, rinsing out the bottles which I then took to another shop which sold stamps. Here I traded the bottles for a stamp and ha'penny change, a technique that I often used when we needed a penny for the gas meter.

After the football coupon was safely posted, my parents'
conversation on Thursday and Friday nights centred on what
they would do if they had a big win. A house with a garden was
their first priority. Good furniture, a set of china crockery that
matched, new clothes for us all, a larder stuffed with food,
repayment of all debts including the redemption of everything
that was permanently pawned, and that unobtainable dream—
a motor car, all featured highly too. I must say my parents were
very generous as they spent their pending fortune. They agreed
I could have a Hornby train set, a Meccano set and a chemistry
set; really big ones costing about five pounds.

'Aye,' my mother assured me many times, 'things will be
different when our boat comes in.' That was one of her favourite
sayings, but she died still waiting for her ship to dock.

On Saturday afternoons, after the English and Scottish
football matches had been played and the results were
announced, the business of checking the coupon began. This
rarely took very long, and usually ended with my father thrusting
away his duplicate copy muttering something like: 'Who could
believe that Hibernian could beat the Rangers—and away from
home too!' If the Rangers, a top of the league team, had beaten
lowly-ranked Hibs, then my father would have had his 'Four
Aways' up.

The biggest pools win my father ever had was when he
correctly forecast eight teams to draw. While we waited for the
dividends to be announced on Monday, the McRobbie
household lived in a state of euphoria such as number 91 had
never before experienced. Dividends varied widely, according
to how many correct forecasts there were, but the eight draws
usually paid close to a thousand pounds, and sometimes more.
The mental spending spree went on all weekend. News quickly
spread around our building that Willie McRobbie had made a
big win, and that the McRobbies were going to be rich. A

thousand quid—that was ten years' wages! Neighbours swarmed into our small kitchen all Saturday night and Sunday. They expected to be given a drink to celebrate the McRobbies' good luck, and in view of his forthcoming fortune, my father had no difficulty in borrowing a couple of pounds, then another couple and another. This was spent on bottles of whisky, crates of beer, port for the ladies, fizzy drinks for the kids, and meat pies, fish and chips, and cakes and buns of all kinds. Our house had never seen such a lavish celebration.

On Monday, the dividends were announced. It was a near calamity, with the eight draws paying only twelve pounds ten shillings per winning coupon, the lowest pay-out ever. Hundreds of people had correctly forecast the results so the winners' pool was thinly spread. By Monday my father had borrowed more than eight pounds, so when his cheque finally arrived, he had less than four left. I felt very sorry for my parents, whose dreams of a new life were dashed. It was back to the harsh reality of struggling to make ends meet.

Betting on the horses was confined to Saturdays, when my father had money in his pocket after being paid on Friday. The bets were laid at an illegal bookmaker's, protected by a network of men who kept their eyes peeled for any appearance by the police. The shop wasn't far from our house, so for most of Saturday my father went back and forth across the road. When he had a win, payment was immediate, but he usually used the money to bet on another horse. While in the house, he pored over the *Noon Record* form guide before writing out his next bet.

It was a rare occasion when he ended up ahead from his Saturday wagers. As he spent more and more money and kept on losing, he became very bad-tempered, and I learned to give him a wide berth on Saturday nights. If the Saturday football match results showed that he had lost there too, then he could become quite dangerous, stalking off to the pub and spending more of the dwindling family income on beer to console himself for his losses. I used to dread his homecoming on Saturday nights after the pubs closed. Huddled in bed with my small brothers in the front room I listened tensely to the dreadful yelling and screaming as he picked a fight with my mother.

When my mother was getting a belting I rarely had the courage to go into the kitchen and interfere. On the few occasions I did so, I got a vicious kick and was told to fuck off. Sometimes after a beating my mother would creep into the front room, sobbing, with Jean in her arms, and come into bed with us. It was hard to sleep under such circumstances.

Oddly, the next day my parents usually made things up. My father would be very attentive to my mother and quite gentle with us kids, and during Sunday the two of them would engage in lengthy post-mortems about their betting. 'I should have backed Blue Blazes,' my father would say. 'I was going to back him, but the form guide put me off. He came in at twelve to one!'

My mother backed the horses too, but her bets were much more modest than father's, usually thruppence a time. She seemed to win more often than he did, and her biggest return came after a successful 'threepenny roll-up'. This involved picking six winners in six consecutive races. As each horse came in, her threepence and the odds it paid were then automatically placed on the next race and so on. Amazingly, my mother picked six winners, and her accumulated total was over eight pounds—four weeks' wages for my father. On that Saturday night it was fish and chips for the McRobbies, and on Monday the factor was delighted to receive four weeks back rent.

This roll-up win and my father's pools success were the largest sums I can remember my parents winning in Glasgow. When we moved to Ayr the Saturday betting continued, and as we were better off than we had been before my parents' bets rose accordingly. My Uncles Tom and Alec (when he was home from sea), also bet lavishly.

When Alec first got home after a long period at sea, he was very flush because he had had little opportunity to spend his accumulated pay, and he wagered sums as large as ten shillings. Consequently when he did win, he won large amounts. The betting shop in Ayr, not far from Green Street, was a sleazy little smoke-filled dive patronised by weedy, furtive looking men with cigarettes hanging from the corners of their mouths. A radio blared constantly with the yammering sound of a commentator whose voice grew more and more hysterical as the horses neared the winning post. I haven't placed more than five bets on horses in my lifetime and have visited race-tracks even less often. For me, the 'sport of kings' has never had any appeal; seeing what it did to my parents gave me a 'fair scunner' for gambling.

The other type of gambling my parents indulged in was playing cards; a particularly cheap form of recreation. Even the poorest home had at least one pack of cards. In Glasgow we had two, but they were so badly marked that we could usually tell the cards by looking at their backs, which gave us a considerable advantage over visitors to our home. This was particularly useful when playing for money, which my parents often did. Their favourite game was Pontoon, which had been a popular game in the army where my father had become quite skilled at it, and on Friday nights (pay night) some neighbours would usually meet at our place to make up a 'school' of up to eight players. Bets were rarely more than a penny, and a ha'penny was more common. My father was more successful at Pontoon than at other types of gambling, and although his winnings were never great, they could reach three or four shillings, with only fairly modest losses.

When we moved to Ayr the card playing became more upmarket. My uncles were keen Whist players and my mother was good too, and occasionally, when only three adults were available, I was asked to sit in and take a hand. But I was never keen on Whist, and invariably earned the disapproval and scorn of my partner. In the boring and lengthy post mortems which took place after each hand, one of the adults tried to teach me the technique of playing the right card at the right time and avoiding throwing away trumps. But the game didn't interest me. I would much preferred to have been reading a book.

EARNING ONE'S KEEP

A boy from a poor family was expected to start working and earning his keep from quite a young age. When we moved from Glasgow to Ayr in August 1939, I had four jobs which I held down while also attending secondary school. From these jobs I earned a total income of eighteen shillings and sixpence—just short of a pound. This was a substantial sum and my father's wage for a forty-eight hour week was exactly two pounds, the average for a labouring man. When I left school at fourteen and began full time work, my weekly salary was 12/6—six shillings less than my part time jobs had brought me.

In Glasgow I didn't work before or after school because I couldn't ride a bike. Hardly any boys in our social strata owned one, so there was no chance to learn on a friend's machine. But to get work as any kind of delivery boy the ability to ride a pushbike was essential, and so the only income I earned was from doing errands for elderly or infirm ladies who lived on the higher floors of our tenement. Their method of contacting me was to wait until I was playing in the communal yard then call down for me to come up and see them, because they wanted me to 'run a wee message'.

I would climb the stairs and be given a written shopping list, plus enough money to pay for the goods. The purchases ranged from loaves of bread to cigarettes. I was a good runner and a quick and efficient shopper, with a keen eye for a bargain, and I often bought things at a price lower than my client had allowed for. In such cases I scrupulously declared the saving and gave it to the housewife in her change. My clients didn't have to wait long before I was back, panting, with their messages, and my reward could be anything from a penny to threepence, depending on the size and weight of the order. Through time, because I was regarded as 'an honest lad', I built up a fair clientele. The canny Scotswomen only gave their money and orders to a lad they knew and trusted, as a strange boy could take their money and that might be the last they'd see of him. In our area there were many boys who would have taken the money before vanishing forever.

I never got any pocket money, and the cash I earned from running messages was my sole source of income. My mother was well aware of these earnings, which I never tried to conceal from her. If I came home with threepence she automatically took twopence from me. Sometimes I was allowed to keep the difference, but often she'd take the whole lot because she needed it to help with the household's precarious finances.

During our annual stay at Grandma's house in Ayr, I earned a small but steady income from 'following the horses'. This involved collecting dung from the streets and bringing it home, where it was unloaded into a big round iron vat in the garden. Water was added to it, and eventually it turned into stinking liquid manure, which was poured over the flower beds and around the fruit trees. Uncle Tom, a keen gardener, paid me a penny for each load of horse manure I collected. The vehicle I used for this was a large packing case mounted between two bicycle wheels and steered by a pram handle. My handymen uncles built this wagon for general carrying purposes, and as it could hold a large quantity of dung I had to work hard to earn my penny.

I took a shovel with me, then set off to look for horse droppings. There were still many horse-drawn vehicles around at that time—mainly delivery carts carrying milk, bread, and coal—but nonetheless collecting a barrowload of dung could take up to two hours. Of course, I wasn't the only person scouring the streets for horse dung as there was keen competition for the prized manure. Often two barrow pushers followed the same horse and cart, waiting for the horse to drop its load, which could lead to a mad scramble to see who could shovel fastest.

A more salubrious money-earning project was finding and selling lost golf balls. There were major golf courses at Ayr and nearby Prestwick, and small boys of my age knew every inch of these, especially the spots where balls were most likely to be lost. We would hang around the edge of the fairways until a golfer sliced a ball into the trees, then on the pretext of helping to find it, we'd sprint ahead of the plus-foured golfers, laden with their heavy bags. Our keen eyes usually located their ball, but instead of shouting that we'd got it, we'd 'accidentally' press it firmly into the ground. It wasn't done just to lift a ball then run away with it, and we'd soon have been banned from the course had we done that, so we strolled around looking helpful while the golfer searched in vain. But after he gave up and moved on, we would return and collect the prized ball.

An excellent place to find lost balls was on a part of the course which involved negotiating a deep gully through which a burn ran. The bottom of the burn was covered with white pebbles, many the size of and shape of a golf ball. We'd wait near it until a pair or foursome arrived then hit out. It was rare when one of their balls didn't plop into the burn, and when the golfers appeared and began peering into the water, they'd ask if we'd seen where it went. We always protested that we didn't know, but of course our hawk eyes knew precisely where the missing ball lay.

One way and another we collected up to a dozen balls at a time, and took these to the club professional's shop where the shopkeeper bought them for a penny apiece. New golf balls cost sixpence, and the shop sold lost balls for threepence, so everybody was happy. Even golfers who ended by buying back their own balls!

During our long summer stay in Ayr, there were more money-earning possibilities than in Glasgow. Apart from being a seaside resort, Ayr was a busy fishing port and home to many deep sea trawlers and Seine Netters, smaller vessels which usually went out for one night at a time and caught herring. At the harbour, boats unloaded their cargo using their derricks to raise the large baskets of fish from the hold. As the cargo was lowered to the dockside, some fish usually spilled from the top onto the ground, and by darting between the rubber-booted feet of the fishermen, small boys like me could grab one or two fish each time a basket was landed. Generally, the fishermen tolerated our scavenging. They never picked up spilled fish themselves, and instead kicked them into the water where hordes of screaming seagulls swooped on them.

On a good morning, it was possible to scavenge as many as three or four dozen herring, which we threaded onto strings by their mouths in lots of a dozen. We then went to the beach, offering our herring for sale at sixpence a dozen. As the same fish cost at least a shilling a dozen in the shops, and additionally the purchasers could be certain that our fish were fresh, we usually found ready buyers for our catch. By the vagaries of the traditional marketing and distribution system, most of Ayr's fish was sent by train to Glasgow, even though after being marketed there some found its way back to the fishmongers in Ayr, where it retailed for more than it cost in Glasgow. I often sold large mackerel to a local fishmonger for a penny a fish, which he then resold for threepence a pound.

I became a herring scavenger from about age eight, and usually gave the money I earned to my mother, although as I got older I started keeping sixpence back for myself. I always brought a dozen herring home, and often some larger mackerel which had spilled from the trawlers' baskets. In our house, the cleaned and gutted herring were fried after being spread flat and coated with oatmeal.

After I turned eleven I stopped eating herring, or any kind of fish, after choking on a fish bone because I was gulping my food down too fast. I was certain I was going to die of asphyxiation until my mother thrust her fingers down my throat and plucked the sharp bone out, but my lacerated throat and gullet were painful for weeks after. To this day I cannot eat fish without minutely inspecting it to make sure it has no bones.

When we moved to Ayr I quickly learned to ride a bicycle as I had several friends who were bike owners. I couldn't afford to buy one myself, even though second hand bikes were available for about thirty shillings, but in most delivery jobs the employer supplied a special bike for work use, fitted with front and back carriers. The space inside the frame carried a metal plate, signwritten on both sides with the trader's name and address.

When I was twelve I got my first job delivering morning papers. It was one of the newsagent's longest runs, which was one reason why I got the job—nobody else was keen on doing the Seafield run, which paid no more than the shorter rounds. Seafield was a wealthy beachside suburb of Ayr, heavily populated by Jewish people, and flippantly known as the 'Holy City'. The homes there were mainly two or three bedroom bungalows, with houses standing in their own front and back gardens. My customers were affluent, and took more papers and magazines per household than the average home did, as well as substantial quantities of the weekly *Jewish News*. Although the name of the business I worked for was McFarlane and Co, the partners who ran it were both Jewish, Messrs. Cowan and Shirren. Cowan was a common Scottish name, and the change from Cohen wasn't a big one, so many Jewish Scots with that name called themselves Cowan. But both my bosses had been born in Scotland and spoke with broad Scots. I never noticed any anti-Semitism in Ayr, and my customers were considerably more generous than the average Scot. At Christmas time, or more commonly on New Year's Day, delivery boys usually received a tip in appreciation of their year's service, the average being about a shilling. But from my Jewish customers I rarely received less than half a crown, so my Christmas bonus came to several pounds.

I always gave good service, and newspapers and magazines were never tossed into a front garden. Instead I dismounted at each gate, running up to the covered porch where I laid the papers on the tiles, covering them with the doormat so they wouldn't blow away. In wet weather I rode the bike dressed in oilskins and a sou'wester. My papers were covered with oilskin too.

The Seafield run was a long and exhausting one, but I didn't mind doing it because I was getting to ride a bike, which I loved, even though my heavy delivery model was scarcely a Raleigh Sportster. The trip out from the shop was an easy one, because the wind was usually behind me. On my return I had to pedal against the wind, which was hard work, and during the frequent gales it was impossible for me to get back in time for school at nine. On such occasions one of the partners took me and my papers in his car and I hopped in and out, making the deliveries.

We weren't allowed to take our bikes home as they were needed by the evening paper boys. So I added an after-school paper run to my pre-school one. This earned me an extra three shillings a week, and as not too many homes had an evening paper delivered the run wasn't a long one. But the partners were still dubious about letting me take a bike home, until finally I made them an offer they couldn't refuse.

The English papers, printed in London, arrived in Ayr at six am every morning. Our bundle was thrown from the moving train, so somebody had to be at the station to pick them up and take them downtown to the shop. The partners took turns doing this by car, but Ayr Station lay on the route I took to work at six thirty each morning. I offered to collect the London papers at six and bring them to the shop—if I could take the bike home and have permanent use of it, seven days a week. The partners agreed, and in addition paid me an extra three shillings a week for starting early and collecting the *Daily Mirrors* and *Daily Sketches* from the station.

At that time, 1939 and part of 1940, we were living in half of a bungalow in Hilary Crescent, one of Ayr's better areas. We'd been accepted as private evacuees by an elderly widower who'd heeded the government's appeal for rural people to take in families from the cities, which might become the target of German bombs. As such we paid rent to the house owner, although we received a small government subsidy. In 1940 my father moved from Glasgow to join us, and he too stayed at Hilary Crescent before we all moved into my grandmother's house in Green Street.

During our Hilary Crescent days I was up at five-thirty, six mornings a week, to make my breakfast before pedalling to the shop (via the station) where I had to assemble the papers and magazines for my round. I usually finished around eight fifteen and cycled home for a proper breakfast cooked by my mother. Then I changed into my uniform and set off for school. I didn't use the shop bike to cycle to school, as most pupils had their own bikes, and I didn't know of anyone else at Ayr Grammar who had a paper run. I would have been embarrassed to park my battered delivery bike beside their gleaming speedsters.

Getting up at five thirty on cold Scottish winter mornings was never pleasant, and in December and January snow and sleet were commonplace. I awoke when my alarm clock went off, long before anyone else in the house had to get up. There was no point in lighting a fire because I would be leaving before it was hot enough to give any warmth. I had a cup of strong tea and a slice of bread and jam for breakfast, and although the tea was warming, I felt the need for something that would put a glow in my stomach.

I was thirteen when I developed a taste for whisky, purely to warm my belly when I cycled off into the bleak Scottish winter to begin my paper round. In Ayr we were better off than we had been in Glasgow, partly because of my financial contribution, and my father usually kept a bottle of Haig's in the sideboard, although it was reserved for special occasions, and for visitors. Before six o'clock in the morning, when nobody was awake, I poured myself a small tot of the whisky, drinking it neat. I replaced it with enough water to bring its level back to where it had been. This led to it becoming very diluted, but my father never noticed when he had 'a wee dram', because he always drank whisky as a chaser after several beers. My Uncle Tom, however, was an experienced whisky drinker, and could actually tell one brand from another. One night he visited us at Hilary Crescent and my father poured him a large Scotch. Tom drank half of it then smirked, 'Haw, I see you're watering your whisky, Wullie.'

My father was mortally offended. To water one's whisky was unforgivable, and a publican caught doing such a thing faced a heavy fine. Willie McRobbie poured a dram for himself and tasted it. Luckily, he'd already had several glasses of heavy so his tastebuds were dulled, and he protested that it was alright. There was no way the whisky could have been watered. Who would do such a thing? My mother couldn't stand whisky, or beer. Her only tipple was port wine. 'There's only Jessie and the kids in the house,' he said.

His oldest kid—me—was sitting at the table doing his homework when this discussion took place. I kept my head down, drawing a map, but no suspicion fell on me, in spite of my red nose. However, from then on I went easy on the amount

I purloined from each bottle, and I must say I missed my early morning dram before leaving for work.

From my paper runs I earned 13/6, but there were other money-making opportunities to be had too. For an extra 2/6 I took on a Sunday paper run. This was fairly easy because the papers weren't delivered until after eight o'clock, so I had a long lie in bed, and apart from that, working on Sunday mornings got me out of having to attend church or Sunday School. However, in spite of doing substantial school homework, and working before and after school on weekdays and Sunday mornings, there was still some time which could be used to 'bring some money into the house' as my mother put it. I had most of Saturday free after my paper round, so I began working for a big grocer's shop, delivering groceries between ten and four. I got half a crown for this, which made me realise that my other employers were relatively generous. Of course, the newsagents recovered my cost by adding a delivery charge, whereas the grocer didn't charge for the service.

The bike supplied by the grocer was different from my newspaper delivery bike. It had a small front wheel, to allow a deep wire carrier which could hold the equivalent of four large cartons to be attached to it. The rear carrier wasn't quite as deep and could carry two cartons. When fully laden with groceries, it was hard work to pedal, and until I'd delivered some of the load it was easier to push it than ride it. Even grown men needed a lot of strength to propel a fully laden grocery bike at any kind of speed. For economy, people bought many things by the stone. Stones of potatoes, oatmeal and flour were common purchases, so one single order could easily weigh fifty-six pounds. Two orders like that loaded the bike with a hundredweight.

Most deliveries were to customers who lived on the top floors of two or three storey buildings, which was one good reason why they opted for delivery. In Ayr, few residential buildings were taller than three storeys, but none had a lift. In fact I doubt if *any* building in Ayr had a lift, and it was hard work dragging heavy cartons up flights of stairs.

One bonus from the grocery delivery job was that while the pay was lousy, the tips were quite good. To minimise the number of trips I made up the stairs, I carried as many cartons or paper bags as I could get my arms around. I think many householders took pity on the tall but scrawny thirteen-year-old lad who rang their bell then stood panting with their order on the doorstep.

Tips were usually a penny or tuppence, or occasionally a thruppenny bit. Threepence was the cinema admission price for a juvenile, so it bought a lot of entertainment. I never declared my tips to my mother, and had I done so, most of the money would have been confiscated and gone into the seemingly endless fund for 'running the hoose'. As it was, my mother took nearly all of the eighteen shillings and sixpence I earned, and I was only allowed to keep sixpence, which was considered sufficient pocket money for a young lad. I was quite proud of the amount I was contributing to our family of seven's meagre income, even before I was of working age. At the time, it was traditional for husbands or working sons living at home to give their entire pay packet to their wife or mother, who would then pay them a personal allowance. The household finances were always in the mother's hands, and it was she who bought the food, clothes and paid the rent. If you needed, say, a new pair of boots, you didn't buy them from your allowance. Instead, the money came from the household's funds which were disbursed on a 'neediest first' basis. Like many working class families, we had no savings account or reserve for a rainy day, and all the money that came into the house each week was spent before next pay day. Often we lived on credit during the two days before pay day when liquid funds had run out.

Anyway, as an income earner, I demanded and received many adult privileges, like staying up late, or having an occasional glass of beer. At that age, I hated the taste of beer, but drinking it was a 'manly' thing to do. And by keeping my grocery tips I had a secret weekly income of about two shillings. This made me nearly as well off as my affluent school chums, who got that much pocket money from their parents.

Looking back, I worked very hard until I was fourteen. But I never found my work a burden. Nor did I resent the fact that few of my school chums needed to find jobs to bring in money for their families. At that time, the Presbyterian work ethic was alive and thriving. Men—and boys—were born to work, and as my parents and uncles often said, 'Hard work never hurt anybody.' Today, I'm not sure if that is always true, but I have remained a workaholic nonetheless.

FATHER DEAR FATHER

During the Great War of 1914-18 my father served as an infantryman from the beginning of hostilities until the November 11th Armistice. Having been a soldier in the army before the war, he was one of the members of the British Expeditionary Force which first faced the German onslaught in France and Belgium. The Kaiser described the B.E.F. as 'a contemptible little army'. Later, the earliest British arrivals in France proudly called themselves 'the Old Contemptibles'.

As a boy, I grew up with names like Ypres, Mons, and the Somme—bloodstained battlegrounds on which millions of British, French and Germans perished in slaughterhouse conditions probably unequalled in any conflict before or after the Great War. There can be no doubt of my father's bravery in action. Early in the war he received rapid promotion to sergeant, although because of the high casualty rate, this was not unusual. His favourite war story, and the one of which he was proudest, concerned an incident which took place just after an unsuccessful assault on the German lines. His platoon commander told Sergeant McRobbie that the unit was to go into action again within the hour. Together, the lieutenant and sergeant entered a large dugout where the weary and battle-scarred soldiers were resting.

The officer's task was to give his men a pep talk after breaking the unwelcome news that they were shortly to 'go over the top' once more. As they entered the darkened dugout, a rifle shot rang out and a bullet buried itself in the timber which supported the dugout entrance, passing between my father and the officer. My father instantly leapt into the dugout, waving a large flashlight around the reclining men. 'All right!' he bellowed, 'Who shot at the officer?'

A weary Scots voice muttered, 'We werenae shooting at the fucking officer!'

My father was a stern disciplinarian and believed that non-commissioned officers were the backbone of the British Army. Commissioned officers had their place of course. They were the ones who went first and led the charges across No Man's Land, but it was the sergeants and corporals who maintained discipline and made the troops more afraid of their own NCOs than they were of the Germans. So when the 'Advance!' was sounded, the men followed their officer without hesitation. Any soldier who faltered or tried to take refuge in a shell-hole was not infrequently shot dead by one of his NCOs.

William McRobbie was only five feet tall, and during the war he became part of what was called the 'bantam battalion', a unit consisting of men no taller than this. When lining the trench parapets, there were some advantages in all the troops being about the same height. The firing steps on which they stood to fire their rifles could be cut into the trench at the same level. During a stand to, the men could rush to any part of the trench and be able to see over the top. Another of my father's favourite stories was how his unit of little men was often relieved by the Scots Guards—all soldiers six feet or taller. If the guardsmen stood on one of the bantam's firing steps, their heads and shoulders would be exposed to the German snipers. The big men pleaded with the little Scots to help them cut out a lower firing step before they departed. In winter, the ground was often frozen solid and it took much hacking with entrenching tools to make any impression on the rock-like earth. But on other occasions, the bantam battalion relieved the Scots

Guards. The little men had no hope of seeing over the parapet if they stood on the guardsmen's steps, and begged them to help them cut higher steps before they left.

As I said before, my father was a stern disciplinarian and was proud of the fact that his men hated him; something which he took as a tribute to his martinet style of discipline. To him, his men's loathing proved he was 'doing his duty'. While growing up in Glasgow I met some of his old comrades who had served under him in France. Oddly, they regarded him with great respect, apparently forgiving his harsh application of military regulations.

Another Great War story told how he went out into No Man's Land to rescue his company commander who had been wounded and left behind in a shell-hole after his unit was forced to retreat. My father got the captain back into the British trenches, from where he was carried back to a field hospital. The officer recovered, but was invalided out and returned to civil life.

In the thirties this man was a prominent and wealthy Glasgow businessman, and he never forgot my father's action, which undoubtedly saved his life. One of the brightest days in our calendar was Christmas Eve. Every year a van would pull up outside our house driven by a chauffeur in a brown uniform complete with peaked cap and leather leggings. He was from Coopers, an upmarket Glasgow grocery emporium roughly equivalent to Fortnum & Mason's in London, and he carried a large wicker hamper which he brought to our front door. This hamper, a gift from my father's former officer, contained unimaginable goodies. The delicacies included salmon in aspic, Gorgonzola cheese, Carr's biscuits, Crawford's shortbread, Keillor's marmalade, Tobler's Swiss chocolates, a large cooked ham, a Christmas cake and bon-bons. It must have cost at least five pounds, and as we unpacked the exotic goodies my mother would sigh, 'I wish he'd give us the money instead. What I could do with five pounds!'

The ex officer's generous gesture typified how out of touch the 'Gentry' were with the lifestyle of the poorer classes. Nonetheless, that 'gentleman' often helped my father out financially when things became desperate. He got work as a waiter at his club on one occasion, and when we were in dire straits my father would swallow his pride, don his good suit and go downtown to see his former OC at his office. He rarely returned without a couple of pounds to keep us going.

After the Great War ended, my father stayed on in the regular army, serving for a time in India with the Royal Scots Fusiliers First Battalion. He became a company sergeant major and boasted that on the parade ground he had the second loudest voice in the British Army. During his service in India, he learned some Urdu, and in Glasgow I grew up with Indian words like charpoy (bed); kip (sleep); dhobi (laundry); imshi (scram); jeldi (quickly); char (tea) and kybosh.

In 1926 my father's military career came to an abrupt end when he and thousands of other servicemen were retrenched for reasons of economy. He fairly quickly got a job with the London, Midland & Scottish Railway Company, driving a horse-drawn lorry which delivered goods from the railway depot to businesses in Glasgow. In his army days he had handled horses, and although he was a small man, he had a way with the huge Clydesdales which pulled the heavily laden carts. He was also very strong. In those days there were no fork lifts, and heavy crates and barrels had to be lifted by manpower alone. Quite often the lorry driver had to load and unload his vehicle on his own.

As a lorry driver, my father's wage was two pounds two shillings, but two and fourpence was deducted from this as a contribution to the national health and unemployment scheme. After being paid to the nearest sixpence, he received one pound nineteen and six, and always grumbled about receiving what he called 'a broken pay'. I think he felt that two crisp pound notes would be less likely to be 'broken' than the mixture of note and coins that he actually got. The logic of this always escaped me; his pay was always broken instantly at the pub, and spent long before next pay day.

My father experienced several periods of unemployment during the depression years of the 1930s, but because there were seven of us in our family, he got more money on the dole than he did when working. After the Great Depression began in 1929, he was laid off from his job because of lack of business. Twice during my Glasgow boyhood he got his LMS job back, but finally had to give up heavy lifting work for good because of lumbago, which he attributed to years of standing in the trenches up to his waist in Flanders mud.

While unemployed, he took various part-time jobs to earn some money. One of these was the part-time waiting post at his ex-officer's club, where he worked as a casual when social functions were held. On such nights he rarely arrived home until after eleven o'clock, but my mother and I keenly waited up for him. He usually brought home paper bags of cakes, buns, scones and other foodstuffs which he'd scrounged after the function was over. Such goodies were a rare treat in our home.

Another source of income my father tried was taking on a Watkins distributorship. Watkins was, I think, a Canadian company which sold its goods door to door through agents who worked on commission. My father was given a large suitcase, crammed with Watkins' culinary products, such as vanilla essence and spices. He took orders from these samples and the company later delivered the goods.

Trying to sell door to door in our part of Glasgow was almost impossible. Nobody had any money, even for goods that were cheaper than shop prices, so father would hump his heavy suitcase to the tram stop and travel to a better part of the city to his allotted 'territory'.

He never earned much money from his Watkins work. There was a pyramid of agents above him who seemed to make a good living from the efforts of the door to door 'footsloggers', few of whom stayed long. And apart from that, my mother used to help herself liberally from his sample case, so he was constantly having to buy replacement stock.

But another part-time job he took on was more profitable. During his army days my father had been a physical training instructor and had mastered the art of ju-jitsu. In the thirties there was a great fad for ju-jitsu as a means of self-defence, and my father taught wealthy Glaswegians at a private gymnasium how to use an opponent's strength to defeat them. He must have been fairly expert at it because he was the subject of a glowing article in a Glasgow evening newspaper. There was a photo of him demonstrating his skills, as he threw a man twice his size and weight over his shoulder.

Willie McRobbie also tried his hand at writing. His manuscripts were carefully written in copybook style on pages from a lined exercise book, and as was the fashion in those days they were sent rolled to publishers. Many of his manuscripts dealt with the subject of duty. My father was an intensely patriotic man, and the fact that the promised 'land fit for heroes' had become a depressed country where crippled ex-servicemen sold matches in the street to stay alive, did not shake his faith in King and Country. He never displayed any Communist leanings. Like many working men, he was a dyed-in-the-wool Tory, who believed that God had ordained the class system; that there was the officer class, and then there were the men, or the masses. He often warned me, 'Never get above your station in life,' although the proudest moment in his life was when I became an officer in the Seaforth Highlanders.

He also admired the fact that I had chosen to take up office work, and not 'get my hands dirty' by doing manual labour as he did. He respected any man who went to work wearing a suit and collar and tie, and would say admiringly of some acquaintance, 'He's getting five pounds a week—and he's never dirtied his hands in his life!'

Despite living in incredible squalor and poverty, my father never lost his love for Glasgow, which he proudly called 'the second city of the Empire', often telling me 'It's a privilege for you to be a Scot and growing up in such a great city. You should count your blessings. At least you have a roof over your head.' But rather than being the second city of the Empire, I thought Glasgow was the arsehole of the world—although it would have been sacrilege to say this. To me Glasgow was a slum city peopled by stunted little men like my father, who wore mufflers instead of collars and ties, men who spoke in one of the most atrocious accents in the British Isles. Men who were too lazy to go upstairs to the communal lavatory, and instead urinated in the kitchen sink. Men who got roaring drunk on Friday and Saturday nights in what must have been the most insalubrious pubs in Britain, then went home at closing time and belted their woman and children.

I was often the victim of violence from my father, and obviously this colours my recollections of him. On one occasion, when dodging a blow from his fist, I tripped and bit my tongue so badly that I needed four stitches. I still have the stitch marks today. I finally stood up to my father when I was fourteen and had become an Army Cadet. Part of our equipment was a long ex-army bayonet which we wore on our belts; our only offensive weapon. Wearing a khaki uniform somehow transformed me, and from a lad who cowered under vicious blows from my father I suddenly became a man. Instead of falling to the floor and huddling there while I got a good kicking, I drew my bayonet and snarled, 'Come and get me!'

My father was a brave man, but my eyes must have told him that if he attacked me I would have rammed the bayonet into his gut with the greatest of pleasure. He backed off, and

153

from then on his power and influence over me ceased. I never paid any attention to anything he said again.

Apart from being intensely patriotic and an ardent royalist, as my mother was, my father, I now realise, was a snob—and very bigoted. He was a Scottish version of Alf Garnett. Willie McRobbie's loyalties lay with Winston Churchill, who for some peculiar reason had elected to become an officer in the Royal Scots Fusiliers during the Great War, and who my father recalled as a good officer, although a Sassenach. He also admired the Prince of Wales, who had served as an officer during the Great War, and in 1917 was appointed Colonel-in-Chief of the Royal Scots Fusiliers. He knew that His Royal Highness had never been placed in a situation of any hazard, being, after all, the heir to the throne, but in 1935 the Prince made a speech stating that something must be done about the plight of the millions of ex-servicemen who were out of work. It was quite a political speech for a member of the Royal Family to deliver. Newspaper commentators said it had been made against the government's wishes. Overnight the Prince of Wales became a hero among unemployed ex-soldiers. My father wrote to him and received a reply from the Prince's secretary, which he proudly showed to everyone he met.

When George V died, Edward became King, but quickly abdicated so he could marry the American divorcee, Mrs Wallis Simpson. The abdication crisis split the nation. Winston Churchill was prominent among the 'King's Men', as was my father, who ardently supported the King's right to marry whoever he chose.

Nowadays, it is difficult to imagine the intense passions the Mrs Simpson affair aroused at the time. My father and mother, living in the lowest strata of the working class, backed the man who was really a royal dilettante, against the nation's elected government. The King had the support of millions of working people from all over the British Isles, and there was even talk

154

of armed insurrection to place the King on the throne.

Although retrenched from the regular army, my father maintained his links with the service by joining the T.A., a volunteer reserve force whose members attended parades once weekly and went on annual manoeuvres at military camps. The Territorials wore normal army uniform, 1914-18 style, complete with puttees, and were allowed to keep their Lee Enfield rifles and bayonets at home. They were not highly regarded by the civil population, but then neither were members of the regular army. By 1935 a revulsion against war had set in. The valorous deeds of 1914-18 had been largely forgotten. Most civilians felt that any man who joined the army and signed up for seven years only did so because he was otherwise unemployable. Joining up was considered a last resort, as for many men it was, and few people wanted to face the fact that soon the army would be needed to contain the Nazis.

In Glasgow, the regimental depot of the Highland Light Infantry was at Maryhill Barracks. Some of the troops undoubtedly earned the title of 'licentious soldiery', often getting drunk and indulging in petty theft such as shoplifting to supplement their meagre two shillings a day pay. Many of the shops along Maryhill Road displayed signs which read, NO DOGS OR SOLDIERS ADMITTED, but in spite of this my father wore his Territorial Army uniform as often as possible.

During the Abdication crisis he and several of his old comrades met to discuss action to support the King. Many such meetings took place in our kitchen in Grove Street, and the old soldiers, up to half a dozen of them, turned up in their 'Terriers' uniform complete with their weapons. They drank beer and in a semi-drunken state would be drilled by my father in our tiny kitchen, doing mostly rifle drill, such as sloping and presenting arms. The men had no ammunition for their rifles, which was a mercy, as my father was an excellent shot. He had represented his unit at the annual shooting contest at Bisley, where only the best marksmen in the army competed, and at weekends I sometimes went with him to a rifle range in Glasgow. At twelve, with my bony shoulder padded by a rolled sock, I fired a rifle for the first time, and later, like my father, became an excellent marksman.

Some kind of military service was part of my father's life during the whole time I lived at home. In June 1940, when Britain faced the possibility of invasion by the Germans, the Local Defence Volunteers were formed. Their 'uniform' consisted solely of an armband, and they carried weapons like shotguns and even air rifles. My father was one of the first to join the LDV, which very quickly became the Home Guard, after which its members were issued a uniform and one of the millions of surplus American rifles which had been bought from the US army after the Great War.

My father was rapidly promoted in the Home Guard and quickly became the Ayr unit's Regimental Sergeant Major. He was issued with a .45 Webley revolver which he kept on top of the wardrobe, supposedly out of reach of the children, although I could easily get hold of it. Occasionally I'd smuggle the revolver from our home then, on a lonely stretch of beach, wearing my Army Cadet uniform, I'd enjoy target practice shooting at tin cans. Even in wartime this was completely illegal. Small arms practice was supposed to be confined to military ranges, but I blazed away across the Firth of Clyde, keeping one eye peeled for the police. I had no problem obtaining ammunition, which I got through a friendly guard sergeant at a military camp where I was working. After using the revolver, I carefully cleaned and oiled it so my father wouldn't know it had been fired.

Willie McRobbie was in his element in the Home Guard. Although he did a full day's work, he got dressed in his uniform almost every night when he got home and went to the drill hall to train the Home Guardsmen. He was highly respected by his officers and the other ranks because he wore the 1914-18 campaign medal ribbons and obviously knew his stuff. I know he regretted seeing the Home Guard disbanded after the threat of invasion became remote.

My father's parentage was a mystery, and I never heard him talk of his father or mother, although he did say he grew up in Aberdeenshire, where there are many McRobbies. As a boy he did farm work, but often used to play with a friend who lived in a big house with French windows and a staff of servants. One of the few stories I heard about his boyhood told how he and the boy of the house were playing cricket when one of them drove the ball through a French window. They went inside and his friend carefully picked up the shattered glass then placed it outside the window. As my father told it, this was so it would be assumed that the window had been broken from the inside by a careless servant.

Whoever brought my father up gave him a hard time. He told how he always had to wash in icy cold water, breaking the ice on top of the barrel in winter. He apparently never had boots or shoes but always went barefoot. When he was working in the fields in winter, he told us how he would place his frozen feet in two fresh cow pats to warm them with the steaming dung.

But his civilian boyhood was brief. Before he was fourteen he was banned from playing with the boy in the big house any more. My mother was sure that this child was his half brother, and that the master of the house had fathered them both. Anyway, at fourteen William McRobbie joined the regular army as a boy soldier, and from then on, it became his life and home.

As well as hitting me, my father continually barked instructions at me too. 'You haven't cleaned your boots, sir! Snap to it!', he would scream, or 'Your hair is too long, sir! Get it cut!' When I joined the army at seventeen I found the harshest drill sergeant a pussycat compared with my father, and as a recruit, military discipline never irked me in the slightest; it was a pushover compared with the quasi-army life of home.

After I became an officer and went home to Ayr on embarkation leave, my father treated me with great respect. I now held the King's Commission and had the single pip of a Second Lieutenant on my shoulders, and he pressed me to accompany him to his regular pub in town—so he could 'show me off', my mother said. His mates, mostly old soldiers from the Great War, treated me with similar respect. It was the first time I'd ever been in a pub with my father, but at nineteen, I was an experienced drinker and could sink eight half pints of beer plus eight whisky chasers in a session and still remain relatively sober. Half a pint of beer followed by half a gill of neat whisky was a standard drink in Scotland. My father had a reputation as a hard-drinking man and boasted he could drink anyone under the table. But possibly because of the euphoria of seeing his officer son, he exceeded his capacity on this occasion, and we had to carry him home. I suddenly realised that my father, the old soldier, had become an old man.

MY LEARNED UNCLES

When he was home on leave, my sea-faring Uncle Alec lived with my grandmother in Ayr. I doubt if he was ever aware of it, but he was a non-stop comedy turn, mostly because he spent the best part of his leave drunk. He was a generous man, who became even more generous when he had been drinking, and my brothers and I were not above exploiting Uncle Alec's generosity. Two of my mother's other brothers, Tom and David, lived at Grandma's house in Ayr too, and on Saturdays we could usually wheedle a penny pocket money from each of them. But it was hard work extracting the penny and we usually had to do some work in the garden to earn it first. But Uncle Alec handed out coins without expecting us to do anything in return, except maybe run down to the shop and get him the *Noon Record*, and it was not unusual to get as much as sixpence from him, especially after he'd had a win on the horses.

But unfortunately, with Uncle Alec it was either feast or famine. When he arrived home after up to a year at sea, he was very flush because he'd only spent his money on cheap duty free whisky and cigarettes. He'd often have several hundred pounds in his pocket, most of which he'd hand over to my mother, who acted as his bank, doling a few pounds out whenever he'd spent all he had.

My mother did her best to conserve his funds. When he came home drunk at night and finally went to bed she would tiptoe into his room and go through his pockets, removing any

159

paper money and adding it to his bank. The next morning he could never remember if he'd had any money in his pocket, and she would give him a few more pounds, warning him that he was going through his funds too fast. But in spite of her best endeavours, Alec continued to spend his money like drunken sailors do, and towards the end of his leave he was reduced to borrowing from my mother or his brothers. His leaves could extend for six weeks or more while he waited to 'get another ship', and he was always very relieved when the telegram finally arrived telling him to report to Liverpool or Glasgow. He didn't enjoy the latter part of his leave when money was tight and he could no longer afford to buy whisky, switching instead to beer.

While at sea Alec was a bottle of Scotch a day man. At duty free prices a bottle cost five shillings, compared with 12/6 ashore. He was a heavy smoker but a duty free tin of cigarettes cost only sixpence for fifty, compared with a shilling for twenty at home, and one reason he resisted taking a shore job was because he couldn't have drunk or smoked to the extent he did at sea. At home, when he was reduced to drinking beer, he was a pathetic sight. He would sit near the fireplace, his glass of Whitbreads on the hob beside him, complaining about the delay in getting a new ship. From the heat of the hob, his beer almost boiled and bubbled, but he never seemed to notice it. Beer alone never made him as drunk as he got when he followed it with a whisky chaser.

Alec's arrival home was always greeted with delight by the family, although after he'd been home for six weeks, my mother was glad to see the back of him. Before World War II he worked mainly as a second engineer. Most of his vessels were cargo ships—tramp steamers often carrying dirty or smelly cargoes, and Alec's status in the merchant navy was well below that of my Uncles Jim and Will, both chief engineers. Will was with the Navy and Jim with the Ellerman Hall Line, which ran the 'City' ships and carried passengers.

My father made fun of Uncle Alec, who he called 'Auld Eck' behind his back. This annoyed my mother as Alec was her favourite sibling, after whom I had been named. Willie McRobbie poured scorn on the type of vessels Auld Eck served on, claiming he could only get work on 'puffers', little cargo boats that served Scottish inland waterways. While we were living in Glasgow, one of Alec's ships docked there for a few days and my mother took me to see it. It was quite large, about six thousand tons, and had brought a cargo of cocoa beans from West Africa. When I saw it, it was in the process of loading a new cargo—sacks of cement destined for Belfast, and a film of grey powder covered most of the vessel. However, by keeping his porthole closed the dust didn't get into Alec's cabin, which was quite large and impressed my mother and I, who took pleasure in telling my father that Auld Eck's boat 'wasn't at all bad'.

Uncle Alec remained a bachelor all his life, even though women found him quite attractive. This was especially so when he became a chief engineer during the war. The status of merchant seamen rose considerably as they helped provide the lifeline that kept Britain going, and members of the Merchant Navy were as highly regarded as those of the armed forces. Indeed, when Uncle Alec came home on his first wartime leave he looked as impressive as any Royal Navy officer with four gold bands on the sleeve of his well-tailored uniform, and a peaked cap bearing a gold crown and anchor insignia. Once when I was walking up the street with him, some young sailors saluted him.

I don't know if Uncle Alec had a girl in every port, but he certainly had a girlfriend in Ayr. Miss McLeish (I never knew her first name) was that relative rarity in Scotland, a woman solicitor, and was obviously well off because she wore a fur coat. She was very keen on Uncle Alec and made it clear that if he would only give up the sea, she would marry him. When he first came home on leave, they often went out together and Alec would return more or less sober, because Miss McLeish chided him about his drinking. But he got stuck into the whisky when he got back, to make up for the time he'd been on his best behaviour, and although Miss McLeish was persistent, she couldn't compete with the lure of the grog. I don't think she ever married.

At one stage during the war, Uncle Alec's ship was torpedoed off the coast of West Africa and he spent several days in a lifeboat before being rescued. When he arrived home he wasn't wearing his glamorous uniform—all his possessions had gone to the bottom of the sea, and instead he wore an ill-fitting suit of civilian clothes which had been issued to survivors by a Seaman's Mission in London. We treated Auld Eck with great respect during that leave. He was a hero and we were agog to hear details of his ordeal. But he would say little about it, except to mutter that it had been very wet, and cold, and that if it hadn't been for the whisky he'd taken with him into the lifeboat, he mightn't have survived.

We finally discovered that before his ship had gone down he had removed the cork floats from his life-jacket and replaced them with flat flasks of Scotch. As he scrambled down a net to board the lifeboat he would have sunk like a stone had he fallen into the water. But he got a place on the boat and survived quite well on a diet of neat whisky. Lack of food didn't bother him as he hardly ate when he was boozing, but he told us it had been very hard to go so many days without a cigarette.

Alec was a very heavy smoker. His normal brand was Capstan, but when he was drinking he often switched to the Gold Full Strength variety which had more 'bite', and not surprisingly, he suffered from a hacking smoker's cough. This afflicted him worst just after he awoke, and sometimes I'd take him up a cup of tea and watch fascinated while he had his morning cough. In his woollen undershorts, he'd sit on the edge of the bed while great heaving spasms of coughing wracked his body. Each spasm started at his feet and a kind of red flush surged up his legs to his thighs until finally it reached his face, which turned puce as he coughed up the phlegm. Sometimes it took fifteen minutes before the fit of coughing subsided and he could talk or drink some tea. In the kitchen below, we always knew when Auld Eck had woken up and risen from his bed by the noise from above. 'You'd better take him up a cup of tea,' my mother would say. 'He'll need it to soothe his throat.'

Once my brother Bill sneaked a slice of bloody liver from the wire meatsafe in the scullery, then slipped up to Alec's room where the old sea-dog was snoring away. Bill gently laid the liver on his pillow and retreated. Downstairs, we heard the hacking sounds of Alec's awakening. But the coughing only lasted for a couple of minutes before it stopped suddenly and we heard Alec clumping quickly down the stairs. He burst into the kitchen and cried out to my mother, 'You'd better come up and have a look, Jessie. I think I've coughed my guts up!'

When he was on a binge in a pub, Alec was an easy target for people trying to sell things. He often brought home a stringload of fish, which he assured my mother were fresh off the trawlers that day, and although this was undoubtedly true, the kind of marine life he bought couldn't be got at any fishmongers'. The fish were usually large and ugly, with dangerous looking spines, like dogfish or catfish which had been snagged in the trawlers' nets. My mother didn't like the look of them, refusing to gut and clean them, let alone cook them.

Alec loved fish and had eaten all kinds of marine exotica, like octopus, during his travels. Holding up a large catfish he would exclaim, 'But them's good eating, Jessie. In New Orleans they're a great delicacy!'

'Well you can cook it yourself,' my mother would reply. 'I'm not touching it!'

My father always scoffed at Alec's fish. 'Only natives eat that

163

kind of rubbish!' he'd state. 'That's not fit for a white man to eat.'

My Uncles Alec, Tom and David had one thing in common, each thinking they knew everything about anything. This riled my father because he was sure he knew even more than they did. The men had some furious arguments during which they heaped scorn upon my father because he 'didn't have a trade'. Alec and Tom were engineers and David was a joiner who worked at a coal-mine near Ayr, but as a horse and cart driver my father had never done an apprenticeship, so wasn't 'qualified'.

Alec, Tom and David prided themselves on the fact that they could 'turn their hand to anything', and indeed they tackled some complex household tasks. They would never buy an item if they could make it more cheaply themselves, and they scoffed at the thought of hiring a plumber, for example. All three knew everything about plumbing, although the taps in our scullery never stopped dripping.

One of my uncles' projects was to make a large sofa and two easy chairs for our front parlour. They built the furniture in the big bedroom upstairs, sawing and hammering away for days, and although they knew nothing at all about upholstering, they weren't deterred. They'd learn. And to their credit they created an excellent three piece lounge suite using a plush, albeit rather violently coloured purple tapestry.

But the problems began when the three men tried to get the sofa downstairs and into the parlour. It was a very narrow and steep stairway, with some awkward turns, and they just couldn't manoeuvre it round the corners. Undeterred, they took the window—frame and everything—out of the bedroom, erecting a block and tackle system in the garden below. The heavy sofa was lowered from the upstairs window onto the ground, the intention being to take it into the house through the back door. Unfortunately, although the cumbersome piece of furniture fitted through the back door, it couldn't pass through the kitchen to reach the parlour. Still undeterred, the men carried it to the bottom of the garden where there was a gate which lead out into a lane. They lugged it all the way round the block to the front of the house where they took out the parlour window. Here, they almost managed to get the blighted piece of furniture into the house before it got stuck fast. To force it any more would have destroyed the upholstery, and in the end there was only one solution. Alec, Tom and David sawed the sofa in two. Once the pieces had been pulled into the parlour, they joined them together again, covering the severed upholstery with a band of material. The finished product didn't look too bad.

My father, for one, was delighted by this incident. 'Bloody qualified tradesmen' he scoffed, 'They didn't have the sense to measure the openings before they built the sofa! That wouldn't have happened if I'd had a hand in it!'

My uncles were always making something or other, and every December, Uncle Tom's major endeavour was to bake the shortbread in readiness for New Year. My elders all despised 'bought' shortbread; it didn't compare with home made stuff, and cost much more too, and I must say that Uncle Tom's shortbread was excellent. The night he 'fired' the shortbread, he took over the entire kitchen. He used several pounds of butter and some shortening, then hand-kneaded the mixture to create large yellow rounds which he decorated at the edges with thumb imprints. The kitchen fire was stoked up with coal hours before 'the firing' so the ovens on either side were as hot as possible. The finished rounds of shortbread were slid into the oven on trays lined with greaseproof paper, then fired. When they were taken out Tom sprinkled them with castor sugar before setting them aside to cool.

Nobody was allowed to eat any of the precious shortbread until Hogmanay, when visitors received a piece with a glass of whisky—or ginger wine in the case of teetotallers and children. I'm sure the ginger wine was really alcoholic. It was made in early December in a large zinc bath, filled with hot water and several bottles of ginger wine essence. The only other ingredient I can remember was sugar—bags and bags of it. After a good stirring, the wine was poured into a variety of bottles and corked. These bottles were put away in a dark place until Hogmanay, by which time some kind of fermentation must have taken place, as I used to get quite high after several glasses of the brew.

My uncles Tom and David were keen gardeners, Tom preferring to grow vegetables while David specialized in flowers. But neither of them liked mowing the lawn with our hand-operated Qualcast mower, so that chore was left to me. Uncle David grew splendid sweet peas, irises, dahlias, rhododendrons, gladioli, marigolds and his pride and joy—roses. In Ayr, there were often flowers in the house, unlike in our Glasgow abode where they were never seen, except in the window box where my mother struggled to grow some little plants.

Tom and David were also keen amateur photographers and had a tiny darkroom upstairs in a windowless attic cupboard. They were wireless enthusiasts too, and subscribed to a periodical called *Wireless World*, building one of the first radio sets in our neighbourhood, using crystals and the 'cats whiskers' system. David, a skilled joiner, built a handsome polished walnut cabinet to house our wind up gramophone and records, and the radio set, whose cabinet he also built, sat beside the gramophone.

Uncle David was my mother's youngest brother, and in his early twenties he was a very good looking young man. My grandmother and mother often said that David could get any girl he wanted, but ironically he finally married Peggy, my grandmother's home help. Peggy was in her late teens and not especially good looking, but propinquity can lead to anything and she and Uncle David began an affair. This was kept completely secret from Grandma, although I think my mother suspected what was going on, and it was she who broke the news that Peggy was pregnant, and that David was going to stand by her and marry her. Grandma was heartbroken. Her handsome baby son was going to throw himself away on a 'skivvy'. She didn't have to attend the wedding because she was confined to bed, but she refused to allow Peggy in the house and instead David found somewhere to rent and moved out.

The other person who deeply hurt Grandma was her oldest son, my Uncle Will. He moved to London after the Great War and married an Englishwoman, never bringing his bride to Green Street to see Grandma. The couple did visit Ayr, but Will's wife stayed at the Station Hotel while he visited his family alone. He always put up at one of Ayr's better hotels and never stayed overnight at his old home, coming and going by taxi—not a common sight in Green Street, except at a wedding or a funeral.

I only met Will about three times, but I remember him because when I was ten he gave me the incredible sum of two shillings (which my mother promptly confiscated after he left). Will's last visit to Green Street, during World War II, was marked by lots of drama. His brothers were angry because he wouldn't bring his wife to meet Grandma, who was ailing and unlikely to live long. But Will refused. His wife was apparently quite a well-born lady and Will did not want her to see the home where he had been born; or perhaps she didn't want to go 'slumming'.

Although I was young at the time, I had a certain sympathy for Uncle Will. In the years I lived at Green Street, I never dreamed of bringing a girl home, and for that matter, I rarely brought any of my friends to the house. It wasn't such a bad house, but the homes of all of my friends were considerably better. This was probably because none of them were part of large families; indeed, most were only children, or one of two offspring. With a four person family it's much easier to keep a house clean and tidy, especially if the dwelling is relatively modern. Our cottage was well over a hundred years old, and was completely overcrowded with six adults and five children living in it.

Two uncles I never met were Gordon and Bertie who were killed during and just after the Great War, but I saw my other uncle, Jim, several times. Like Will, he married an English woman, moving to Birkenhead to be near the head office of his shipping company. He had two daughters, Margery and Jean, who were raised in England and spoke with English accents.

I liked my two girl cousins and their funny piping English voices, and I met them on their several visits to Ayr. Their mother, my Aunt Muriel, dressed them in the styles favoured by Princess Elizabeth and Princess Margaret Rose. When Uncle Jim brought his wife and family to Ayr they occupied the big upstairs bedroom where the seven McRobbies normally slept. During their visit we really had to crowd up so Jim's family could have some comfort and privacy. In the small kitchen we ate in relays, and Jim's family, who were late risers, being on holiday, had the table to themselves at breakfast—which was cooked and served by my mother.

Aunt Muriel was a very tall and superior type of woman, rather like an actress of the time, Hermione Gingold. But unlike Uncle Will's wife, she did condescend to stay at her husband's old home. I quite liked her as she was extremely forthright. She thought I was very intelligent and 'wasted' in Scotland, telling me 'You must move to England soon. You would do very well there.' This didn't endear her to my mother, because in 1940 at age fourteen I was making strenuous efforts to get away to sea. Jessie McRobbie didn't like the idea of her eldest son braving the German U-Boats like two of her brothers did, and discouraged any plans for my leaving home.

Uncle Jim rose to the highest engineering position with the Ellerman Hall Line, supervising all the company's engineer officers. His most striking physical feature was a glass eye which was fitted after he lost the real one in an accident. In those days, glass eyes were fairly primitive and wearing it gave him trouble. When he went to bed he took it out and placed it in a glass of water. He had false teeth too, which he also removed and put in a glass.

In his early days at sea, the stokers were Lascars and the stewards Goanese. Rightly or wrongly, the British crewmen regarded the 'natives' as being untrustworthy and not above lifting valuables from officers' cabins. When Uncle Jim turned in for a nap, he placed his eye and teeth in their glasses then warned the stewards that although he might be asleep, his eye stayed awake and would watch everything that happened in the cabin. If there was any attempt at pilfering, the eye would see it and arouse the teeth which would leap from the glass and bite the culprit. He also advised the stewards that the teeth had been trained to go for the testicles. Uncle Jim said he never had any of his gear stolen.

IF SCOTLAND STOOD ALONE

Before World War II, many Scots refused to accept that Scotland was part of Britain, except geographically. England was the land of the Sassenachs, a traditional enemy for centuries, and most Scots had a low opinion of the English as fighters. They were convinced that the backbone of the British Army was the Scottish regiments, and that the Scots, a warrior race, would bend the knee to no foe.

In June 1940, via Dunkirk, the bulk of the British Expeditionary Force in France narrowly escaped the blitzkrieg which forced France to surrender to the German forces. Within weeks Holland, Belgium, Luxembourg, Denmark and Norway had all capitulated to Germany. At the time, Prime Minister Winston Churchill made his famous BBC broadcast announcing Britain's intention to continue the war by fighting on the beaches, in the streets, and on the landing fields, ending with the rousing declaration, 'We shall *never* surrender!'

In the kitchen-living room at 55 Green Street, Ayr, home town of poet-philosopher Robert Burns, my three uncles and my mother and father listened intently to the 9pm broadcast. Churchill's assurance that the war would be continued from London was received with scepticism by this section of his Scottish listeners. My Uncle Alec, in his Merchant Navy officer's uniform, downed his sixth neat whisky before facing the gravity of the situation. He said to my father, who had donned his old Territorial Army uniform to listen to the broadcast, 'You know,

Wullie, a lot of countries have surrendered, and now the French have given in. Things look bad for us.'

'Aye,' said my father, 'if the English surrender next, it'll take us a long time to win this war.' There were nods of agreement. If England capitulated then Scotland would have a hard struggle to defeat Germany alone.

My mother added, 'If the English give in, do you think the Americans will help us?'

'Of course they will!' Uncle Tom declared. 'There's a lot of Scots in America. Like Andrew Carnegie.' He refrained from naming any others, probably because he didn't know their names, but steel magnate Carnegie had endowed public libraries all over Scotland, including one in Ayr, and was a familiar Scots-American tycoon.

Uncle David added, 'Then there's Canada, and Australia and New Zealand. They're full of Scots. They'd help us.' I thought the war situation was looking brighter by the minute.

'Then there's India,' added my father. 'There's four hundred million Indians. And some bonnie fighters among them. Jerry can never beat the whole British Empire!'

We glanced at the map of the world which featured on an insurance company calendar above the mantelpiece. Large parts of the map were coloured a reassuring red, while the brown area that was Germany didn't look very big at all. Even when it included Austria, Czechoslovakia, Poland, Holland, Belgium, Luxembourg, Denmark, Norway and France.

'And there's the Russians,' said Uncle Tom. 'Old Joe Stalin's not going to stand by and let Scotland fight Jerry by ourselves. I mean, Glasgow's not called the Red Clyde for nothing.'

The shipbuilding areas around Glasgow's River Clyde had voted several communist-sympathising MPs into the British parliament, and it was felt that Scotland had paid its dues in the interests of Soviet-Celtic relations.

The discussion about the prospect of Scotland—and its

allies—winning eventual victory over the Nazis went on until midnight. It was accepted that thirty-eight million English couldn't be relied upon to maintain resistance to Hitler once things got tough, but four million Scots could do the job.

'Just look at history,' Uncle Tom said authoritatively. 'We can hold Jerry up at the border for ever. I mean, for four hundred years the Romans couldn't conquer Scotland. They had to build Hadrian's Wall to keep us out.' Nobody mentioned that less than two hundred years before the despised English had in fact conquered Scotland. But it wasn't the time to introduce a negative note, especially when the adults were getting stuck into the Haig's with a vengeance.

After the grandfather clock in the lobby struck twelve, there was general agreement that the war between Scotland (and its allies) and Germany would be a long one. Uncle Tom said 'At the weekend I'll dig in the sweet peas and the hollyhocks, and the lawn too. I'll put the whole garden under spuds. We won't starve, Jessie.'

My mother, who was housekeeper for her three brothers as well as her husband, five children and her bed-ridden mother, nodded saying, 'I think we should get some hens. Then we'll have plenty of eggs.'

Uncle David promised he'd build a hen house and run at the weekend. Thus with a plentiful supply of potatoes and eggs, 55 Green Street would be ready to face a long war.

At this point my father, who fancied himself as a light baritone, broke into a rousing rendition of 'Scotland the Brave!' and his wife and brothers-in-law joined him in an outburst of patriotic fervour. I left the boozy Scottish Nationalist gathering, confident that Hitler would bite off more than he could chew if he tried to invade Scotland.

A CHEERY BIDDY

In many ways, my mother was a remarkable woman. She wasn't the product of a slum upbringing, and although she came from a family of nine children the Hewitt cottage, where she grew up, was a reasonably spacious place. Nonetheless, it must have been a tight squeeze to fit nine kids and two adults into a house with three bedrooms, one parlour and a kitchen-living room. However, my mother's father had died long before I was born and some of my uncles left home at an early age, which gave more living space to those who stayed at home.

The fates of my mother's sister and seven brothers is in some ways representative of what happened to many Scottish families whose children were born around the turn of the century, when Britain still had an empire.

My Uncle Gordon was killed in Flanders during the Great War. Uncle Bertie served in the army too, then went to Australia after the war to investigate the possibilities of the Hewitts emigrating Down Under. But soon after he arrived the family received a report that he had died of black-water fever in the West Australian goldfields, and never heard any more about him. My mother's only sister, Jean, met a Canadian soldier during the war and married him, subsequently emigrating to Canada. Uncle Will served in the Navy during the First and Second World Wars, and was finally killed at sea, while Jim and Alec went to sea as engineers, spending World War II on merchant ships. Jim later married an Englishwoman and went

173

to live in Liverpool. Tom, also an engineer, worked for a company in Ayr, and along with my Uncle David looked after my grandmother. My mother, Jessie Hewitt, met her husband during the Great War, and later moved to Glasgow to start her own family.

My mother's parents were respected merchants in Ayr where they had a grocer's shop in Main Street. There was a belief in our family that the Hewitts were related to William Ewart Gladstone, the great nineteenth century British prime minister. The Ewarts and the Hewitts were supposed to be kinfolk and Grandma Hewitt claimed a definite relationship, although I never found any proof of this.

After my grandfather's death the shop was sold, and my grandmother lived on a small annuity, with financial contributions from some of her sons. In the family tradition, my mother opened a little shop when she arrived in Glasgow. It was in Balmain Street, opposite the primary school, and it opened all hours, selling confectionery, cigarettes, staple groceries, stationery and magazines. But it didn't prosper. My mother told me the business failed because she 'gave too much tick' and too many customers failed to pay for their credit purchases. She and my father had lived above the shop, and when it closed after the Great Depression began, they moved only a few hundred yards away to the room and kitchen at Grove Street where I was born.

Through having run the shop for several years, my mother was well known in our neighbourhood. Many of the occupants of our building had been her customers, and owed her money which she occasionally tried to recover. But she never pressed her creditors too hard; she knew their financial position was no better than ours. Nonetheless, she kept all the 'tick books' from the shop, which recorded her former customers' debts. Each customer had a small exercise book in which the shopkeeper wrote each item purchased, and its cost. A running

174

total was kept and when it became too high—reaching say a pound—credit was cut off until some payment was made. At Grove Street, my mother would occasionally bring out the tick books and talk about how rich we would be if everybody paid their debts.

Jessie McRobbie's single greatest asset was her optimism. She was what was known as a 'cheery biddy', always looking on the bright side and ready to help cheer someone up, and only rarely did the horrors of poverty and slum life get her down. Our cramped kitchen-living room was seldom without a neighbour or neighbours who had dropped in for a 'wee chat'. These neighbours, always women, often said 'I hope you can cheer me up, Jessie. Things are very bad with us.' My mother would make the obligatory cup of tea while she listened to what were often heart-rending tales of misery. At weekends I used to sit at the kitchen table reading while a neighbour poured out her heart to my mother. Often I only pretended to be absorbed in my magazine. I was much more interested in the real life dramas being narrated by a neighbour, and I kept my ears wide open.

Some of the sordid details that were unfolded went over my head, but I knew when the women were discussing something juicy because they always spelled out the key words. This was pointless as I was a good speller and could easily work out that the neighbour was up the D-U-F-F, even though I didn't know what that meant. Eventually I discovered from older friends that this meant that someone was going to have a baby. During one drama when I was eavesdropping, I learned that the neighbour was up the D-U-F-F but that Fergie (her husband) wasn't the F-A-T-H-E-R. It transpired that the man who had got her pregnant was Ram Singh, an Indian pedlar who regularly called upon the housewives in our area.

There were many Indian pedlars who worked the Glasgow slums. They always wore a turban and carried two large pigskin

175

suitcases crammed with gaudy fabrics of every kind. It was a common sight to see them kneeling at doors while they spread their colourful wares in front of an attentive housewife. Sometimes the pedlar was invited to bring his suitcases inside and spread his fabrics across the kitchen table, although this wasn't done very often as the Indians had a reputation for being skilled seducers of women. Indeed it was rumoured that some pedlars would accept sex as payment for their wares.

This was what had happened in the case of Fergie Watson's wife, but unfortunately she had become pregnant. As Mr Singh was of a distinctly dusky complexion, Mrs Watson's husband could hardly fail to notice that the child was not his. It was some time before I managed to work all this out, not that it was ever very clear to me, because I knew nothing about the act of conception. But I did gather that Mrs Watson was somehow going to produce a baby that she didn't want, and that she was seeking my mother's advice on how to prevent the birth.

Jessie McRobbie was never a back yard abortionist, and her interest in obstetrics was confined solely to bringing babies into the world. But she apparently knew a thing or two about unwanted pregnancies, and gave Mrs Watson certain advice, which must have worked as a few days later she came beaming into our house and gave my mother a big cuddle. More importantly to me, she also gave my mother a tin of cream biscuits.

Another reason for my mother's popularity with the neighbouring women was because she read tea cups, and after say three women had drunk their tea they would ask her to read the cups. My mother took this fortune telling task very seriously, first swilling away any remaining tea so that only the dregs were left, then announcing what the patterns of the wet leaves meant. She nearly always confirmed that there was 'money in your cup', which was what her audience wanted to hear. Quite often travel was foretold too, but this was only forecast when my mother already knew that the subject was planning to make a train or bus trip somewhere. Most of her predictions were of a pleasant or happy nature—her audience didn't want to hear anything gloomy, but instead expected to be cheered up. And my mother's subjects always told her when one of her forecasts came true, as indeed they often did. The arrival of the gas man to read the meter and leave a cash rebate was fulfilment of the 'money in your cup' reading, as was finding a threepenny bit in the street.

My mother also told fortunes from playing cards, and these sessions were particularly entertaining because she had the gift of the gab. She was an excellent story teller with a flair for dramatic presentation, and sometimes, when her friends couldn't afford the price of a cinema ticket, they would club together until my mother had the threepence needed for admission to the front stalls. She then went to a matinee and when she got home three or four neighbours would be keenly awaiting her arrival. After cups of tea had been served, the group would sit around our fireplace while my mother narrated the story of the film—something that she continued to do after we moved to Ayr.

To hear her relate the story of 'The Maltese Falcon' in broad Scots dialect, complete with verbatim passages of dialogue, was a memorable experience. She also stood up and acted out some parts. Watching my plump mother mimic Peter Lorre when he was being slapped by Humphrey Bogart was a hilarious sight, although her entranced audience didn't think so. The time she took to tell the story equalled the length of the film, so her avid listeners got their money's worth, and the consensus was that my mother's narration was 'as good as seeing the picture yourself.'

Jessie McRobbie was a great knitter, often working to order for neighbours, who supplied her with wool and paid her a small sum for making the garment. She also crocheted clothes for small children, and could knit complex patterns like Fair Isle, turning out quality work at great speed. When she was sitting down, I rarely saw my mother without her knitting needles in her hands and a ball of wool magically changing into part of a pullover under her skilful fingers.

In the thirties, wool was mostly sold in long hanks, or skeins. It was available in balls too, but they cost more than skeins, and the knitter's first task was to wind these lengths into more manageable balls. From an early age I was given the task of standing in front of my mother, with my arms widespread and a thick hank of coloured wool hitched round each of my thumbs. My mother then wound the hank into a ball ready for her needles. This was a tiresome chore, for which I was spurred on by the veiled threat of not getting new knitted socks if I didn't help out.

Among her other domestic accomplishments, my mother was a good seamstress. Her most treasured possession was a treadle operated Singer sewing machine with which she could make dresses, shirts and even boys' pants. She made a lot of our clothes and also sewed for wealthier people who knew how good her work was, and although her income from knitting and sewing was never large, it helped keep us going.

Another source of income came from doing washing and ironing for people who could afford to pay to have it done. My mother had a regular clientele, some of whom brought their washing in a motor car, collecting it later when it had been done in the communal wash house in the yard below our house. This wash house, called the steamie, featured a big boiler which was filled from a tap then heated by a coal fire. The steamie was shared by about twenty-four families and was in almost constant use. But there were very few arguments over whose turn it was to have use of the boiler. The women seemed to have a roster system which they all observed, and Mrs McRobbie always had Monday mornings from eight until noon. Mrs Lynch's

178

slot was from noon until three, Mrs McGinty's from three until six, and so on, day by day.

When doing the washing, each woman brought her own bucket of coal down to the steamie. On Mondays my mother was first to have use of the wash house, and I would carry down a bucket of coal, and some sticks and old papers for kindling. I'd light the fire and get it going, then fill the boiler ready for the first load of washing. Next, I'd fetch the big wicker basket of clothes, and my mother would follow with her Sunlight Soap and other laundry aids. Once downstairs, she stayed there until the washing was finished. She didn't like climbing stairs, claiming that it brought on her palpitations.

After getting her started, I had to rush off to school. But I got out at noon for an hour for lunch, and by this time the washing had been put through the communal wringer and was ready to be hung out to dry. I'd do this before scoffing my lunch and running back to school.

Drying the washing was often a problem. If it wasn't raining, the clothes could be pegged out along communal lines in the back court, but a close eye had to be kept on them, or some might be stolen. Another wash day hazard came from children who played football or rounders in the yard. A muddy ball belted into the centre of a customer's clean white sheet meant my mother had to re-wash it. As dozens of kids played in the yard— footballers getting mixed up with rounders players, or girls with skipping ropes weaving between pitcher and hitter—this was quite a problem.

When it rained, which it often did, the washing had to be dried in the kitchen. The drying device was a pulley, bolted to the ceiling, and lowered by a cord tied round an iron cleat in one wall. On the pulley was a central length of timber and four lengths of cord over which the washing was hung. Afterwards, it was hoisted back up to the ceiling again.

Hoisting a load of damp washing was heavy work and

beyond my mother's strength. But I mastered it at an early age and learned how to lift the pulley an inch or so at a time, snagging the cord in the cleat and taking a deep breath before raising it a little bit higher. Letting the washing down was almost as hard. If you missed snagging the cleat, the pulley 'ran away' and the heavy load came crashing down—often dumping the clean clothes on the invariably dirty linoleum floor. While the washing was suspended from the ceiling, large items like blankets hung down to about head height, and tall people had to duck their way between these items as they moved around the kitchen. The air in the small room became humid and steamy as the clothes dried, and when my father came home from work he complained that the place smelt like a Chinese laundry.

On washday, when I got home from school in the afternoon I'd unpeg the washing from the lines in the yard and carry it upstairs, or lower it from the pulley. My mother could then start on the ironing.

Our family wash was fairly easy to handle. None of us boys wore underpants, and our shirts didn't need ironing because we always wore a jersey over them so that only the collar showed. Our pillows didn't have pillow slips, and we never had sheets on our beds, sleeping instead with a blanket next to our skin. We didn't use a tablecloth or exotica like table napkins either, so all in all the family wash wasn't very extensive. In fact, the bulk of the ironing came from my mother's paying customers.

When doing washing for her clients, my mother had no hope of getting a vacant slot in the wash house roster, so I helped her carry the extra washing to the local municipal bathing and washing facility. The centrepiece of this establishment was a large indoor swimming pool which could be used at no charge. There were also a number of individual bathrooms for hire at threepence apiece, including the use of a clean towel, soap and a bathtub full of hot water. It was in one of these tubs that I had my first full length bath. In another part of the building there were a series of washhouses which could also be hired for threepence. Here, my mother did her clients' laundry.

After the washing was done and wrung out, I'd hump the heavy basket back home. Then the really hard work began, for me anyway. In our front room, along with the sewing machine, there was a massive instrument of torture called the mangle. It had a series of rollers between which damp articles of laundry, such as sheets, pillow slips, tablecloths and any garment which didn't have buttons were fed; buttons would have been crushed by the immense pressure the rollers exerted. The pressure was created by me turning a large handle causing the rollers to draw the articles into the machine where they were wound round and round until they could be wound no further. Tension was maintained by several heavy iron weights which hung from the bottom of the device.

Turning the handle to wind the washing in was a back-breaking task, and I hated the mangle. But it did do an excellent job, and sheets that had been put through it looked as if they had been hand ironed. Without it, I doubt if my mother could have got through her clients' laundry using only a fire-heated flat iron on the kitchen table. This type of iron soon lost its heat, especially when it was pressed over a damp cloth, and had to be returned to the fireplace to reheat regularly. To speed things up, my mother used two irons—one heating while the other was in use. Gas-operated flat irons were available, but we had no such luxury.

There were few luxuries in my mother's life, but one thing she did insist on was that she drank her tea from a cup and saucer made of fine bone china. All our other crockery was thick, cheap delft. But mother had a china cup which was washed separately from the rest of the crockery then placed on a high shelf. In spite of this, it still got broken frequently because it was so delicate.

The first present I can remember buying my mother was a replacement bone china cup with a gold line around it. It cost me two shillings and represented weeks of hard saving. She scolded me for being so spendthrift, and also for concealing so much money from her, but I knew how much she liked her special cup.

In Grove Street, I heard a lot of female gossip. It is sometimes said that women's conversation deals with the 'small change' of life, but I never felt that way about it. To me women seemed to discuss the important subjects. I found men's conversation, which seemed to be mostly about football and race horses, completely uninteresting.

Oddly, the women in our neighbourhood talked a lot about royalty and the artistocracy. Most of the housewives were ardent royalists, and the two little princesses—Elizabeth and Margaret Rose—were discussed endlessly, and their frocks analysed and the cost of copying them estimated. The two royal children were fashion trend-setters for other little girls all over Britain. When King George VI was crowned my mother was proud of the fact that she had lived under five sovereigns—Queen Victoria, King Edward VII, George V, Edward VIII and George VI. In her lifetime she lived well into the reign of Elizabeth II too.

It always struck me as incongruous to listen to my mother and a gaggle of her neighbours sitting in a kitchen that was squalid to say the least—while they animatedly discussed the social life of the Duchess of Argyll, or Lady Astor and whether they were going to winter in Florence or Cannes.

OUR MYSTERIOUS LODGER

Incredible as it may seem, our overcrowded room and kitchen in Glasgow also accommodated a lodger. Gerald was something of a mystery man. He was in his fifties, worked nights, and spent the daytime sleeping which suited the household routine. As he paid five shillings a week (or half our weekly rent) for the use of a bed in our front room, he was a welcome source of income.

Bill, Jean and I left for school just before nine o'clock in the morning. At that time, my infant brother David was moved from the bed he shared with Bill and me, and put in the cavity bed in the kitchen along with baby Gordon. This left the main room free for Gerald to use undisturbed. When we left for school Gerald was asleep, and by the time we got home in the afternoon he had already left for work. I only became aware of his routine when I was kept home from school ill.

Gerald rarely came home from work before three in the morning. He let himself in with his own key then undressed and got into his pyjamas without lighting the gas lamp; enough light from the street filtered through the net curtain for him to see what he was doing. Gerald's wearing pyjamas was a touch of class. My father and us boys slept in old shirts. But Gerald dressed immaculately in the daytime too, wearing expensive looking suits always accompanied by a collar and tie. His well-tailored overcoat was in a navy blue melton material and his brown shoes were highly polished. All in all he looked the image of a distinguished businessman. My father said Gerald had been an officer during the Great War.

I always marvelled at how Gerald could leave our house looking so spruce and well turned out. When he woke around noon he used our communal toilet before washing and shaving at the kitchen sink. Then my mother made him a cup of strong tea which he drank at the kitchen table. He never ate anything. Soon after, he would emerge from the front room immaculately dressed and carrying a smart leather case, about briefcase size. He also had a Malacca walking stick which my father told us was a sword stick. Gerald would then say goodbye to my mother and stride out of our squalid home and into the street, where he always looked out of place. Even the rent collectors and insurance salesmen weren't as well dressed.

The only nights Gerald didn't go to work were Sundays. But he didn't sleep at our place when he wasn't working. He would get up at about noon on Sundays, perform his ablutions and get dressed. Shortly after twelve, a rather glamorous platinum blonde woman in her early forties would call for him in a sleek motor car. It was a Riley, quite an upmarket car, and the woman wore a full-length fur coat, sheer silk stockings and earrings. She looked very much a lady. I never learned her name, but she was not too proud to come into our hovel, which impressed me. My mother used to make our visitor a cup of tea, and the women would chat pleasantly while Gerald got into his overcoat. Then he would escort the lady out to the car, which she drove. A small crowd, mainly boys, usually gathered round the Riley to admire it—private cars were a rarity in Grove Street. My father said the lady was Gerald's 'fancy woman', and I presume he stayed with her because he never returned to our place until the early hours of Tuesday morning.

The McRobbies often discussed what Gerald did for a living. He always had a thick wad of one pound notes in his wallet so was very rich by our standards, even owning a Bank of England five pound note. It was a large note, printed on crisp white paper, and had to be folded three times to fit in a wallet. Gerald showed it to us one Sunday and it was the first fiver I had ever seen. Working men rarely earned more than five pounds a week, and if they did, they received their money in one pound notes. To offer a five pound note to a shopkeeper in our part of Glasgow would have caused consternation. Even as late as 1954, when I was living with my wife and two children in London for a year, five pound notes were rarely seen in working class areas. When my wife tendered one at a local Woolworth's she was escorted to the cashier's office where she had to write her name and address on it before it would be accepted.

Possessing a five pound note was proof that Gerald was a wealthy man, and my folks couldn't understand why he lodged at our place when he could have afforded much better accommodation. No mail addressed to him ever came through our letterbox, but on several occasions I did see him using a public phone box in New City Road, not far from our house.

My father was sure Gerald was a confidence man of some kind, albeit a high class one. He spoke with an educated Scottish accent and was courteous and gentlemanly in his behaviour. In our front room he slept in a big iron-framed double bed. He had his own sheets and pillowcases which my mother laundered for him at no charge. With Gerald's big bed, the massive heavy mangle, my mother's treadle Singer sewing machine, a wardrobe (one side of which was for Gerald's suits, overcoats and underwear) and a table and two chairs, the small front room was packed.

Sometimes when Gerald came home in the early morning, he would be wearing shiny black pumps instead of the lace-up brown shoes he had on when he left our house. The pumps, made of thin leather, were called dancing shoes. My father was sure he worked at a dance hall, and suspected that he might be one of the professional male dancers who sat in a 'pen' and could be hired for a shilling a bracket of dances. Women hired such men not just because they needed a partner—women dancing with women was commonplace—but because a real professional also gave the woman tuition while they danced, acting as instructor as well as partner. Female partners were available for hire too.

Going dancing, or 'jiggin', was an important pastime for young couples. It only cost a shilling to get into a dance hall, which was open until midnight, and it was a great way to meet someone of the opposite sex. The girls dressed in their best frocks and the boys made themselves look spruce, their hair slicked back with Brilliantine.

My father said that if Gerald worked at a dance hall then it would be a high class one, not the kind frequented by lads and lassies from the slums, and his dancing theory was backed by the fact that Gerald never went out on Sunday nights, when the halls were all closed. My mother believed that Gerald was a professional Master of Ceremonies, and some mornings she found traces of makeup on his pillow. But Gerald himself never gave any clues to his occupation. He politely resisted my mother's expert probing, which she couldn't push too hard, not wanting to risk losing his five shillings a week. Plenty of poor families would have crowded into one room to make the other one available to a lodger for five bob.

Apart from the clothes in the wardrobe, Gerald's only other possessions were two large pigskin suitcases which he kept under his bed and were always locked. I was intensely curious about their contents, and although I had no intention of trying to steal anything from them, I wondered what Gerald kept in them. He never opened a case while anyone was in the room. However, when he came home in the early hours I was often awake, and through half closed eyes I watched him slide the cases from under the bed then put something in them. From tugging them out and lifting them when Gerald wasn't there, I knew they were very heavy.

At my grandmother's house in Ayr there was a wooden box filled with keys of every kind, including dozens of suitcase keys, the accumulation of years. Nobody knew what locks they had once fitted. When we were in Ayr one time, I helped myself to a selection which looked about the right size to open Gerald's cases. Back in Glasgow I waited until I was alone in the house. This didn't happen very often, but occasionally my parents went out on Sundays, taking Bill and Jean with them and leaving me to look after my infant brother and the baby.

I felt very nervous about trying to open Gerald's cases when my chance finally arose. He had left with his fancy woman and wouldn't return until early Tuesday morning. My parents were out too, and unlikely to be back for at least an hour, although I couldn't be sure that no-one would return, and I was dry-mouthed at the thought of being caught red-handed with Gerald's open case. I would have got the belting of a lifetime from my father had I been discovered.

I struck it lucky with almost the first key I tried, flipping up the locks on the case and raising its lid. Inside was a mass of black and white photos. They were all of naked men and women copulating, or indulging in oral sex, and at only ten years old and nowhere near puberty, they didn't stimulate me in the slightest. In fact, I thought the pictures were disgusting and was bitterly disappointed. The men in the photos were nearly all bald, and the women were very plump and looked like prostitutes. I thought the men's swollen penises looked grotesque compared with my own small organ and those of my friends. They were the first dirty photos I'd ever seen, and I was unimpressed.

There were several hundred photos in the case, secured in groups by rubber bands, but I didn't even consider taking one and keeping it. In our house, hiding anything was impossible—as I'd just proved. Instead, I locked the first case then tried my keys on the other, which opened with the last key on my wire ring.

Its contents were even more disappointing. It was packed with little black cigars, about four inches long with a very pungent smell, secured in bundles of ten with a twist of calico. I removed one from a broken bundle before locking the case and sliding it back under the bed.

It was some days before I tried to smoke the little cigar, and on my own at the end of a lane where nobody could see me, I lit it with the aim of having a few puffs. Until then I had only ever smoked cinnamon sticks. I hadn't even tried a cigarette, and Gerald's little cigar was difficult to light, feeling almost damp to the touch. I had to suck like mad before I got it glowing at the tip, and by that time my head was swimming and seemed to be swelling to twice its normal size. The smoke didn't make me feel sick, but it made my bowels contract and I had to dash home to use our lavatory, after stubbing out the mysterious cigar and slipping it into my pocket.

Late that night, after we'd had our evening meal, I gave the cigar to my father, knowing that when he was desperate he'd smoke anything. When he asked where I'd got it from I said I'd found it. 'That's a Burmese cheroot,' he said. 'We used to smoke them in India.'

My father lit up the cheroot and inhaled deeply. I watched his eyes water before he started coughing and finally spluttered, 'It's bloody strong!' He only took a few puffs before putting the cheroot out and carefully placing it in a tin box on the mantelpiece. 'I'll have a wee smoke of that again,' he said, his tone unusually cheerful. He smiled at me benignly then said, 'How about we have a game of Snakes and Ladders? Jessie, you can play too when you finish the dishes.'

I was very surprised. My father rarely played any game with us, except when he'd had a few drinks and was in a good mood. After too many drinks he was in a bad mood. Tonight he was on top form and he hadn't had a drink.

For a few nights, the atmosphere in our house was unusually pleasant following father's homecoming. After a few puffs of the cheroot he would survey us kids with a benevolent smile, and openly flirt with my mother, trapping her at the sink and giving her squeezes and cuddles. He also became very loquacious and talked at length about his army days.

When he had finished Gerald's cigar, smoking the last bit with the aid of darning needle, he said to me, 'Where did you find that cheroot?' I told him I had found it down a nearby lane, adding that an Indian man had thrown it away. 'Oh,' he said, 'keep your eye out for another one. It makes a nice change from a fag.'

Next day after Gerald had left for work, I opened his suitcase and purloined another cheroot. I sneaked down the lane with some matches and lit it, taking a few puffs before stubbing it out. I avoided inhaling or holding the smoke in my mouth, but nonetheless our street looked brighter after puffing on the cheroot. After tea I presented it to my father, who was very pleased.

When he'd lit up and had a few deep draws, he tried to get my mother to have a puff, but she refused. I only ever saw my mother try to smoke once, when a woman neighbour pressed a scented cork tip cigarette upon her. My mother puffed primly on the cigarette and my father, who was home at the time, laughed and said she looked like 'a coo wi' a straw hangin' oot o' its erse!' Although she didn't smoke, my mother loved the aroma of a cigar, although she did not appreciate father's cheroot. 'It makes a terrible smell!' she complained. 'It stinks out the whole hoose.'

Looking back, I realise that I was unwittingly responsible for getting my old man stoned. Gerald's 'Burmese cheroots' were most probably bhang, the Hindu name for Indian hemp, a narcotic known outside India and the Far East as marijuana.

During my army service in the East I often saw bhang smoked and remembered the distinctive odour from my boyhood.

In Britain in the thirties, few narcotics were illegal. Cocaine, morphine, heroin and other drugs were freely available from chemist shops on prescription, and cost was only a few pence. There was no social stigma attached to using drugs. People who couldn't afford to pay for a doctor's prescription could buy a wide variety of patent wine 'tonics' from grocers' shops as well as chemists. Most of these tonics were laced with heroin, cocaine or laudanum (tincture of opium).

In the latter years of her life, my God-fearing Presbyterian grandmother was soothed by regular draughts from her 'bottle', a concoction she obtained from our chemist on permanent prescription. The eight ounce bottle cost sixpence, which included a twopence refund, and I bought it regularly for her from Kay's the Chemist in Ayr. The medication was almost pure laudanum and for several hours after her draught, Grandma felt no pain.

Another narcotic that was freely available was snuff which could be bought from tobacconists. Even in our poor neighbourhood, many people carried little tin snuff boxes, from which they snorted when they felt like a lift. In the thirties, Conan Doyle's Sherlock Holmes stories were very popular, and Sherlock regularly shot up on heroin or cocaine, which never perturbed his medical companion, the good Doctor Watson. The first Western nation to make the possession and use of certain narcotics illegal was the United States of America. In 1914 the Harrison Narcotics Act was passed. It was aimed specifically at opium and its derivatives, and consequently drug-using Americans switched to Mexican marijuana. The first federal law outlawing marijuana was not passed until 1937. Britain lagged behind the USA in outlawing drugs, and I cannot recall any report of prosecution for using drugs either before or during my army service. I assume it must have been 1947 before narcotics began to go underground in the United Kingdom.

Returning to our lodger, Gerald, and his suitcase of bhang cheroots, I imagine that he probably sold these at the dance hall where he (presumably) worked. I doubt if he was in any danger of prosecution for supplying marijuana. At that time, no Glasgow policeman would have known what the weed smelt like. Where he did risk arrest was for selling pornographic photos, the penalties for which were severe.

Gerald lodged with us for about three years before departing suddenly from our lives.

One Sunday around noon, Gerald's lady friend was sitting in our kitchen drinking a cup of tea while he got dressed in the front room. My father was home and he casually lit up the butt of one of Gerald's cheroots (by this time I had purloined about six of them for my father). When Gerald came into the kitchen he took a sniff of the smoke and turned ashen. He asked my father, 'Where did you get that?' and he replied 'Oh, Alex found it. An Indian fella threw it away.'

Gerald stared at me and it was obvious that he knew I had been into his cases. He didn't say anything except to tell his lady friend that she should hurry, as they had to be going. He hustled her out of the house and that was the last I saw of either of them.

The next day, when I got home from school at lunchtime, my mother was distraught. Gerald and his friend had arrived just after nine o'clock when he had announced that he was giving up his digs, paying my mother ten shillings in lieu of notice before loading his suitcases and clothes into the Riley. My mother was shattered. 'I'll never find another lodger like Gerald,' she moaned. 'He was such an easy-going gentleman. And his money was always on time.'

We tried to find a replacement lodger. My mother put a sign in our front window, but it was mainly women who enquired about the room, and she told them it had been taken. She would never have a woman lodger. She said they were too much trouble, and too fussy. Most of the men who looked at the room were fussy too. They didn't fancy sharing a room with three small boys—plus the mangle and sewing machine. So the room, or anyway, the bed, was never let again.

While our household suffered financially from Gerald's departure, my father (although he didn't know it) had an additional reason to regret Gerald's leaving. My supply of Burmese cheroots dried up, making him quite testy. 'Has that Indian fella stopped smoking?' he often asked me. 'Or are you not looking for his cheroots any more?'

I said I thought the Indian had gone away. But I'd keep an eye out for him.

'Aye,' my father sighed, 'you don't get a good smoke like that every day. They did me more good than Capstan.'

SALT IN YOUR PORRIDGE

In Scotland, cooking, serving and eating porridge was performed according to a ritual that hadn't changed for generations. For a start, only oatmeal was used. There were 'convenience' products, such as Scott's Porridge Oats, or Quick Quaker Oats, which could be cooked more quickly, but such packaged offerings were scorned by most households. Apart from being untraditional, packaged porridges cost considerably more than basic oatmeal.

In Ayr, where my mother cooked for four adults and five children, porridge was served seven days a week for breakfast, and the oatmeal was purchased in bags weighing a stone. One bag usually lasted a week. The porridge was always cooked in a big cast iron pot that hung from a hook over the coal fire, never in an enamel or aluminium saucepan on the gas stove. A gallon or so of cold water was brought to the boil in the pot, and after it had been bubbling for five minutes, a handful of salt was added. By a handful, I mean exactly that. A large jar of raw salt stood beside the stove and was used liberally in all cooking.

In a house without refrigeration or an icebox, salt was also used as a preservative, especially in summer. We ate a lot of herring, which we got for nothing by scrounging it from the harbour when the fishing fleet docked and unloaded its catch. Fish that wasn't eaten immediately was filleted and rubbed all over with salt, before being placed in the meat safe, a large box covered with fine wire mesh to keep the flies out. After salting, fish could be kept for a long time before it began to glow in the dark—a sign that it was going off.

During porridge making, salt was used to provide flavour. After the boiling water was salted, the oatmeal was poured in and stirred constantly with a big wooden spoon called a spurtle. Metal spoons were never used to stir porridge. This was the most time-consuming aspect of the cooking process. To get the porridge to the right consistency, it had to be stirred almost constantly, and if the cook had other things to do, someone, usually a child, was instructed to stand by the pot and keep up the good work.

The cooking went on for twenty minutes or more, during which time the height of the pot was adjusted to keep the porridge simmering gently. At the ideal height, the surface was covered with little bubbles which swelled and burst, like lava in a volcano.

When it was finally judged to be ready, the porridge was ladled into large plates. But it wasn't served immediately. No way! The plates were carried outside and set along one or two windowsills. This allowed the essential cooling process to begin, which was completed when a thick skin had formed on top. Under the skin, it stayed very hot, and would burn your tongue unless cooled with milk.

When the plates were brought to the table, a pinch of salt was sprinkled over the crust and milk added. Like many kids, I hated adding salt to my porridge and much preferred sugar. But adding sugar to one's plate was an unforgivable offence. You didn't *have* to put salt on your porridge. That was permissible, but woe betide if you were caught putting sugar on it. Sweetening porridge was considered unmanly, and was certainly not done by a true Scot. Porridge was a Spartan dish which had sustained warriors for generations during the clan wars and when fighting the English, and we weren't supposed to *enjoy* eating it: kids were fed it so they would grow up strong and healthy. Cereals like corn flakes and shredded wheat, to which sugar was added, were for the English and other soft races. True Scots always started the day on porridge.

After I got a full time job at fourteen, I ate breakfast with my uncles as I started work at the same time as them. While they ate their porridge, the men usually had their heads buried in the morning paper, which they divided between themselves. Until cups of tea were served, the sugar bowl was deliberately left off the table so there was no temptation to sprinkle some on the porridge. But I developed a system of excusing myself for a minute then sidling across to the food cupboard where the sugar bowl was kept. A quick dab and I had a fair pinch which I surreptitiously sprinkled over my porridge when I got back to the table.

Occasionally I'd be spotted and Uncle Tom would growl, 'Jessie, your boy's put sugar on his porridge!'

My mother, who was in the scullery preparing the second breakfast course, would rush in and throw her hands up in horror at this culinary sacrilege. But there wasn't much she could do, and I was able to enjoy my sweetened porridge.

We had two English girl cousins, daughters of my Uncle Jim, who lived in Liverpool with his English wife. On a visit to Ayr, the two girls, their mother and Uncle Jim had breakfast with us and were served porridge. Aunt Muriel requested honey for herself and daughters as they always took it at home. My uncles Tom and David could scarcely conceal their disgust that their nieces were being raised on sweetened porridge. Uncle Jim still put salt on his, but let his family do as they pleased. After the visitors had left, Uncle Tom said scornfully, 'Honey on their porridge! I suppose you can't expect any better from an Englishwoman.'

At nineteen I became an officer in the Seaforth Highlanders and porridge was served in the mess. Most of the Scottish officers put salt on their porridge in the traditional way, but we had a few English officers who had opted to join a Highland regiment. They sprinkled sugar on theirs.

I must confess that I went along with the majority and salted mine to show that I was a true Highlander, although born in the Lowlands.

My uncles would have been proud of me!

FOR AMUSEMENT ONLY

In the 1930s, Sunday in Scotland was a day of abysmal boredom for active young people, which I used to dread, counting the hours until the Sabbath was over. The Church of Scotland, and its offshoots like the 'Wee Free Kirk', decreed that the Lord's Day was a day of rest during which no work could be done. But it was not a day of rest *and* recreation. Sundays were *not* for pleasure. Children were banned from playing any kind of sport, even hopscotch, and we weren't even supposed to yell, shout or make any sound of merriment. So, what did we do on one of the two days when there was no school? We went to Sunday School.

Our Sunday School was held in a cavernous temple of religion called the Grove Street Institute, not far from our house. I was forced to attend both morning Sunday School and afternoon bible class, and, to crown my day, had to go to the Band of Hope at night too. I had to wear my best clothes— which never looked very new—and this meant I couldn't do anything that might get them dirty or torn. Not that there was anything to do. We weren't even allowed to play marbles.

On Sundays the shops were all shut except for a few 'open all hours' places. This meant we couldn't go into the city and cruise stores like Woolworths and Marks and Spencer, indulging in some 'wabbing' (shop-lifting).

It was my school chum, Lionel Watson, who introduced me to shop-lifting. Prior to his tuition I'd only ever stolen edibles like biscuits or boiled sweets from Woolworths temptingly accessible display counters. But Lionel was highly skilled at the art of lifting goods without being spotted. I never actually saw him pick anything up, but when we got outside the store, he would produce items such as combs, propelling pencils, playing cards, toy cars and bottles of Brilliantine from his pockets.

Lionel tried to give me his booty, but there was no way I could have gone home with anything of value without being cross-examined about how I had acquired it. If I'd claimed to have bought it from money I'd earned by running messages, then I would have got a belting for not handing over the cash, and if it was suspected I'd stolen something then I would have got a belting for that too. At home, there was no place to hide anything. It would have been discovered instantly by Bill or Jean, who had noses like bloodhounds when it came to ferreting out anything I tried to conceal. So usually I stole only edibles, which I ate before I got home.

But Lionel, whose parents gave him quite a lot of pocket money, could take anything home and it was assumed that he'd bought it. Lionel was well off by my standards, but to him shoplifting was a challenge and a diversion. However, on Sundays even this diversion was denied to us. On Sundays *everything* was closed, including the picture houses, pubs and those dens of iniquity—the dance halls.

At the time, the Lord's Day Observance Society was very powerful, and its members devoted themselves to opposing any relaxation of the strict non conformist laws governing entertainment on Sundays. When a liberal local authority proposed to amend the law to permit say, Sunday night film shows, the Society took them to court and usually won. Even in cosmopolitan London, the Society managed to restrict the Sunday opening of cinemas until eight pm, when the last church services were over. Reformers who wanted to introduce what was called the 'Continental Sunday' were castigated for trying to turn Britain into a dissolute nation like France, Italy or Spain, where Sunday was a day for pleasure as well as religious observance. Such nations were, of course, Catholic countries, so that explained everything.

There were lots of Roman Catholic families in our neighbourhood in Glasgow, and they had many, many children. The Catholics didn't observe the Lord's Day as strictly as the 'Proddies' did. However, we rarely mixed much with the Catholic kids because they went to their own schools and on Sunday to their own chapel, and apart from that, there was always antagonism between Protestants and Catholics. Sometimes this flared into street fights between boys of opposing religions.

On Sundays, the Catholics had to get up at the hellish hour of six o'clock to attend early Mass, but between services they were allowed to run around and play like they did on other days. I envied them their freedom, but most of all I envied them for having that marvellous ritual called confession. They could do all kinds of wicked things during the week, then wipe the slate clean on Sundays by telling the priest what they'd done. They always received forgiveness, and all they had to do to atone was mutter a few words of gibberish over and over, or count a string of beads. The lucky buggers could keep sinning for ever! Or so I thought. In my boyhood I considered turning Catholic to escape from the horrors of the Sabbath. My mother nearly had a fit when I told her I might 'turn', ordering me not to play with the Doherty, McMullin or Flaherty boys—all from Catholic homes.

While the Sabbath was strict in Glasgow, it was much more rigorously observed in Ayr. My grandma, God-fearing Presbyterian woman, didn't even like my uncles working in the garden on Sundays, although she had difficulty in getting them to don their best suits and go to the kirk. The 'no amusements on Sundays' rule was strictly enforced. All our indoor games were put away for the day, and we couldn't even play Snap—or horror of horrors—open a deck of playing cards. We were allowed to read, providing the material was suitable, and the Bible or John Bunyan's *Pilgrim's Progress* were prescribed over comics or anything light-hearted. I hated Bunyan's dreary tome! But I read it for lack of anything else, because I was a compulsive reader.

After my grandma became bedridden, the restrictions on Sunday recreation eased considerably. Additionally, the outbreak of war in 1939 meant that working on the Sabbath became commonplace at munitions factories, shipyards and industrial plants. But the war didn't result in much relaxation of the strictures against amusement. The shops, pubs and cinemas stayed closed, which made Sundays a dreary day for servicemen and women who thronged garrison towns like Ayr.

In 1944 I was in the army, stationed at Inverness. As a major concession, the church arranged free Sunday film shows in the town's largest cinema for servicemen and women. However, these shows were preceded by a long and dull religious service by a Church of Scotland Minister. The troops began queuing an hour before the service began to guarantee their seats for the film, so the minister always had a packed house. Anyone who wanted to watch the film had to endure the service. Soldiers of every faith, as well as atheists and agnostics, sat stolidly through a lengthy sermon, standing up to sing dreary hymns and bowing their heads during prayers.

The only films we saw on Sundays in Glasgow were short, silent features at the evening Band of Hope meetings. These were garishly hand-coloured films about the evils of strong drink, interspersed with glass slides shown on the Magic Lantern. But at least they provided something to do to fill in the dreary and interminable hours of Sundays.

In spite of the prohibition on playing games, we did manage some clandestine recreation. Boys took their marbles secretly from their home and gathered at the end of lanes or behind deserted factories where they wouldn't be seen playing with them. Childhood pastimes such as these had definite seasons when a certain game was 'in'. The marbles craze could last for six weeks, then die overnight, and it would be impossible to give them away. Suddenly a yo-yo craze began and every child had to have one. Then it was Hi-Lo, a rubber ball attached to a kind of table tennis bat by a length of elastic, which some kids could keep bouncing off the bat for a thousand or more times. Another craze that came and went was for spinning tops, or 'peeries'. Shops sold whips to whip these with, but we preferred to use a length of tightly-wound cloth with a knot on the end called a 'pugee'. Using coloured chalks we'd draw circles on the top's surface, which produced colourful changing patterns as the toy spun round.

One craze that withstood the vagaries of fashion in the 1930s was collecting cigarette cards. These were issued to make up sets, usually of fifty different cards, and covered everything from footballers and cricketers to wild flowers and railway locomotives. For a penny, you could buy an album which had a slot for each card. Once you had several complete sets you could take them to a big store in the city and exchange them for a wide range of goods.

When we lived in Ayr, my grandmother wanted a Westminster chiming clock for the mantelpiece. The particular one she liked was available in exchange for forty completed albums of Kensitas cigarette cards. With one card in each pack of twenty cigarettes, this meant buying a minimum of two thousand packs of Kensitas to fill the albums. But it wasn't as simple as that. Many packs had duplicate cards in them, and getting forty complete sets was very difficult.

Uncle Tom smoked Gold Flake, David bought Churchman, and my father and Uncle Alec (when he was home from sea) smoked Capstan. But Grandma urged them all to switch to

Kensitas until she had enough cards to get her clock, and they complied, reluctantly, with the result that she got her timepiece about a year later.

I played a fairly major part in helping to get the albums filled. Cards we had in excess of our requirements could be swapped, and I brought many sought-after cards home to complete another album. In addition, I often hung around outside a newsagent or tobacconist's shop and asked customers for their Kensitas cigarette cards. That was how many boys built up their cigarette card collections.

One type of recreation that was, surprisingly, available to children and adults on Sundays was slot machine gambling. In Glasgow, almost every small shop had one or two fruit machines. These only accepted brass tokens, which could be bought from the shopkeeper for a ha'penny, and every machine bore a notice which warned FOR AMUSEMENT ONLY. However, this was not the case. If you had a win, you could buy goods from the shop for your tokens. It was illegal, but all the shops did it, and I found it remarkable that in Presbyterian Scotland, one of the few pleasures available on the Sabbath was gambling on Las Vegas type slot machines.

A SCHOOL ROMANCE

After I left primary school at eleven, I sat the exam for a scholarship to the fee-paying Allan Glen's school, one of the best in Scotland. Hundreds of boys from all over the country took the exam, and there was great jubilation in Grove Street when it was announced that I had won one of the two coveted places. My parents basked in the glory of having produced a son who would attend the city's most prestigious public school; until grim reality shattered their euphoria. Although the scholarship covered tuition fees, my parents had to supply my uniform, as well as sportswear and school books, which had been free at primary school. Another expense was daily tram fares to and from school, as well as money for lunch. Allan Glen's day boys did not carry cut lunches, but ate at table with the boarders.

There were numerous 'incidentals', and a guinea here and there soon swelled the total beyond my parents' budget. After careful calculation, they determined that it would cost a hundred pounds to send Alex to Allan Glen's for the first year alone. This was my father's exact annual income.

To his credit, my father pursued every avenue in an attempt to find the hundred pounds. He looked at taking out a loan, but had no collateral and couldn't hope to meet even the most modest repayments. He visited his old wartime company commander who had often helped him when he was in dire financial straits, but there was a vast difference between giving father a couple of pounds to keep him going, and donating a hundred pounds towards his son's education. His old CO also pointed out that I would be at Allan Glen's for several years, and said that it would be unfair to let me attend for one year then have to take me away.

Finally, my father was forced to admit defeat; there was no way I could take up the scholarship, and in the end it passed to the boy who had come third, to the delight of his parents. I felt no great regret at not being able to go to a 'snob' school; at least I had won the scholarship. In any case, I was going to Woodside Academy, which although not as prestigious as Allan Glen's, was a very good school in one of the better areas of Glasgow. The teachers at Woodside Academy even wore gowns and mortar boards.

My teachers at Woodside knew about the Allan Glen's scholarship and why I hadn't been able to take it up, and were very considerate. When I got a place in the house second eleven football team I needed football boots, stockings, shorts and a shirt. Such an expense made my mother turn pale, but by digging into his stock, the sports master managed to lend me everything I needed, so I was able to play wearing the proper kit.

When World War II started we moved to Ayr, where I went to the local grammar school. There were less pupils than at Woodside, but it was a co-educational school, and at age thirteen girls became a major distraction in my life. I had the handicap, for a suitor, of being the youngest in the class. Some of my fellow pupils were as old as sixteen, and the youngest girls were all at least a year older than me.

The favours of the prettiest girl, Fiona Dunbar, were eagerly vied for by all the boys; not only was Fiona very attractive, but she was brainy too and regularly came top of the class. To distinguish myself in the lovely Fiona's eyes, I became a swot. I'd always been a good student, but I'd never really exerted myself, and to woo Fiona I got really stuck into my studies.

I came equal first with Fiona in the first term examinations. This didn't entitle me to sit alongside her in class—the girls had one side of the classroom and the boys the other—but it certainly made her pay attention to me. In the second term exams I came top, beating my rival by one mark. With hindsight, I realise that this was a mistake. Fiona treated me very coldly. She'd been Queen Bee all through her schooldays, and now an interloper from Glasgow had burst upon the scene and knocked her off the top spot. I had to find another way of winning her favours, and to do this I started a class newspaper.

The *Third Year News* was an eight page, half foolscap publication over which I had total control, writing every item. The stencils were typed for me by the accounts girl at the newsagency where I worked, and I set the 'headlines' in larger print, using rubber type from a John Bull printing set. There were no photos or drawings.

I coaxed the headmaster's typist into reproducing about fifty copies of my paper on the school duplicator, and the first issue of the *News* caused quite a sensation. It was a highly irreverent publication, in fact it was a scandal sheet, heavily larded with juvenile innuendo. Personal paragraphs named boys who were keen on certain girls in class, and vice versa. The progress of various class romances were charted in a column titled 'Holding Hands', and some of the 'Big Men' in class were lampooned, which was potentially dangerous for me. Riskiest of all, and what made the journal eagerly sought-after, were items which took the mickey out of the teachers.

But the paper was a clandestine publication for pupils' eyes only, and after the typist duplicated the fifty copies I forgot about the inky stencils. Before I left she tossed them in the waste paper basket.

I later discovered that the school typist had run off a few more copies, which were distributed to various teachers, and I would have been in deep trouble had the staff, and in particular our English teacher, Andrew Leckie, not had a good sense of humour. At first, none of them let on that they had read the *News*—I think they were as intrigued as the pupils by the torrid teenage romances that my paper reported on. Items which dealt with supposed romantic affairs between teachers were pure supposition on my part, but occasionally I scored a bullseye. I had long suspected that our rather glamorous French teacher, Miss St Claire, and our maths teacher, Mr Kramer, were keen on one another, and I printed this as fact. Within a month the couple announced their engagement. News of this was conveyed to Class 3A by Mr Leckie at the start of an English period. 'You will be pleased to know,' he said, 'that Miss St Claire and Mr Kramer are engaged to be married.'

There was a gasp from the class, and Mr Leckie added, 'The happy couple would like it to be known that their announcement was in no way hastened by its premature publication in a scandal sheet which is believed to be circulating in this school.'

He looked me in the eye briefly then lowered his head. I knew he was well aware of who edited the scandal sheet although in the paper I didn't name myself as editor. No action was taken about the *News*, which I published every two months until I left school. From the remarks they made, it was apparent that the teachers were still reading their copies and enjoying them, and I quickly discovered that most people didn't mind how much they were satirised, as long as they got a mention. This applied equally to teachers and pupils, so I ensured that everyone in the class and all the staff were mentioned at least once in each issue. I'd learned a fundamental lesson of journalism—people like seeing their name in print.

The person who was mentioned most frequently in the journal was its *raison d'etre*, Fiona Dunbar, and by printed innuendo, I could say things to her I didn't have the nerve to say face to face. At that stage I'd never been out alone with a girl. But Fiona basked in having her status as the most popular girl in class confirmed in print, and warmed to me, especially when I slipped back a place after the third term exams and she was top of the class again. I think my concentration on extra-curricular activities had affected my school work.

I was rarely short of material for my paper. Among the boys there were two camps, one led by sixteen-year-old Donald Rodd, who carried his clout because he shaved. Indeed, by four o'clock when school ended his dark jowls needed a second shave. Roddy was an expert on jazz music and had a vast collection of records. His other hobby was boxing and he bought magazines like *The Ring*, talking knowledgeably about the sport. I only saw him box once, but in the schoolyard at breaks he often shadow boxed and showed us the finer points of footwork, ducking and weaving, etc. He said he couldn't box with anyone at school because he was a semi-pro and it would have been unfair to fight with amateurs.

Roddy's rival was another sixteen-year-old, Hughie Sharp, who had a strong following because he had access to a supply of pornographic ditties of the sort that schoolboys love to read. Most boys kept at least one salacious poem in their wallets, and on the way home from school Sharp and his group detoured to the Low Green—a large park in Ayr—for a poetry reading. In the middle of the park, where they couldn't be overheard or surprised by any adults, the boys huddled together while Sharp read out his latest piece of porn.

I became a member of Roddy's group, preferring him to Sharp because he wasn't always boasting about his romantic conquests. Hughie constantly bragged about his sexual prowess, assuring us that he had scored with several girls in class; although he never claimed he had made it with the virginal Fiona Dunbar. She turned up her nose at him, and it was Roddy who finally scored with her. When she began going steady with him, I felt no rancour. If Fiona had to go out with someone, I would rather it was with my friend Roddy than his rival Hughie Sharp. Anyway, Roddy invited me to join him and Fiona at a milk bar where we used to hang out.

After I started the class newspaper, I became very popular. I was assiduously wooed by Hughie Sharp, who wanted me to join his group and abandon Donald Rodd—and for a time I kept a foot in both camps. Sharp had the attraction of his porno material, while Roddy was Fiona's 'steady', and I was quite happy to be courted by the two biggest men in school.

Finally Sharp issued an ultimatum: it was him or Roddy. I couldn't belong to both camps, and decided to stay loyal to Roddy—and Fiona, after which things became very strained. During breaks in the school yard, we gathered in our respective groups and glowered at one another. Threats of a punch-up were made by Sharp's pals, but we were confident of the boxing prowess of our leader, Roddy, who would quickly clean up Sharp while we dealt with his chums

In the end it did come to fisticuffs. The spark was ignited by Fiona when she got bored with Roddy's talk about jazz and boxing, and their romance began to wither. For Roddy, their eventual split was a tragedy of Grecian proportions. He had been 'jilted'—his actual words. His mates had to work hard to help him through a period of black despair, and I could sympathise with him—what a blow to lose the lovely Fiona!

But worse was to come, and a few weeks after the split Fiona was seen walking hand in hand with Hughie Sharp! To be jilted was bad enough, but to be dumped for a despised rival was a mortal blow, and Roddy's honour could only be satisfied by a fight. He let it be known that he was ready for a showdown, and an emissary from Sharp's camp arranged the time and place for the match.

After splitting up with Fiona, many of Roddy's group had defected to Sharp's camp. The only two followers Roddy had left were myself and an Italian lad, Bruno Tomasini—scarcely enough to provide a defence during the bout with Sharp. But Roddy said that he was unconcerned by his lack of supporters. He was quietly confident he would clean up Sharp in the first round.

On the afternoon of the big fight all the boys in Class 3A marched to the Low Green. I was looking forward to seeing Roddy box, and although Sharp was bigger and heavier than him, Roddy had expert ringcraft. It was to be a bare knuckle fight as Sharp had refused Roddy's request that they wore boxing gloves. My duties as second thus involved little more than holding a towel and a can of water in case my champ needed a drink.

As Roddy had predicted, the fight didn't last long. After the referee called 'Seconds out!' Roddy went into a crouch before ducking and weaving around Sharp, who barely moved, waiting until Roddy came within reach of his long arms. Ten seconds into the fight Sharp landed a blow on Roddy's left eye, closing it almost instantly. Our shaken champ ducked and weaved even faster until Sharp delivered an upper-cut to his chin which came close to knocking him out. The referee stopped the fight while Bruno and me worked on the champ. But he was obviously unfit to fight, and I threw in the towel for Roddy, who raised no objection as Bruno dabbed at his black eye and the cut above it.

Sharp was lifted shoulder high and carried off by his exuberant supporters, leaving the myth of Roddy's boxing prowess shattered. As Bruno and I escorted our groggy champion home, Roddy confessed that he had a glass jaw. To overcome this, he said he led with his chin. The logic of this tactic escaped me, and having a glass jaw seemed to be a serious handicap for a boxer, although Roddy assured us that some legendary fighters had the same problem. He reeled off their names, the dates of their fights and titles they'd won—

just as he'd always done when he'd been the unchallenged champion and boxing expert. Roddy's other excuse for his defeat was not being able to wear boxing gloves. He claimed gloves would have made a difference. We loyally agreed that they would have.

The fight took place on a Friday afternoon, so it was Monday before Roddy made an appearance before the class, with his magnificent black eye and large square of plaster over the cut above it. The fickle Fiona Dunbar was most concerned about her former boyfriend's injury. I had great pleasure in telling her that *she* had been the cause of the grudge match between Roddy and Sharp, and her eyes sparkled at the news. She glanced tenderly at Roddy, completely ignoring Sharp, who had adopted the lofty manner of a victor. After school Bruno and I walked home with Roddy. We were joined by Fiona almost immediately, and within seconds Roddy was carrying her school case. Sharp and Co were standing nearby and Sharp's jaw dropped when the lovely Fiona slipped her hand into Roddy's. So—Roddy lost the fight—but won the girl, at least for a while. Fiona believed in playing the field.

After Bruno and I parted company with the reunited couple, we pondered the ways of women, both agreeing that they weren't worth bothering about to console ourselves for never having had a girlfriend. I was too young and Bruno was too fat. He wore thick pebbled glasses and his nickname at school was 'Musso', as he looked rather like a young Mussolini.

Not long after the big fight, the real Mussolini declared war on Britain, and the days following Italy's entry into the conflict were traumatic for people of Italian descent living in the United Kingdom. Most Britons were incensed at the Italian dictator's action in joining the Nazis. All over the country Italian-run shops and cafes were smashed by rampaging mobs. Most towns had at least one ice cream or fish and chip shop run by Italians, and Ayr had several, including one run by Bruno's family at the bottom of High Street. The Tomasinis lived above the shop with their extended family, including some aunts and a grandmother as well as Bruno's parents and sisters. On the night of 10th June the family huddled in terror in their flat while a mob smashed the windows below and looted the shop, breaking display cases and destroying the furniture and the refrigeration. The police were kept busy racing from one Italian shop to another, but as the station was quite close to Bruno's cafe the mob was quickly dispersed and the Tomasinis came to no harm.

I knew nothing of the night's drama until I read about the rampage in the morning newspaper, as there were no Italian shops in Green Street. That morning, I left earlier than usual for school. Part of my daily routine was to pick up Bruno at the family shop and cafe, which lay half way between my home and school, and as we walked to school we would discuss the homework we had done. Bruno would help me with algebra while I gave him a hand with his English and grammar.

When I reached the cafe it looked as if it had been blasted by a bomb. The windows had been hastily boarded up but the gutter was piled with shards of broken glass, empty confectionery boxes, shattered milkshake glasses and pieces of broken mirrors. I ran round to the back entrance where stairs led up to the living quarters and banged on the door until I heard Mr Tomasini's frightened voice. I told him who it was and he let me in, slamming the door behind me and quickly bolting it. Upstairs, the family were in a state of shock. Bruno was white-faced and had been crying, as had everyone else. His mother greeted me with a kiss and said she was very pleased to see me, but when I asked if Bruno was ready to go to school she looked horrified, saying there was no way any of the family would leave the house that day, and perhaps not for several more. But I told her that the looters had been hooligans who had used the declaration of war to raid shops and steal scarce items like chocolates and cigarettes—nobody hated the Italians.

I finally convinced Bruno's parents to let him go to school, saying I would look after him and walk home with him after school as usual. So, with our schoolbags over our shoulders, Bruno and I strode up High Street. He was very nervous, but I was spoiling for a fight, disgusted by the behaviour of some of my countrymen. To attack the inoffensive Italians whose forefathers had been in Scotland for centuries was not fair play. It wasn't British. As we strode up the street in our yellow and black school blazers, nobody paid the slightest attention to us. When we reached school Bruno braced himself. I think he expected to be greeted with racist cries such as he'd heard the night before, but our schoolmates behaved normally, except for displaying some embarrassment. They were well aware of the events of the previous night.

The first period was taken by our English teacher, Andrew Leckie. After roll call he addressed us in his lilting Highland tones, saying 'I am sure we all want to express our sorrow at last night's disgraceful looting of Italian premises in our town. I am pleased to see that Bruno Tomasini is with us as usual, and I am sure you will all make sure that he is looked after for the next few days. Now, bring me your homework, please.' Sitting alongside me, poor old Bruno's eyes filled with tears.

After school, Roddy insisted on walking home with us, and outside the gates we were joined by Fiona Dunbar. She said she wanted to walk with us too, and gave Bruno the full force of her violet eyes before asking if he would like to carry her school case. He was powerfully affected—it was the first time she'd deigned to even talk to the 'fat four-eyes' as Bruno was sometimes called. As we stood at the gates we were joined by two of Fiona's girlfriends, and then, to my surprise, Hughie Sharp and his cronies appeared. They said they were going down to the harbour for some reason, so they'd come with us if nobody objected. So off we went with Bruno escorted by three girls and nine boys, walking three abreast down High Street. Nobody can be more cruel to one another than children, but on that day in June 1940 I felt closer to my school chums than I'd ever been.

SMART BOY WANTED

I left Ayr Grammar School on my fourteenth birthday, 9th December 1940, and the following day I started my first job, working as an office boy at Ayr Slipway for 12/6 a week.

I got the job through a classified advertisement in the *Ayrshire Post*. Although World War II had been going for over a year, and Britain had suffered the disaster of Dunkirk the previous June, jobs were not easy to find. The aftermath of the Great Depression still lingered, and in 1940 there were over half a million people in Britain on the dole. It was 1941 before the nation went into a 'total war' situation and the unemployment slack was finally taken up.

The advert I replied to was headed SMART BOY WANTED. In those pre-sexual discrimination days, it was permissible to nominate the gender of a required employee, and I was one of several lads interviewed by a harassed clerk who came from London to oversee the administrative side of the Slipway's expansion. The Clerk, a dapper Londoner, told me later that I had been the outstanding applicant. Although only fourteen, I had completed third year at Ayr Grammar School and was by far the youngest in my class. I left school because I had gone as far as I could go. There was no higher class to move up to, and to continue my education I would have needed to go to a school which took pupils to matriculation standard. Anyway, between Woodside Academy and Ayr Grammar, I felt that my education had been pretty good. I'd done three years of French and

German and got good marks in both subjects so, on the surface anyway, I was more polished than the average fourteen year old school leaver. Mr Hearne, the Slipway clerk, was an old public school boy and was impressed by my linguistic ability and consistent top marks in English, history and geography. He was even more impressed when I told him I had enrolled at night-school where I would study accountancy, bookkeeping and the principles and practices of commerce two nights a week. But the clincher was the fact that I spoke 'educated' Scottish. When he began working in Ayr, Mr Hearne had great difficulty understanding the Lowland accent, and occasionally he used me as an 'interpreter'. Although I was only a lad, I quickly became indispensable to him.

The other reason I had no regrets about leaving school was because I wanted to begin my adulthood. There was no financial gain in starting full time work, and my income dropped six shillings a week when I started at the Slipway. Instead, I sought the job because as a ship repair yard, the Slipway was to play an important role in the war effort. What was called 'The Battle of the Atlantic' had begun, and British and Allied shipping was being sunk at an alarming rate by the German U-Boats. Many ships which were torpedoed but didn't sink managed to limp back to the west coast of England and Scotland. Repairing them and getting them back to sea was a matter of top priority.

In 1940 all British ship repair yards were taken over by the Admiralty, and as an Admiralty agent the London Graving Dock Company was appointed to run Ayr Slipway and introduce the latest repair techniques. Many English executives were transferred from London to oversee operations in Ayr.

At fourteen I was as patriotic as the next boy. I joined the Army Cadets in 1940, training at nights and weekends, while my job at the shipyard made me feel that I was doing vital war work. The Slipway could only cater for vessels up to about three thousand tons, but these included Royal Navy frigates which came from as far as the Mediterranean to undergo repairs, and every day I was going aboard damaged ships (to deliver mail to the crew). Hearing first hand reports about the war at sea was heady stuff for a lad, and working at the Slipway was much more exciting than being a junior clerk in a lawyer's office.

Prior to my appointment there had been no office boy at the Slipway as before its wartime expansion the yard hadn't had much work. There were originally less than a hundred yard workers and about six office staff. Within a year these figures had risen to eight hundred yard workers and an office and drafting department of about forty. I was able to create my own little empire, expanding the stationery store, organising the mailroom, stamping out the brass checks which the workers hung on boards when clocking on and off, and undertaking many other tasks for which nobody was directly responsible.

Wartime conscription was taking most able-bodied men into the armed services, but shipyard workers were in an essential occupation, and like coal miners could neither be conscripted nor volunteer for active service. In the office most workers were very young, like me, or too old to be called up. More than half the staff were women.

I quickly ingratiated myself with the female staff who taught me office skills, including how to type, letting me use their machines when they were at lunch, or after hours. The switchboard operator showed me how to operate the telephone exchange, which became quite extensive, and included my favourite—the priority line to London. I also picked up some shorthand from the stenographers. The women were intrigued that a boy should want to learn such essentially female skills as typing and shorthand, but even at fourteen I had ambitions to be a journalist. I put my name down for one of the rare cub reporter vacancies on the *Ayrshire Post*, but was told to re-apply after I could type competently and write shorthand.

At the Slipway, I made myself useful in many ways. One of

the small jobs I did was to change the typewriter and adding machine ribbons, which none of the female staff liked doing. When a ribbon needed to be changed, I was called on the intercom. I also looked after the staff at morning and afternoon tea breaks. As office boy I didn't have to perform that traditional chore of making the tea as I was busy from morning until night with more essential tasks. Instead, someone in each department took turns to make the tea for their group, and my task was to go round the office and collect orders, and money, for such items as doughnuts and cream buns. I then cycled up to the town to make the purchases.

In wartime, buying sweet things wasn't easy. Rationing was in force and while goodies like doughnuts weren't restricted, they were in very short supply. Cakes were an 'under the counter' item, reserved for regular customers, and when they were made generally available it was usually only at a certain time of the day and not for long. Housewives knew these times and began queuing for the delicacies long before they were put on sale. When buying things for the office staff at the Slipway I had no time to queue as I had to get back to work, but I had a number of 'contacts' in bakers' shops who supplied me with scarce goods.

The reason I had such contacts was because I could get access to valuable supplies of tobacco and alcohol. When I delivered mail to the crews of ships undergoing repair, I always sought out the chief steward and gave the post to him. As well as delivering mail, I volunteered to take the crew's letters to the Post Office, which I visited twice a day anyway, and for this and other small services, such as advising crew about the best pubs and dance halls in town, I was on good terms with many chief stewards. These officers controlled the ship's stores, including the grog and tobacco.

When a ship came into port its duty free liquor and tobacco store was sealed by Customs and placed in bond. After this, nothing in the store was supposed to be used until the ship left port and passed the three mile limit, although on most cargo ships veteran stewards concealed a quantity of duty free goods somewhere on board. These goods were then sold (illegally) to the crew at duty free prices.

During the war, a bottle of very scarce Scotch cost twelve shillings and sixpence from a licensed grocer, while the duty free price was five shillings. A number of stewards sold me bottles of Scotch for ten shillings, which I then resold to selected people for the standard 12/6. Profit was not my motive. If it had been I could have got much more than 12/6 for a bottle of whisky, which sold for two pounds or more on the black market. Instead, the ability to provide Scotch at the regular retail price enabled me to do deals with various traders who sold other scare items. The proprietors of three baker's shops were among my customers, as were some tobacconists and confectioners, so I always received favoured treatment when shopping at these places.

I also got many gifts of scarce items like evaporated milk, bully beef and tinned fruit from the ships. In the Slipway mail room, which was my domain, I stored my stock of goodies in a locked cupboard to which I had the only key. I often took items home and gave them to my mother, who never asked any questions about how I came by such delicacies.

My quasi black market business kept the Slipway office staff supplied with cakes to accompany their morning tea. I also obtained cigarettes and pipe tobacco from the ships—they were 'under the counter' items in the shops too, and I selectively supplied these to some office staff, including the general manager who had great trouble buying his favourite brand, Players. I don't think that was the only reason why my salary was raised to seventeen shillings and sixpence within six months, but it was probably a factor. Soon after, I got another rise to one pound five shillings. My father, who was then an excavator driver, earned just over three pounds.

I liked working with the female staff in the office and doing little jobs for them, and was always willing to take on extra work if it gave me experience in some new skill. Our switchboard operator's hours were from nine to five thirty, but our hard-driving general manager liked to start work at eight, and he often stayed at his desk until after six. He used the phone constantly, talking to head office in London. Once I'd learned how to operate the switchboard (the old plug-in type), I volunteered to stand in for the switch girl until she arrived at nine, and to stay on each night until the GM left.

After I passed the commercial subjects in my first year at night-school, Mr Hearne promoted me to the Timekeeping and Wages Department where I was one of four clerks. My salary jumped to two pounds ten shillings weekly. A month after my fifteenth birthday I was doing the same work as the other three clerks, who were all much older than me.

Two of my colleagues were in their fifties, and the other was a youngish Scots-born Italian with the classical name of Marc Antonio. Because Italy had become an enemy, Italians, or Scots of Italian descent, were not conscripted into the services. It was believed they would be 'unreliable' if their unit faced Italian troops, as the British Eighth Army was then doing in North Africa. Instead they were 'directed' into essential occupations, which is how Marc Antonio, who had a degree in Modern European Languages, came to be working as a clerk in a shipyard. The fact that he was married to a Scottish woman, and had two Scottish children, didn't alter his quasi-alien status.

Like me, Marc could get through his work very quickly, and we escaped from the office frequently, mostly to discuss problems with yard workers whose time cards didn't add up correctly, or were wrongly filled in. Each worker filled out a daily card on which he was supposed to write how many hours he'd spent working on each ship, and what he did during that time. Apart from being essential in calculating his wages, the cards were used by the costing office to charge the worker's time against the appropriate ship.

Although Marc was as patriotic as the next Scot, his university education had taught him to think objectively, and he scorned the wartime propaganda which took the place of unbiased news. He was one of the most influential men I ever met. At fifteen, I started thinking for myself, largely due to Marc's teachings. It was he who pointed out that the British Army's 1940 retreat via Dunkirk had been a defeat and near disaster, instead of the 'victory' it was still being portrayed as in 1941. I was sorry when the military brass belatedly realised that a man like Marc could be of more use to the war effort as an interpreter than a clerk. He was conscripted into the army where he became an intelligence officer and was sent to North Africa.

At the Slipway, I liked getting out into the yard and talking to the workers. My own men, meaning the trades who were on my wages ledger and whose pay I looked after, included the riveters, welders, shipwrights, fitters, turners and plumbers. Visits from the office staff were regarded with suspicion by the workers, who felt that the collar and tie brigade were spying on them, but I was regarded as one of the workers. I often arranged subs for men who had just begun work and were waiting for their first pay. From my Glasgow upbringing I knew how precarious a working man's finances could be, and I usually took the man's sub to where he was working, slipping it to him privately so nobody would know he was flat broke.

On Fridays a number of raffles were drawn at the yard, and on request, I regularly pulled the tickets from the tin, announcing the winning numbers. One raffle I drew cost two shillings a ticket. This was pricey, as most of the raffles, for a bottle of whisky or some beer, only cost sixpence a go. I was curious about the prize at stake in the two shilling raffle, but when I asked what it was, the men became evasive and started sniggering. Eventually, a sixteen-year-old rivet boy told me that every pay day one of the workers raffled his wife and the holder of the winning ticket was given an hour in the bedroom with her. Her spouse had no difficulty in selling a hundred tickets at two shillings each, which gave him ten pounds—about twice his weekly wage. In Ayr at that time, prostitutes charged a pound for a 'short time'. Really high class ones got two pounds or more, and after the arrival of the American forces prices soared to around five pounds. Another yard worker raffled his pay packet each week. This contained less than four pounds, but at a shilling a time he had no trouble selling enough tickets to make at least a fiver.

About the time of Marc Antonio's departure I became unhappy with my job. I had gone as far as I could go, and although the genial Mr Hearne was paying me well above the maximum salary for my age I decided to take another job, which had the dual attraction of a higher salary, plus complete autonomy. People employed in an essential occupation couldn't leave their jobs at will, although it was possible to move on to work in another essential area. The job I applied for was with a local firm of builders and civil engineers, all of whose work was for the Royal Air Force, and hence essential. I got the post because of Mr Hearne's excellent reference, and also because manpower was becoming scarce as more and more older age groups were being conscripted into the armed forces. My salary was a mighty three pounds ten shillings a week.

I became site manager for William Govan and Sons at a radiolocation post being built at Irvine. I was the only employee in the site office—a small timber hut in the middle of a desolate moor some miles from the town—although there were about two hundred workers on site. Many of these were rambunctious Irish navvies, and it was considered an unsuitable location to place a woman office worker who would have been the only female around.

My duties included keeping all time and wages records and paying the men each week, as well as receiving and checking goods and materials onto the site. My immediate superior, who shared the office with me, was a genial pipe-smoking civil engineer, who gave the various foremen their instructions. Hughie Green, a Glasgow University graduate, was a true eccentric, with a drooping ginger moustache and an irreverent attitude to authority. Some of Hughie's irreverence rubbed off on me, and in later years got me into a great deal of trouble, notably in the army, where I faced court martial on three occasions.

But I saw very little of Hughie, as he also oversaw work on four other sites around Ayrshire. When he did visit, he spent much of his time poring over plans and fiddling with his slide rule as he worked out specifications for the next stage of the project's construction. He spent a lot of time talking to head office too—usually abusing someone for not having essential materials delivered as promised.

We were often visited by RAF officers who came to check up on our progress. Usually, the officers brought a bottle of whisky with them which was shared with Hughie—and myself. I looked older than fifteen and the men regarded me as an adult, although a young one. To my delight, during discussions Hughie would often say, 'You'll have to ask Alex about that. He's the boss out here.'

Hughie liked the way I ran the site because I knew how to handle the hard-drinking Irish navvies. On Friday afternoons, when I was locked in the office making up their pay packets, they used to gather round and urge me to hurry up as they wanted to get their pay and go to the pub. I told them that wage paying began at four o'clock, and that their money would be ready by then, and not before.

The hut stood, unanchored, on four piles of bricks, and when the navvies became impatient they put their shoulders to one side of it and tilted it, causing loose furniture to slide across the floor. Hot coals also shot from the cast iron stove onto the wooden floorboards. When this happened, I opened the window and yelled at the mob, telling them that if they set the hut on fire I would make sure their pay packets went up in the blaze. Then they began singing 'Why Are We Waiting?', or worse, Irish songs. But for the most part I got on well with all the workers. There was rarely a mistake in their pay, and to them, being paid correctly and on time was my main function.

The radiolocation post was completed in six months and handed over to the RAF, after which the company transferred me to another project, this time a large barracks under construction at Doonfoot. I was once again site manager, and got a pay rise to four pounds ten shillings. My father was one of the workers on this project and I made up his wages as a mechanical excavator driver. At sixteen I was earning more than him.

My father was never comfortable with the fact that I was *au fait* with his earnings. He warned me I must never tell my mother how much pay he got when he worked overtime. Like me, he was supposed to hand his full pay packet over then get an allowance for his personal expenditure. When he worked overtime he kept some extra money for himself.

At Doonfoot, as fast as huts were erected and made habitable, the army moved into them. The first unit to arrive was a battalion of the Liverpool Regiment, and I quickly made friends with the guard sergeant and regimental police who manned the barracks entrance. Beside the guardhouse was the armoury in which the unit's ammunition was stored. This was manna to me because I had become an under officer in the Army Cadet Corps, and we were always short of training material like practise grenades and blank ammunition. I got on good terms with the English guard sergeant and guardhouse personnel by buying a copy of the *Daily Mirror* every morning, and giving it to the sergeant. During the war the *Mirror* was known as 'the Forces newspaper' and was very popular for its pin-up photos and a comic strip which dealt with the sexy adventures of a girl called Jane. Because of paper rationing, only a few *Mirrors* reached Ayr. But by using contacts I had made as a paper boy I was always able to procure a copy, and in return for this, the guard sergeant kept me supplied (quite illegally) with blank ammunition and Thunderflashes for use by my cadet unit. On cadet training exercises my platoon could always make the most noise as we blazed away with the army's ammunition.

As soon as I began working and earning money, I rarely spent a night at home. Two nights a week were reserved for night-school classes and another two for Army Cadet training. On the other three nights I went to the movies with fellow cadets. Home was too crowded for any recreational pursuits, and even finding a quiet place to read was rarely possible.

Although I was sixteen and my two closest friends were seventeen, going out with girls played a relatively minor part in our lives. None of us had a steady girl or particularly wanted one, although sex was rarely far from our minds and most of our adolescent conversation revolved around it. We all carried that symbol of manhood—a French letter—in our wallets, so we were prepared if we ever got lucky. But Scottish girls of our age were not free with their favours.

When the barracks were completed, I moved onto a new job at Prestwick Airport. After the war Doonfoot became a Butlins Holiday Camp—which may or may not say something about the Spartan amenities in such places!

PLAYING AT SOLDIERS

Between the ages of fourteen and seventeen I experienced a deep yearning to get away from home and leave Scotland. In Ayr, I would walk along the rocky Newton Shore by myself and gaze longingly across the Firth of Clyde in the general direction of North America. This wish to get away from home was at times almost overwhelming, and coloured all my thoughts.

After I started work at the Slipway, I wrote to Cunard in Liverpool and applied for a job as a cabin boy on the *Queen Mary*, which had just been converted into a troopship. To my delight, I got a reply saying I had been accepted. All that was needed was my mother or father's permission, and one of their signatures on the enclosed form. I was euphoric. I was going to sail the world in the magnificent *Queen Mary* which I'd watched being built in the 1930s at John Brown's Clydeside yard! It was too good to be true.

My father refused to sign the form, saying he would leave it up to my mother. But she wouldn't even consider letting me go to sea at fourteen. There was a war on and there were dangers at sea, especially on a big boat like the *Queen Mary* which the Germans would be keen to sink. In fact, I would have been perfectly safe on her. The world's largest and fastest ocean liner survived the war unscathed, even though she never had a naval escort. Nothing could keep up with the mighty Queen when she travelled at full speed, and no U-boat had a hope of getting her in its sights.

My mother stood firm against my pleadings, cajoling and threats, and instead agreed to let me join the army when I was seventeen. I needed her permission because youths couldn't be conscripted into the forces until they were eighteen and a half. I snarled that the war would be over when I reached seventeen, and I'm sure my mother hoped that it would be. She had lost two brothers in previous wars and had two more at sea in 1940; she didn't want to risk losing her oldest son as well. So I resigned myself to waiting until I was older before I could leave home, and morosely concentrated on being the office boy at a shipyard.

As a lad I'd had more ambitious career plans than being a clerk. Before I left school I'd wanted to be a psychiatrist. As a boy, people often confided in me and told me their problems, and quite often I was able to cheer them up. Even my mother gained solace after she'd discussed her worries with me. But when I made enquiries about becoming a psychiatrist, I was told that I would first have to matriculate, which would keep me at school for a further three years, and would then need to spend a further five years studying medicine at university to become a doctor. After that it would still be three years before I could practice as a psychiatrist.

This ambition was financially impossible, and hence short-lived, so my next career choice was to become a vet. I discovered that this only took three years at a veterinary college, but that I would also have to matriculate before I could be accepted. I'd always loved animals and had a way with them, but couldn't have pets at home because of the cost. When I mentioned buying a white mouse for sixpence, my father said sardonically, 'What do you want a white mouse for? There's plenty of grey ones running around the house.'

When we moved to Ayr there was a garden, and I was able to build a small hutch for various pets. I got some white mice, although my mother drew the line at a rat, and I also bought a couple of guinea pigs. I had some goldfish too, and kept a few birds, mainly ones that had been caught by our evil cat, who was a cunning hunter. We'd always hear the commotion from inside the house when the cat caught a bird. The other birds would screech and chirp and I'd rush outside and occasionally manage to boot the attacker away from its victim. Often the creature looked stone dead, but before burying it I always went inside and sneaked an eyedropper of whisky from Grandma's bottle. I'd prise the bird's beak open and let a couple of drops of whisky run down its throat, and it was amazing how often they came round and began chirping furiously. If the bird had a wound from the cat's teeth or claws, I'd bathe it and nurse it back to recovery.

Although I liked solitary pursuits, I had plenty of friends and never lacked company. From fourteen, the Army Cadet Corps took up a great deal of my leisure time, and almost every weekend my friends and I went out on field days, or military type exercises. We were merely playing at soldiers in the way that boys of that age often do, but we took it very seriously, drilling with our nineteenth century South African War rifles.

To make our training exercises more realistic, I managed to acquire a working World War I Lee Enfield rifle. As well as firing blanks, it could also take live .303 ammunition, which I got from a friendly army guard sergeant at the military camp where I was working. At the time, the army was training troops at battle schools, where live ammunition was fired over the men's heads by expert marksmen, the object being to let soldiers experience what it was like to be under fire.

I thought this was an excellent idea, so at a deserted country estate near Ayr, I set up my own Sunday battle school. It was completely contrary to regulations, both civilian and military, to fire weapons outside a firing range, but that didn't bother me, and I had guards posted around the estate. Anyway, if anyone in authority had appeared I would have claimed I was only firing blank ammunition.

During their baptism of fire, my 'men' sprawled in a trench while I blazed away at them with my rifle from about forty yards. Fortunately, I was a good shot and never hit any of them, although I did have one big scare. The day after a Sunday battle school exercise I arrived home from work and my mother said dolefully, 'One of your cadets is deed, Alex.'

I nearly died myself. Had I unknowingly shot one of my cadets and left his body behind on the estate? My God—I was in deep trouble. But my mother added, 'It was Tommy Dunlop. He fell down the mine shaft this morning.'

I felt an immediate surge of relief, and spared no thought for poor Tommy, who was a pit boy at a nearby coal mine. Later, I found out that he had been skylarking at the top of the shaft when he missed his footing and plunged hundreds of feet to his death.

After I had recovered from my shock, I got dressed in my cadet's under officer uniform and cycled to the home of a fellow officer, Bill Murdoch. We decided it would be proper for us to call on Tommy's family to express our condolences, and we pedalled to the little council house where Tommy's tearful mother was pleased to welcome her son's officers. She gave us a cup of tea and asked if we would like to see Tommy, who was laid out in the bedroom. Bill wasn't keen to view his first corpse, but I signalled to him that we should. One was expected to accept an invitation to see the deceased, and I knew Tommy's mother would have been offended if we'd said no.

When we tiptoed into the bedroom I got a shock. Despite the undertaker's efforts, Tommy still looked like a lad who had fallen several hundred feet to his death. His corpse was swathed from neck to toes in a tight winding sheet, but blood had begun to ooze through the white cloth, and although Tommy's head had been pulled together by means of a steel plate on the top of his skull, his shattered face still looked like a jigsaw puzzle.

Worst of all, the undertaker had laid him out so he looked about six feet tall. In reality, Tommy was a little fellow.

His mother sighed, 'It disnae look like him at all. does it?', and we were forced to agree.

After we'd viewed the body Bill and I went to the home of our commanding officer, Major Gowrie, a schoolteacher who'd been an officer in the Great War. We told him of Tommy's untimely death and suggested that we provide a cadet guard of honour at his funeral. The Major agreed, and left it to Bill and me to make the necessary arrangements. This wasn't a simple task. That night we had to find twelve lads who could get time off work to parade at the funeral next morning, and before the squad appeared in public we needed to give them some quick instruction on how to do the slow march.

As we talked with Major Gowrie he said, 'You chaps look rather shook up. I'm sure the death was a shock to you both', and we agreed that it had been.

I told him about viewing Tommy's body, and he was very concerned. 'You poor fellows!' he said. 'How terribly grisly! My God, I think you deserve a whisky.'

He got out a decanter and poured three stiff ones, and we drank to our fallen comrade before downing the neat whisky. Gowrie insisted that we have another, which we did. Meanwhile, he reminisced about his feelings on seeing his first dead body in Flanders in 1916, and poured himself a third large Scotch. He kept saying how terrible it was about Tommy and seemed to be more upset than Bill and I were, which surprised us—we were the ones who had seen the corpse.

Eventually we managed to get away from him, pleading that we had a lot of calls to make and that night, Bill and I split up, cycling round the homes of lads who were members of our cadet unit. At each house we had to tell the story of Tommy's death and, under morbid prompting, relate how we'd viewed the body. The various parents were shocked. Most of them said

I must need a drink, and I scored several whiskies, a gin and a tot of rum before I rendezvoused at Bill's home about midnight. Luckily his parents had gone to bed so they didn't see their drunken sixteen-year-old son and his plastered friend as we sat down to polish off a bottle of beer from Bill's father's stock.

The next morning the funeral party assembled at the cadet drill hall where Bill and I inspected the cadets before marching them to the church. On the way we practised slow marching, which must have puzzled the onlookers. It was a dismal squally day, and I remember thinking that it was better to be buried on a rainy day when even the trees were weeping, and when under the ground was a snug place to be, than on a fine sunny day.

When we arrived at the church I was surprised to see Major Gowrie in his dress uniform, carrying a sword. He had given no indication that he planned to attend the funeral, and when I marched up to him and saluted I realised that he was almost staggeringly drunk. But he was still able to enunciate clearly, and announced, 'I'll inspect the squad. We must put on a good show.'

We did put on a good show, and my only concern was for our commanding officer, who teetered alarmingly as he stood alongside our squad while we waited for the coffin to be carried out. We stood in two rows facing one another and when the coffin passed between our ranks we reversed our rifles and bowed our heads. The solemnity of the occasion was only marred by one cadet who exclaimed in a hoarse whisper, 'Jeeze—did you see the length of the coffin? You could get two Tommys into that!'

Later in the week there was a photo of the funeral in the *Ayrshire Post*, and the caption read, CADETS HONOUR FALLEN COMRADE. One could have thought that poor Tommy had been killed in action.

Our time as cadets was not usually solemn, and I had a busy social life, centred mainly upon cadet functions and dances. I organised fortnightly dances for cadets, servicemen and women and their partners in Ayr Town Hall. This involved quite a lot of work, including hiring a good band. The two best bands around were the dance bands of the Royal Scots Fusiliers and the RAF dance band from Prestwick Airport, some of whose members had worked for famous English bands such as Joe Loss's and Geraldo's. Keen dancers 'followed' certain bands, and having the RSF or RAF band on the bill guaranteed a sell-out night.

To avoid paying a professional compere's fee, I took on the role of MC, and although I couldn't dance, I had a good line of patter which went down well with the dancers and their partners.

Despite getting out and about in Ayrshire on cadet marches, I wanted to travel further afield, and in particular I was keen to see England. This would be the first foreign country I had visited, and to me and my elders, England *was* a foreign country. My father had been there during the Great War of 1914-18 and my Uncle Alec's ships often docked at English ports, but my mother and Uncles Tom and David had never made the leisurely two hour drive.

I first saw England when I was sixteen, although it wasn't a planned excursion. At that age I was a fairly seasoned drinker, as were my cadet pals, although as juveniles we weren't allowed in pubs. The legal drinking age was twenty-one, but we nonetheless managed to secure a reasonable amount of scarce liquor, mainly because my best friend, Bill Murdoch, worked for a licensed grocer. During wartime, people drank whatever kind of alcoholic beverages they could get hold of, and when we had a party, usually at the home of a friend whose parents were away for the night, we brought an exotic supply of grog, most of which we poured into a baby's enamel bath with a few bottles of fruit cordial. The ingredients of these lethal punches could include such diverse drinks as South African port, Australian Emu wine, Cherry Brandy and, if we were lucky, one or more bottles of Scotch.

We usually made about two gallons of this powerful mixture—enough to get a dozen teenage boys and girls powerfully drunk—and one Saturday night we had a tremendous binge at the home of an attractive blonde girl, Ethel Paterson, whose wealthy parents were away on holiday. The Paterson home was a large two storey villa which stood in its own grounds so we could make as much noise as we liked, with the radiogram turned up full blast. Jitterbugging was all the rage then and we threw our partners over our shoulders and slid them between our legs with great abandon. Bill Murdoch and I had been at a cadet party before going to Ethel's and we were both in uniform. We felt very much men of the world as we smoked our heads off, downed the grog and chatted up the girls with the confidence induced by alcohol.

At about eleven the punch ran out, but the resourceful Ethel managed to find the key to her father's drinks cupboard. We couldn't touch his scarce Scotch or gin, as he would certainly notice if any was missing, but at the bottom of the cupboard there were six bottles of creme de menthe which Ethel said nobody ever drank. In fact, the sickly green liqueur had been there since before the war, and we soon got stuck into it. After that the night passed by in a daze.

When I awoke the next day I was lying on a pile of straw in a goods van in a railway siding. Bill Murdoch was sprawled beside me, and looked terrible. We both had the mother of all hangovers. I shook Bill awake and we stumbled from the van and had a look around. I presumed we were somewhere in Ayr, but couldn't locate any familiar landmark, so we tidied ourselves up and walked around the lines, trying to find some sign that would tell us where we were. This wasn't easy. During the war, road and rail signs were removed to make it difficult for any German invaders to find their way around. The one thing

232

we knew was that we were in a very large railway depot. We stumbled on until we came upon a uniformed railway worker, and feeling rather stupid, we called out to him. 'Hey, Jock—can you tell us where we are?'

In a very thick English accent he called back, 'You're in Carlisle—and you shouldn't be on railway property. So you better buzz off.'

We were dazed. Neither of us had any recollection of how we had got to Carlisle, but we were in England for the first time. We found our way to the city centre, and had just enough money for a cup of tea and a bun. We had to hitch-hike back to Ayr, although this wasn't too difficult as we were in uniform and most drivers readily gave soldiers a lift. Apart from our youth, we looked no different from real soldiers, despite only being cadets.

When I got home on Sunday I told my mother that I'd been out on a night training exercise, which wasn't unusual, and she made no comment except to remark that I looked worn out. I felt absolutely knackered, but I had been in my first foreign country. Many years later, when I was in Britain with my Australian wife and two small children, we visited my parents in Ayr. We had a car, and took my mother and youngest brother Gordon for a quick drive to Gretna Green. It was the first time either of them had been to England!

THE JOYS OF SEX

Like most Scots of my generation, I received absolutely no sex education. Indeed, even asking a question relating to sex led to a scolding and a command not to be so dirty, and I realise now that our questions about sex were acutely embarrassing for my parents.

I had heard various incomprehensible warnings about the evils of self-abuse, playing with oneself, or onanism from various ministers of the cloth, and had been told that such self abuse could cause blindness, consumption, even insanity. The old time ministers certainly didn't spare the fire and brimstone when it came to warning boys against wanking. But my knowledge of sex was slight, and when I discovered the pleasures of masturbating I had no idea that this was the inelegant name for what was such an enjoyable diversion.

Until I reached puberty my penis was merely a handy water pipe. I thought us boys were much better off than girls who had to sit down to pee. We could do interesting things with our waterlogged organs, like write our names in the snow, or see who could pee the highest or furthest. But after puberty, I realised that I had a source of constantly renewable pleasure—which didn't cost a penny. It certainly beat the hell out of stamp collecting, another solitary pursuit that I indulged in.

From thirteen I had what seemed to be a permanent erection. It would appear even when I wasn't thinking about women, and I was especially stimulated by the motion of buses or trains. It was incredibly embarrassing because the bulge in my pants was very conspicuous, and I was forced to carry a light raincoat or briefcase at all times to hold over my groin when I walked along the aisle to get off a bus.

When I began masturbating I didn't need any fantasy figures for stimulation—the manual action was enough. But soon I began to focus my imagination upon movie actresses and then more obtainable girls, like my classmates. All the boys and girls in the class were older than me and reached puberty long before I did. I frequently had to dissemble to hide the fact that I didn't know what my chums meant when they talked about 'tossing off' or 'pulling their pudding', and I didn't get most of the dirty jokes which circulated behind the lavatories in the schoolyard. I'm sure my chums assumed I had discovered the pleasures of onanism. I would have been the butt of their scathing jokes if they'd realised that I didn't know how to handle myself.

Our class at Ayr Grammar School was a hotbed of teenage sexual tension, and during breaks, the subject of sex dominated our conversations. The boys consisted of two groups—those who'd done it with a girl and the ones who hadn't—although many tales of conquest were mere sexual bragging. Nevertheless, having some kind of sexual encounter with a girl was the major objective in all our adolescent lives, and until we reached nirvana, we talked about it incessantly. I often wonder what the girls were going through while they coped with their burgeoning sexuality.

Before I left school, I bought my first French Letter. Well, actually I didn't buy it. I never would have had the nerve to go into a chemist's shop and ask for one, and instead my friend Donald Rodd sold me one for ninepence. I carefully tucked it away in my wallet so that if I should get lucky, I was prepared.

My earliest sexual experiences were of a voyeuristic nature. I had a friend of my age who lived opposite us in Green Street, and Alan's interest in sex was as intense as mine. We often went for walks along the greens of Prestwick golf course, a favourite trysting spot for RAF men from the nearby airport and their girlfriends as the terrain adjoining the course was rugged, with lots of concealed gullies where couples could frolic unobserved. That is, except by teenage voyeurs such as us who were skilled at getting as close as possible to a couple to observe them. It was during these spying missions that we first glimpsed what a couple did when they copulated, although we couldn't see very much. We weren't game to get *too* close, as we were sure the airmen would be furious if they caught us watching them and their girls. In reality, no man caught in the act was likely to pursue us, and if he did we had a head start while he pulled his trousers up from around his ankles.

We saw many couples in horizontal congress, and from this got a rough idea of the mechanics of copulation. But we still weren't certain of exactly where *it* went. We knew it went between the woman's thighs, but precisely how it found the right spot wasn't obvious from a distance, and one of my fears, if I was lucky enough to find a willing female, was being unable to put 'it' in the right place. Alan felt the same way, but said that perhaps the girl would know, so that stage could be left to her.

Apart from stalking courting couples on the golf course, other opportunities for voyeurism abounded in wartime Ayr. There were large numbers of Polish troops and Free French sailors in the area, and these continental men were sexually uninhibited compared with most Britons. I once saw a French sailor having sex standing up in a shop doorway in broad daylight on a Sunday afternoon. When I paused to gape at the couple, his Scottish girlfriend hissed over his shoulder, 'Piss off, you dirty wee boy!' I didn't mind the 'dirty' but was annoyed at being called wee. Later, curiosity drew me back to the shop entrance, where the evidence of the couple's activities was present in the form of a used condom lying on the ground. It was the first time I'd seen a Frenchman use a French Letter.

The sand dunes at the furthermost end of the town shore were another favourite spot for fornicating couples. I had a friend called Morrie Cowan who was two years older than me and intensely interested in sex, as I was. He was a skilled stalker and we were able to get much closer to couples around the sand dunes than we could on the golf course. It was there that I was able to observe the tremendous vigour that went into intercourse, and it was Morrie who told me that sex used up as much energy as a five mile run. I believed him. I always felt weary after masturbating, although I was usually horny again within half an hour.

Morrie also introduced me to the pleasures of masturbating in company, instead of doing it surreptitiously in the lavatory or under the bedclothes. He was an only child who lived with his parents in a big two-story house in Racecourse Road, a better part of town, and upstairs he not only had his own bedroom, but a study and bathroom too. His parents never visited his quarters so he could do what he liked.

Morrie had a huge collection of pornographic photos and magazines, which he called his 'stroke books'. When he masturbated he spread selected magazines around the floor, and after some cajoling, he persuaded me to join him in masturbating simultaneously. The combination of the pornographic images, plus Morrie's lascivious accounts of girls he had made love to, were highly stimulating.

Morrie knew I was still a virgin and was keen to help me 'become a man'. He said he knew several accommodating girls who would make themselves available for a small fee, but the idea of paying for sex turned me off completely. I wanted my first conquest to be a nice girl. The problem was that a nice girl didn't go all the way with a boy until he married her—or that was what I firmly believed.

I was almost fourteen and still at school when I had my first real sexual experience with a girl. Her name was May McKenzie and she was sixteen and in my class. May was reputed to be quite free with her favours, and several boys claimed they had gone all the way with her, although she wasn't regarded as a slut. One winter's night in 1940 I was coming home from the pictures when May got on the bus and came and sat beside me. She had been visiting an aunt. I knew she lived in a little farm on the outskirts of town, about half a mile's walk from the bus terminus, and although my stop was before hers, I offered to stay on until the terminus and walk her home. May said she would be glad of my company as street lighting was minimal during the wartime black out.

I found no difficulty in chatting with her, and we mainly talked about school. May said she supposed I was as smitten by Fiona Dunbar as all the boys were, but I sycophantically said I didn't think she was half as attractive as May was. She let me hold her hand and trace little circles in her moist palm with my forefinger, something that older boys had assured me aroused girls.

When we got off the bus May said I could put my arm round her waist if I liked, and by the time we reached the gate that led to her farmhouse, we had stopped several times to kiss passionately. As we stood in the dark by the gate, May asked if I'd ever done it. I confessed that I hadn't, but told her I would very much like to, and was very horny as I pressed myself hard against her belly. She knew I was not yet fourteen, and wasn't surprised that I was a virgin. She murmured, 'Would you like to do it?'

Hallelujah! I'd never dreamed it would be so easy. And to have an older woman to guide me, with no embarrassment about finding the right place. I babbled that I'd love to!

May gave me a long kiss, her wet tongue snaking down my throat, before asking me briskly, 'Have you got a French Letter?' Overcome with rapture, I assured her I had, and she murmured, 'Have you ever put one on?' I told her that I hadn't, but May said

238

she'd do it for me, apparently relishing the prospect of teaching a young virgin the ropes.

I whispered hoarsely, 'Will we do it standing up?'

'Not on your Nellie!' she replied. 'Come on, we can go in the barn.'

She led me through the gate and we walked quietly to a small hay barn. I was stiff as a poker and my heart pounded in fevered anticipation as we lay down on a hay bale and started kissing passionately. Soon May undid her blouse and unhooked her bra, and as she drew my face against her breasts I was almost overcome with the stimulation. I got even more excited when her experienced fingers undid the buttons on my flies. 'Hmm,' she crooned, 'you've got a big one for your age.' She breathed in my ear, 'Give me your French Letter and I'll put it on.'

I tugged out my wallet, then with trembling fingers extracted the Durex. I'd often taken it out of its little paper packet and studied it, but had never unravelled it, as I was sure I'd never be able to roll it up so neatly again. May extracted the condom with practised fingers and told me to lie back while she put it on for me. I reclined in a daze of joyous anticipation, and as she rolled it on I almost fainted with bliss.

I felt the hard ring roll down to the base of my penis then May suddenly muttered, 'Oh, blast!'

'What's the matter?' I mumbled.

'It's broken off. It's come apart.'

'But it's on,' I cried, 'I can feel it.'

'Part of it's on,' she said. 'The rubber must have perished. How long have you had it?'

About a year I said, and she sniffed. 'Well it's no damn good! You can't put it in. It would slip off and you'd put me up the duff.'

I was devastated. 'I could hold it on,' I babbled, 'I'd make sure it stayed on.'

She sniffed again. 'Forget it. I'm not taking the risk.'

I sprawled all over her, begging and pleading, almost grovelling at her feet, and finally she said, 'All right—you can do it on my belly.'

This wasn't what I'd been anticipating, but it was better than nothing, and as she pulled her skirt up I scrambled on top of her. Before I began to thrust on her belly I muttered, 'But what about you?' I had a vague notion that girls also got some pleasure from sex.

'Don't bother about me' she said, 'just hurry up and come. My folks will be worrying.'

Within seconds, I had ejaculated into the clinging French letter.

Afterwards I felt a definite sense of disappointment. I'd had more thrilling climaxes doing it with my hand, but I kissed May passionately, assuring her it had been wonderful. She pulled her skirt down and re-hooked her bra saying, 'Next time get a bigger size.'

I had no idea condoms came in sizes, but my ears pricked up at her 'next time', although sadly we never got together again. May was courted by Hughie Sharp, an older boy at school, and they began going steady. My hopes were dashed, but I never lost my regard for her, and although they knew she was free with her favours, the boys at school all respected her.

For me, my adolescent years were marked by almost constant sexual frustration, as everyone seemed to be scoring except me. I had fumbling encounters with various girls, although mutual masturbation was as far as I got. But I didn't complain—at least I now knew where to put it—and where it went, although it was not until I joined the army at seventeen that I finally lost my virginity.

THE PRESTWICK AIRPORT TIMES

The three civilian jobs I had before joining the army in 1944 were all closely involved with the war effort. At Ayr Slipway I worked with the Royal and Merchant Navies, while my job at William Govan & Sons involved working alongside the RAF and the British Army. My third job led me to meet those marvellous men, the airmen of the US Army Air Corps and the US Air Transport Command. Through this job I also met Hollywood greats such as Bob Hope, Bing Crosby and Dorothy Lamour, who visited Britain to entertain the US forces.

After America entered the war in December 1941 it began a massive build up of its forces in the United Kingdom, culminating in the Allied assault on Normandy on D Day, 6th June 1944. At the time Britain was described as America's 'unsinkable aircraft carrier', situated safely off the coast of Nazi-held Europe. But well before any American ground forces began assembling in Britain, the US Army Air Corps established itself at bases on England's east coast from where their Flying Fortresses flew on daylight bombing missions over Germany.

Before the bombers could begin these missions, almost everything needed to equip the bases was flown in from the USA, including the aircraft and personnel. The pilots who ferried the planes and other equipment to Britain belonged to the US Air Transport Command. From 1942, almost every plane that was flown from the USA landed first at Prestwick Airport after the long flight across the Atlantic.

Prestwick, only four miles from Ayr, had been a small aerodrome for civilian light aircraft and RAF Tiger Moth training biplanes before the war. In late 1940, after the USA agreed to supply war material to Britain under a lend lease agreement, American-built military aircraft were flown into Prestwick by men and women pilots of the RAF Transport Command. The aircraft included the famous Douglas DC3 (called the Dakota by the RAF) transport planes and fighting aircraft such as the Lockheed Hudson and the Boeing B24 Liberators. The USA was not then at war with Germany so the aircraft were painted with RAF colours and flown into Prestwick by Britons.

Prestwick became a particularly important wartime airport because, due to a meteorological freak, it was fog-free all year round. This came about because Prestwick faced the Isle of Arran, whose mountains caused thick Atlantic fogs to lift above the town—before dropping on its eastern side, where they reduced visibility to nil.

Many aircraft which flew from Gander, Newfoundland (the nearest point to Britain's west coast) were at the extreme limit of their range when they reached the UK, and it was essential that there was sufficient visibility to make landing possible on their arrival. Prestwick Airport could always be relied on for clear weather. For some reason, the German Luftwaffe never bombed the airport. They were possibly unaware that the American Flying Fortresses, which were pounding their factories daily, arrived in Europe via Prestwick, as did their spares and other equipment.

Prestwick also became the base for the fledgling British Overseas Airways Corporation, the airline born out of the pioneer Imperial Airways. BOAC kept flying during the war, although its passengers were exclusively VIPs involved in the war effort, and the fact that BOAC had a base at Prestwick was my reason for seeking a job there. I was sixteen at the time and hoped to get work with the airline as a junior steward. This would have let me get out of Scotland and see the world, but alas, as I eventually discovered, BOAC didn't allow personnel to fly on its overseas routes until they were eighteen. I knew I could join the army before then, so it was a matter of filling in time until I reached the right age.

The job I got was with Scottish Aviation, the company that employed the civilian workers at Prestwick Airport. Between the mechanics and technicians who serviced all kinds of aircraft and its administrative staff the company employed many hundreds of workers. Because of my past experience I had no difficulty in getting a job in the accounts department. The deciding factor in me taking the post was the opportunity, as a sideline, to produce an airport newspaper. The executive who engaged me, a Mr Binnie, was the father of a girl who had been in my class at Ayr Grammar School, and by one of those quirks of fortune, his daughter had brought home a copy of my school newspaper, which he remembered favourably. He told me he had been toying with the idea of launching a periodical, mainly for the airport's civilian staff. 'You know, something to keep them in touch with one another: we have lots of shift workers who never meet many of the other employees. I'd like something chatty, with lots of personal items. No war news or anything gloomy. Just cheer-up stuff that doesn't read like it comes from management, like you did with your school paper.'

It was a marvellous brief, although it carried no extra pay. But Mr Binnie was sure I'd manage to produce a fortnightly journal during working hours, and was impressed by my references believing, rightly, that I'd 'eat the work'. I got through my week's workload in three days, leaving me plenty of time to produce the fortnightly journal. The company supplied the paper and I printed it on their duplicator.

The *Prestwick Airport Times* was well received, and I soon began to get contributions from staff members. As an employee I wore an ID badge which allowed me entry to the restricted airport area, permitting me to go virtually wherever I wanted in the complex. Being the paper's editor had a certain cachet, and I was warmly received all over the airport. People were generally eager to see their name in the print.

After two issues I began to extend Mr Binnie's brief to include items about the RAF and US Army Air Corps personnel. The easy-going Yanks were delighted to supply items for the paper and I increased the print run to give them a few hundred copies. I wrote articles like 'How To Understand Scottish', which the Americans loved, and also included a column about how to meet Scottish girls, which they liked even more, as did the female workers at the airport.

With the RAF, things were not so free and easy, but I cultivated a couple of contacts, including a Women's Auxiliary Air Force officer. She gave me some items about airport romances involving the WAAFs and the Americans, and altogether it was quite a spicy little journal. Fortunately, Mr Binnie didn't object to my covering the interests of the air forces either.

'Good stuff!' he said. 'It gives everybody a giggle.'

He had remarkable trust in me and never asked to see the paper's contents before I printed it, although I always took a copy to him before I distributed it elsewhere. He would drop what he was doing and chuckle his way through the paper. 'Good stuff!' he beamed. 'Very good stuff. Keep it up.' In my later life in journalism I often longed for an uncensorious publisher like Mr Binnie.

One of my 'scoops' was a report on the arrival of Bob Hope and his troupe at the airport. They had come to entertain the US forces in Britain, but stayed at the American officers quarters for a few days to recover from their turbulent flight across the Atlantic. During that time they gave a concert for the airport's civilian workers, as well as shows for the Americans, RAF and WAAF personnel.

Bob Hope's arrival in Britain was big news, but at first it was kept hush hush. I'm not sure if the Americans thought the Germans might bomb any base where Hope made an appearance, but nothing about his tour was released immediately, and for some days I had the story all to myself. Press reporters were not allowed on the base except with special permission and for a special reason. But I had no difficulty in getting an interview with *Mister* Hope, as he preferred to be addressed by reporters, and he treated me as if I was representing the *Times* or *Daily Mirror*. Heady stuff for a sixteen year old!

In my report I wrote that Bob Hope was as funny offstage as he was on (later, I found from interviewing famous comedians that this was not always so). Hope used no cue cards and was an excellent ad-libber. His troupe consisted of Frances Langford, a voluptuous blonde singer who really belted out a song, and Jerry Colona, a comedian with a big drooping black moustache which was his trademark. The three were backed by Les Brown and his Band of Renown. They had no minders, except an officer from the American USO which organised such tours by Hollywood stars, and the troupe carried no costumes or props, only a microphone and an amplifier which could, if necessary, be operated from a truck battery. They were the first Hollywood stars I'd met, and I liked them all.

Some time later, Bing Crosby arrived, and I was surprised to find that he was bald. Offstage, or offscreen, he didn't wear his hairpiece. I didn't get an interview with him as he left the airport shortly after his arrival, but I did manage to see him at a reception in the American officers' mess. He looked tired and morose, and my American contact told me he had been quite irascible after a long bumpy flight in an unpressurised transport plane.

The arrival of Dorothy Lamour and her troupe was more productive, interview-wise. She was happy to talk to anyone from the press, and frankly I think she confused my *Airport*

Times with the *New York Times*. Naturally I asked about the road movies she had made with Hope and Crosby, but I got the impression that she wasn't keen to talk about her co-stars, preferring all the questions to be about herself. I didn't ask for her autograph, nor did I ask Hope or Crosby for theirs. Some instinct told me that it was unprofessional for a reporter to ask an interview subject for an autograph, or to show any awe of their fame.

The fondest memories I have of wartime Prestwick are not of interviewing movie stars, but meeting the men of the US Eighth Army Air Corps. I admired them tremendously. On their arrival they were everything I expected Americans to be—very gung-ho, ebullient and cocky—but friendly and anxious to be liked by the British. After they had finished their tour of duty, bombing Germany, they sometimes went home on leave via Prestwick. They were different men then. Months of living in hazard had changed them, and their cockiness and ebullience had gone.

I talked with many of them and they were often highly critical of their equipment, which surprised me. The Yanks seemed to have everything fighting airmen could need: the finest aircraft and equipment and plenty of it, produced by America's industrial might. They had their own ice cream plants on their bases and endless supplies of Coca Cola, candy and cigarettes from their PX stores, and they could even buy scarce nylon stockings, which British girls would sell their bodies for—as many did.

But, the veterans told me bitterly, they never had enough of an essential called a 'walking bottle', which was a portable oxygen supply. Their bombers flew at over 20,000 feet which made extra oxygen essential. Each crew member plugged his face mask into the aircraft's main oxygen supply, but when a man had to move from one part of the plane to another, to attend to a wounded gunner for example, he used a portable oxygen tank into which he plugged his face mask. From this 'walking bottle' he drew his oxygen supply while away from his position.

I was astonished to learn that these vital bottles were in short supply, and that some bombers took off without even one on board. The airmen had complained, but due to some glitch in the system the supply of bottles reaching the bases was still insufficient. I was amazed. I thought the Yanks had everything.

I wrote an article about this deficiency, not that I expected it would do any good. My small journal would never be read by the US Army brass, although it was being read by at least one newspaper reporter on a mainstream daily paper as copies went out of the base, taken home by civilian workers. A reporter on the Scottish *Daily Express* saw a copy and he contacted me about my walking bottle article. Whether or not my article was used as the source, I don't know, but the *Express* later ran a feature article on equipment shortages in the US Army Air Corps. The article included details about the lack of portable oxygen bottles.

It would be nice to round this story off by saying that there was an immediate increase in oxygen bottle supplies. I have no way of knowing this. But I do know that returning Americans stopped complaining about equipment shortages of any kind. By 1943, American industrial output was moving into top gear as the invasion of Europe drew nearer.

I liked and admired the American aviators. The men I saw were going home; many of their comrades returned by sea in coffins, or were buried in English cemeteries. I thought these were among the bravest servicemen anywhere in the world, and I hated to see them ripped off by British civilians. One thing the Yanks couldn't buy at their PXs was whisky, or 'Scaatch' as they called it, and when they got hold of it on the black market they were often swindled by civilians. The going black market price for a bottle of Scotch was five pounds—about seven times its retail price, and the Yanks paid this price readily—they were highly paid compared with British servicemen and many civilians. But confidence men soon targeted them. The con men supplied bottles of Scotch filled almost to the top with cold tea. A thin layer of paraffin wax sealed off the tea then an ounce of real whisky was added to top up the bottle, which was then expertly re-sealed to look as if it had never been opened.

Before handing over his money, an American buyer would uncork the bottle then sniff or taste its contents to make sure that it really was whisky. Some had previously bought bottles full of cold tea, so they were aware of that trick. In my paper, I reported on the paraffin wax scam and warned the Americans to be careful, also giving them other 'buyer beware' advice which they cut out and stuck on notice boards in their quarters.

The only hazard I found it difficult to warn the amorous Yanks about were the local girls. How could I tell them that tarts from all over Scotland had swarmed into the Prestwick area to catch and preferably marry a Yank, who would take them back to the Hollywood dreamland that was the USA. Even if that dream didn't materialise, having an American boyfriend ensured a girl of a steady supply of scarce cigarettes, candy bars, canned foodstuffs—and nylons.

Many girls who were dated by American servicemen weren't exactly the flower of Scottish womanhood, and I was ashamed when I saw a girl obviously on the make clinging to the arm of her Yankee boyfriend. But how could I write this about my own countrypeople? Like many Scots at the time, I just had to put up with it and hope that the Americans were aware that many of the females they dated were not truly representative of Scottish women.

In the main, my time at Prestwick Airport was a happy one. When I turned seventeen I volunteered for the army and three months later I was 'called to the colours'—as the military term has it. Mr Binnie was sorry to see me go, saying 'I don't expect I'll find another editor like you, Alex. I'll miss your wee paper.'

He added with a sly grin, 'And I don't expect I'll find anybody else who would work for nothing. But still, it was good experience for you, wasn't it?'

It certainly had been, and I thanked him before going off to become a soldier.

A LOWLY RANKER

I'm sure no happier recruit ever joined the army than me, as I boarded the train for Inverness to report to the 30th Training Battalion at Cameron Barracks on 20th March 1944. At long last, I was getting away from home. The years of yearning were over, and at seventeen I would see the world.

As a volunteer I was entitled to join the regiment of my choice, and my father was keen for me to join his old regiment, the Royal Scots Fusiliers. But their regimental depot was in Ayr, and the thought of joining the army then being stationed in my home town, even for a short time, was too horrible to contemplate. I wanted to get as far away as possible, so I joined the Seaforth Highlanders whose depot was at Fort George in Inverness-shire.

I loved the army from the start. It had luxuries like hot running water, which meant that I could have a proper shower every morning. We certainly had to get into the ablutions block early because the hot water quickly ran out, but at home in Ayr and Glasgow there had been no bathroom at all, and to get hot water for washing and shaving involved boiling the kettle.

My father always jeered at me for shaving in hot water, calling me a sissy. 'In my day we shaved in cold water, and were very glad to have it!' he'd scoff. In Ayr, I also liked to wash in warm water, and my father would bark at me 'You're a softie, sir! When I was a boy I had to break the ice on top of the water barrel before I could get any water at all!'

I was glad to get away from the old man and into the army where even commandos unashamedly used hot water, and after the Spartan regime of my sergeant major father, my new life was a breeze. I can honestly say that I never had a moment's homesickness, or found the army discipline irksome. Some of the conscripted recruits suffered very badly from homesickness, especially those from wealthier backgrounds who missed all kinds of amenities that I'd never had. Most missed their mother's cooking, but I didn't. I'm not disparaging her 'guid plain fare' as she called it, but I found army meals were often more adventurous.

Lots of recruits missed not being able to sleep between sheets, as only officers had them in the army. The other ranks got three blankets and slept on one with two on top, plus their greatcoat in winter. I'd always slept like that, but the army blankets were thicker and warmer than the ones at home.

I did suffer financially when I joined the army. At Prestwick Airport I had earned four pounds ten shillings a week of which I gave three pounds to my mother. As a private soldier my pay was three shillings a day. From this I made an allotment of 7/6 a week to my mother, the army retained 2/6 a week to pay for barracks damages or any fines that might be imposed upon me, and I got 12/6 a week to live on. Certainly I didn't have to buy any clothes or footwear, and there were some concessions like cheap cigarettes and beer at the NAAFI, but it was a struggle to survive between pay days. I envied the lucky lads whose mothers didn't need any of their pay and who got the full eighteen and sixpence in their hand each week.

I breezed through the first six weeks of basic training when the sergeants and NCOs gave the raw recruits a really tough time—to break them in to the army system. The training consisted of a never-ending round of bellowing, hectoring, tirades of abuse and heavy sarcasm from the NCOs as they taught us the basics of drill, weapon handling, laying out our kit for inspection, saluting—and instant obedience to the orders of a superior officer. To us, this meant everybody from lance corporals upwards.

My three years in the cadet corps stood me in good stead for my new way of life, and I was never admonished for being slow to learn. I learned nothing new at basic training. In fact I had to play down my military knowledge to avoid being tagged a know-all by the NCOs. When we were introduced to the Bren light machine gun, the cockney instructor, Sergeant Bellow, made one of the traditional sexual/weaponry jokes the NCOs liked to pass on to recruits. After he'd disassembled the gun and named each part, he asked, 'Now, you 'orrible lot, which part of this 'ere gun is also known as the Ladies' Delight?'

Quick as a flash I said, 'The body locking pin, Sergeant.' I'd learned that the first time I stripped a Bren gun, when I was fifteen.

My comrades sniggered but Sergeant Bellow gave me a black look. I'd stolen his punch line. 'Ho, ho!' he sneered. 'So we've got a smart arse in the platoon, 'ave we? Wot's yer name, private?'

'McRobbie, Sergeant.'

'Your first name, laddie!'

'Alex, Sergeant.'

He slapped his sides. 'So it's not a smart arse we 'ave—it's a Smart Alec!' He roared with laughter and my comrades dutifully tittered at his wit.

'Orright!' the Sergeant barked, 'So—Private Smart Alec—you know all about the Bren gun, do you?'

I said cautiously, 'Just a little bit, Sergeant.'

'Right,' he smirked, 'so let's see you put the fucking thing back together again!'

I dropped behind the gun, which was in six pieces including the little firing pin. I reassembled it in twelve seconds then leapt to my feet and stood to attention.

He gave me a long hard look, but for a moment he didn't say anything. Then he said, "Ow much does this gun weigh, private?'

'Twenty three and a half pounds, Sergeant.'

'Good. Now pick it up.'

I picked up the gun by its carrying handle.

'Now raise it above your 'ead.'

I did this then he roared, 'Now double march right round the range and don't lower the gun until you get back 'ere!'

Right round the training range was a good half mile, but I was back in fifteen minutes, still with the heavy gun held above my head.

Sergeant Bellow surveyed me as I stood panting. 'You don't look very winded,' he leered. 'So—'ave another run round the range!'

When I got back the second time I managed to look more exhausted than I really was. 'Right!' he barked, 'Put the gun down and fall in with the squad.'

I returned to the ranks and the instruction continued. I was sure I was in Sergeant Bellow's black book and that he'd give me a hard time, but he didn't. In fact within two weeks I was appointed an acting unpaid lance corporal, a kind of sergeants' dogsbody who was assigned to march the platoon from place to place while the sergeant followed at his leisure. I knew the drill commands backwards as I'd been giving them for years. When we went on the range to fire the basic infantry weapons— the rifle, Bren gun and Sten gun, I scored top marks. I had used all these weapons, and was familiar with priming and throwing hand grenades too.

On completion of our six weeks basic training I was ordered to report for company commander's interview, which usually meant trouble. I was marched into the company office by the company sergeant major and ordered to halt before the OC's table. The major said affably, 'Stand easy, Corporal. I've been studying your record and the reports by your NCOs and platoon commander, and I'd like you to know that your record has been marked PO—that means potential officer. So when you are posted to your PTC your officers will keep an eye on your progress. Once you've been in the army for six months and completed your training, you could be recommended to appear before an officer selection board.'

I was delighted. Back in the hut I shared with twenty nine other recruits, I broke the news to my pals, but none of them were envious. Their comments were along the lines of 'Don't forget your old mates if you become our officer!'

Although I quickly became a lance corporal, I never threw my weight around—not that lance corporals carried much weight. Using the military knowledge I'd gained in the Cadet Corps, I was able to help some of the less able lads with the intricacies of rifle drill, laying out their kit for inspection, or correctly wearing their equipment. Amazingly, in 1940, after decades of compulsory free education, some of the recruits couldn't read or write. They had to attend special classes run by the Army Education Corps, so they could at least read a map, or write a simple message. One nineteen year old from Tyneside, Enoch Lane, was an especially slow learner and smarter recruits often took the mickey out of him for his illiteracy. But I came down heavily on anyone who teased him.

Enoch thought I was a gentleman. He was slavish in his devotion and beamed with pride when I said he could be my mate along with another lad, Harry Pepper, who we called the Professor because he had matriculated. Being mates simply meant that we went together as a threesome when we visited the NAAFI for a pint of beer. For the six weeks of Basic Training we weren't allowed to leave the barracks and go into Inverness. Our sergeants said it took that long before we knew how to wear our uniforms properly and not disgrace our unit.

Enoch had a steady girlfriend in Durham whose letters he

asked me to read to him. She used scented pink notepaper and wrote in block capitals, trying, I think, to make it easier for him to read her words, although the big ones like MISSING still stumped him. Her letters were mainly very sweet, mostly about everyday things and how much she missed him, although she urged him to write back to her, even if his letter was only a few words long.

One night Enoch decided to write his first love letter. I encouraged him and got a writing pad and pencil, before leaving him to it. After about an hour I wandered back and sat on his bed beside him. 'How's it going?' I asked.

He chewed the end of his pencil. 'Not too good' he said, thrusting the pad towards me. 'This is all I've managed to write.'

At the top of the page of lined paper were the words DEAR SWEATHEART in block capitals.

He looked at me imploringly and asked, 'Do you think you could write it for me? I'll tell you what I want to say.'

I said I'd do it and suggested we went to the NAAFI where we could get a table and not be overheard. We got a beer each and I tore off the page he'd written, starting a new one DEAR SWEETHEART. I said I'd use block letters so she'd think it was him writing, and asked what he wanted to tell her. He thought for a moment then said, 'Tell her I'm missing having cuddles with her.'

I wrote something suitably flowery then awaited his next words. He took a pull at his beer then said, 'Tell her I'm really missing her fud.'

I said, 'You mean her food?'

'No, her fud—F-U-D—fud.'

I said, 'What's her fud?'

He looked coy, then blurted out, 'You know—her pussy. That's called her fud. When I fuck her I go up her fud.'

I was familiar with most euphemisms for the vagina, but fud was a new one. It sounded very unattractive, but Enoch assured me that in his region, it was quite an elegant term. I wrote some romantic lines but couldn't bring myself to use the word fud. Instead I got rather carried away and wrote how eager he was to be back home and entering her Temple of Delight.

After I'd filled a whole page I read it out to him. 'Eh lad' he enthused, 'that'll make her wet her knickers! Maybe it was best that you didn't mention her fud.' I addressed the envelope, then he stamped and posted it. A week later he got a reply which I helped him read. His sweetheart had been thrilled by his letter and 'his lovely words'. But, she complained, 'Don't you want to fuck me any more?'

At seventeen I placed women on a pedestal, and was shocked to read such a word written by one. I never used four letter words when ladies were present, and still don't today. I believed that a nice girl never said fuck, or wrote it, even to her lover. But here was Enoch's girl, obviously a nice North of England lass, not only using the word fuck, but writing about her desire to feel his big cock inside her again.

After the shock of reading Enoch's sweetheart's earthy love letters, my belief in female wholesomeness was further shattered. I was detailed to take a squad of men to clean up the toilet block in a camp which had been occupied for most of the war by Wrens, the women's naval auxiliary. The Wrens were regarded as the cream of the women's services. Many of them were 'high born' young ladies and they were often rather snooty, tending to only associate socially with officers. With my ten men, and armed with buckets, mops and scrubbing brushes, we went into the Wrens' deserted toilet block to clean it before the camp was taken over by the army.

I was shocked to find the walls and doors of the toilets covered with graffiti. This was standard in male toilet blocks, but these obscene drawings and words could only have been written by women as no men had been allowed into the camp.

There were crude depictions of erections, usually at the moment of ejaculation, with legends such as 'suck him off, Jenny Wren!' scrawled in lipstick underneath. One of my men, Fergie, a big raw-boned Highlander, shook his head sorrowfully then sighed, 'Well, Corporal—women—they're just like us, aren't they?'

Another encounter that shattered my naive conception of what women were like took the form of a men v women hockey match. I'd never held a hockey stick before joining the army, but I found I had a natural aptitude for the game. The rules were very similar to soccer, but I was much more dextrous with the stick than I was with my feet, and within a few months I had been appointed team captain.

The first time we were beaten was when we played against a women's army auxiliary team, and before we took to the field I warned my men that there was to be no rough stuff, like we commonly used when playing against men. The ATS team looked rather fetching in their sports skirts, and my men had difficulty keeping their eyes on the ball. But by half time my rugged troops were in a pitiful state. We'd never played against such ruthless and vicious opponents, and we had numerous gashes on our ankles from deftly wielded sticks. A couple of men even had cuts on their heads, and several players were in agony after being hit in the balls. One strapping Scot said he wouldn't go back on the field without a steel jockstrap. 'These bitches are *murder*!' he complained, 'And the bloody ref is on their side!'

To ensure neutrality, the referee was from the air force— but she was a WAAF sergeant, and there was no doubt that she favoured the women's team. Our frequent cries of 'Foul!' were ignored and the mayhem continued. We lost eight to one.

Sport and recreation became particularly important in our lives after the D Day assault on France. Under normal circumstances, service people in Britain got seven days leave every three months, and I had been due for my first week's worth in June.

However, after D Day, all leave was cancelled. The generals had no real idea of how many casualties might be suffered during the invasion of France, but with memories of the slaughter that took place during the Great War still vivid, they felt that they might have to throw every available man into battle. This would include, if necessary, half-trained soldiers like my unit. At least we knew how to shoot.

It was around Christmas 1944, when the war in Europe was going well for the Allies, before the leave restrictions were lifted and I got my first home leave. During the freeze on leave most of the troops were in low spirits. The married men suffered most, especially our staff NCOs, many of whom had served in North Africa, Italy or Burma and had already spent several years with no home leave at all.

Our two company sergeants, Bellow and Dyer, were very despondent as they both had children, whom they had had little chance to see. One night I was in Inverness at a pub with my mate Harry Pepper when Sergeant Dyer joined us and bought us a beer. After several more drinks which he insisted on paying for, knowing our impoverished state, he became unusually talkative. 'This no fucking leave business is terrible!' he said. 'I suppose you lads aren't happy about it either?'

We agreed that we weren't too pleased about not being able to get home. 'Aye,' he said, 'the CO says we've got to do something to keep the men's minds off it. Plenty of sport and army education lectures for your off-duty time.'

He snorted, 'The only sport I want is to get home and prong my missus!'

We laughed dutifully then I said, 'Why don't we put on a show? In the Mess hall. We could do it—if we could get some time off.'

He stared at me. '*You* could put on a show?'

'No bother,' I said confidently. 'I'll write the script and Harry can paint the backdrops—he did that for his amateur dramatic society.'

'Have you ever put on a show before?' Sergeant Dyer asked.

'Yes,' I lied grandly, 'Often. There's nothing to it. There's a lot of talent in the company.'

I had never staged a show in my life, but I felt that if the script was right—and was funny—then I'd soon learn the mechanics of production. I'd seen several ENSA shows which toured military installations to entertain the troops. Some of them weren't very good because they had no localised humour which pertained to the unit they were entertaining, and they mostly used old vaudeville routines which everyone knew already.

Sergeant Dyer must have been convinced that I was a budding impresario as he talked to our Company Commander about the project and the Major gave it his blessing. I reckoned I could produce a show in six weeks. It would be staged in the big mess hall which could seat six hundred people, and had a proscenium at one end. The performance would be for the whole battalion.

I was allowed to use the company office typewriter after working hours, and over three nights I hammered away at the keys until I had written the script for a two hour show. It was to be non-stop comedy, with no boring baritones singing 'The Road to Mandalay' or actors reciting 'Gungha Din'. I called it 'Cameron Barracks Capers'. Basically, it took the mickey out of the army and in particular its training system. It was written from the viewpoint of the lowly recruit and I went as far as I deemed it safe when lampooning our officers and NCOs.

My next task was to find a band to back the performers. From the Cameron Highlanders Pipe Band I managed to gather together enough musicians who could play instruments other than the bagpipes—and who relished the opportunity to do so.

With the Pipe Major's help I assembled a band consisting of a pianist, drummer, trumpeter, saxophonist and a bass player.

The next problem was finding the talent. There were few people available with any experience, but I'd written the script in the form of a radio show along the lines of the BBC's 'It's That Man Again', so the performers could read most of their lines into a microphone, instead of trying to memorise them. Using the battalion duplicator, I ran off sufficient scripts for all the 'artistes'.

Organising costumes was the next challenge, and although they could be hired from a theatre in Inverness, this cost money. But the CO came to the rescue and said that the battalion welfare fund would meet this cost, so I was given time off training and supplied with a truck to go into Inverness. The Colonel had become very enthusiastic about the project, and I had to tactfully resist his desire to attend one of our rehearsals, which took place every night.

With the aid of the battalion signwriter, Harry Pepper got stuck into painting the backdrops, and although our unit's paintshop only had four colours—khaki, red, black and white, they did wonders with them. All I needed then was a troupe of dancing girls—something sexy was essential in an army show— and female performers for some of the sketches.

With this in mind, I sought an audience with the ATS Captain in charge of the women soldiers. Knowing of the Colonel's interest in the show she was keen to help. 'But you won't do anything to demean my gals, will you Corporal?'

I assured her that I wouldn't and that everything would be in the best of taste. Luckily, one of her 'gals', Shirley, had been a professional dancer before enlisting in the ATS, and she undertook to assemble and drill a good looking line of 'kickers'. The women soldiers were delighted to get out of uniform and appear in fishnets and short skirts to entertain the troops, although I suggested to Shirley that she didn't show the scanty costumes to her Captain before the performance.

I ran off several hundred programmes on the duplicator, beginning with the words, 'With the kind permission and assistance of the Commanding Officer, Lieut Colonel Bernard McLachlan, DSO, MC.' I was not above a little crawling when it was for a good cause, and was well aware that the CO's reaction to my irreverent humour would decide how the show was received, by our superiors anyway.

On the big night, the mess hall was packed. After the opening fanfare, the first sketch showed the recruits receiving their inoculations, then, while they could hardly raise their swollen arms, being given a strenuous hour of physical training—a sore point with every recruit. The army's theory was that vigorous exercise helped circulate the vaccines into the bloodstream, but the recruits felt they should be given forty eight hours of light duties to recover from the painful after-effects of the inoculations.

From the wings, where I was performing the duties of stage manager, I peered out to watch the front row where the CO sat with our officers. He roared with laughter as the sketch lampooned military stupidity, and from then on the audience guffawed unrestrained all through the show. We got many calls for encores and Lord knows how many curtain calls we took.

The next day the Colonel sent for me and asked that we repeat the show for two more nights. 'Lots of the staff couldn't get in last night', he said. 'Apart from that, I want to see it again and invite some officers from Scottish Command—and some Navy and Air Force chaps too. I'll show them how we put on a show at Cameron Barracks!'

For the second performance, many officers who lived in the married quarters brought their wives, and I think the ladies appreciated our ribaldries even more than their husbands did.

Altogether, the 'Cameron Barracks Capers' was a great success. The Colonel wanted me to prepare another show, but at the time I suddenly contracted peritonitis and was rushed to hospital. Some tainted cat gut was used to stitch up my wound which then festered, so I had to be cut open again then re-stitched, all of which kept me out of action for about two months, including time for convalescence.

When I returned to my unit all my fellow recruits had finished their basic training and been posted to their regimental Preliminary Training Centres.

I was posted to the Seaforth Highlanders PTC at Elgin, not far from Inverness, and after three months I was a fully-trained soldier. I was ready to join one of the battalions of the Seaforths, and preferably our 1st Battalion which was in Burma, fighting the Japanese. Our 5th Battalion was in Europe but the war against Germany looked like it would soon be over.

But my hopes of going abroad were soon dashed. My Company Commander sent for me and told me that as a Potential Officer I would not be posted to my regiment. Instead, I would proceed to the War Office Selection Board in Edinburgh for psychological and other tests to see if I was really officer material. I bitterly resented this. If I was selected for officer training I would need to spend six weeks at a pre-OCTU then another sixteen at an OCTU before I received my commission. In six months the war could be over. My Company Commander was sympathetic. 'But,' he said, 'the army needs officers more than it needs another soldier in the field. Once the veterans are demobilised, we'll be very short of officers for a while. So—off you go to WOSB. I'm sure you'll pass.'

I did pass, and I was very glum about it. But I didn't go straight to pre-OCTU. Instead, I contracted cerebral spinal meningitis and was rushed to an infectious diseases hospital in Inverness. I was placed on the dangerously ill list and remember the awful agony of receiving lumbar punctures—the most painful medical procedure I have ever experienced.

During my first forty eight hours in hospital I came out of a state of delirium to find my father sitting by my bedside. This gave me quite a shock. I realised that I must be very ill indeed for him to have been sent for, and the fact that he was wearing his good suit and a collar and tie disturbed me even more. He usually only wore this outfit at weddings and funerals.

We had a brief and strained conversation. He told me he'd made the trip to Inverness after receiving a telegram saying I was on the danger list and not expected to live. The army had provided him with a free rail voucher, and the British Legion gave him free accommodation in Inverness. He had little to say, except that my mother was worrying about me. I told her she shouldn't, and that I'd be back on duty in no time. In fact I spent four weeks in hospital then another six convalescing at Leys Castle in Morayshire.

In those days, complete recovery from meningitis was fairly rare, and sufferers were often left with varying degrees of disability. Fortunately for me, penicillin had just become available. Its limited production was reserved for members of the armed forces, and a course of injections led to a complete cure, although I think its use to treat meningitis was in the experimental stage then.

After finally being declared A1 again, I left for the pre-OCTU in Wrotham, Kent. I was pleased to finally get out of Scotland, even if it was only to southern England, a poor consolation for not sailing off to the Far East and the exotic Road to Mandalay, where, I later discovered, flying fishes *do* play.

OFFICER MATERIAL

My main memory of my six weeks at the 148th pre-OCTU was the incredible cold. The winter of 1945 was an especially bitter one right across Europe, and snow and fog even halted the Allied thrust into Germany for several weeks. In fact, I have never been so cold in my life as I was during my stay in Wrotham. Winter in Northern Scotland was almost balmy compared to the freezing temperatures in England that year.

Completing six weeks at pre-OCTU didn't mean a soldier automatically went on to OCTU and became an officer; we could be returned to our units at any time, for a variety of reasons. Discipline was harsh, and physical training and simulated battle exercises were strenuous. But worst of all the spit and polish at Wrotham (the 'bullshit'), was oppressive. The most minor infringement of uniform-wearing regulations resulted in a demerit. Too many demerits, and a man was sent back to his unit. Also, the officers were absolute bastards, which was a new experience for me. Our recruit training NCOs had been positively benevolent compared with the NCOs at pre-OCTU.

At pre-OCTU we were treated even worse than new recruits. This was particularly galling for the more mature cadets, many of whom had been senior NCOs who had seen action in various theatres of war, and been decorated for valour. But when NCOs entered pre-OCTU, they removed their badges of rank, and as probationary cadets we were all equally lowly.

Getting through the first two weeks of assessment was the hardest, and that was when many cadets were returned to their units with the curt notation, 'unfit officer material'. But things improved after that as we began to be taught some useful skills. One week was spent learning to drive most types of army vehicle, from 15 cwt trucks to three tonners and Bren carriers. The army insisted upon all officers being able to drive, and having never had the chance to learn before, so I welcomed this opportunity, passing the final test easily. During another week we learnt how to handle motorbikes, not just riding them on the flat, but up mountains, across rivers and through mud, snow and sand. I loved that week and the motorbike soon became my favourite mode of transport.

We learned advanced map reading and how to follow a prismatic compass reading, got lectures on military law, and were instructed on how to deal with men brought before us for misconduct. We learnt to fire weapons which hadn't been included in our previous training: the PIAT anti-tank projector; the two inch mortar and the officer's personal weapon—the revolver.

In spite of this packed schedule, we had a reasonable number of free days, such as when we were waiting to be called for a test. In the bitter cold, these days off were hell. We couldn't go to the NAAFI because it didn't open until after the last parade for the day, but sitting around in our freezing Nissen huts was impossible as we weren't allowed to light the heating stove until five thirty. Our kits were laid out on top of our beds and couldn't be disturbed, so we weren't even able to relax, but had to stand around, stamping our feet and slapping our gloved hands against our hips to keep some circulation going in our fingers. It was too cold to bare our hands to play cards.

On our second 'free' day I said to my frozen fellow cadets, 'I've had a gutful of this. My feet are freezing. I'm going for a march, which'll at least get my feet warm. But I need eight men to make up a squad. I can't march around by myself or I'll be pulled up for sure.'

Eight men volunteered—the other six were doubtful about leaving the precincts of the hut in case they were summoned for testing—and outside, I ordered my squad to form double file. With myself at the rear I marched the men through the camp. We marched smartly, arms swinging, eyes front, no talking, and when we passed an officer I gave the 'Eyes right!' and saluted him. Nobody paid any attention to us. Squads of men were marching all over the place, each under the command of an NCO or a senior soldier, and we marched briskly out of the camp, past the guardhouse and the sergeant on duty. He didn't even look at us, presuming we'd been ordered to go somewhere else. On the snow-covered road to Wrotham village, I kept the men marching at attention. Many army vehicles passed us, some containing officers, and it was essential we looked purposeful with someone in command.

Near Wrotham we came to a pub called the Bull and Bush. After glancing back to make sure no vehicles were coming, I gave the order 'Left wheel!' The squad marched through the pub forecourt, from where I directed them to the side entrance before I fell them out and we rushed inside.

It was beautifully warm, with a coal fire blazing in the fireplace, and as the pub had just opened it was empty too. Mine Host was glad to see us. We ordered pints of beer, warmed ourselves before the fire, and lunched on bread, cheese and pickles before boozing moderately until closing time at three. When I'd marched the squad back to the camp, falling them out at our hut, the men who'd stayed behind couldn't believe we'd spent the day at the boozer—and got away with it. If we'd been found out we would all have been instantly RTU'd, and as the instigator, I could well have been court-martialled. The army liked its potential officers to display initiative—but not too much of it.

During the final two weeks of the four month course at OCTU, my 'initiative' came close to having me RTU'd. There, cadets trained in what were called syndicates, with an officer in charge of each group. This officer took a keen interest in us as individuals and every four weeks he had a lengthy private meeting with each of us, giving us a grading and a written report on how we were progressing. Unlike those at pre-OCTU, the OCTU officers were gentlemen, and the NCOs were intelligent men with a keen sense of humour.

Our OCTU was in a hutted camp surrounding Alton Towers, an historic old pile in Staffordshire. The officers there were from a unit called the Artists Rifles, which had originally been formed during the 1914-18 war. It drew its recruits from the City of London financial area, and most of its men were Jewish. They had been bankers, stockbrokers or in the theatre in civil life. My syndicate officer, Major Gershwin, had previously been an actor, and spoke rather like Laurence Olivier.

During World War II, the Artists Rifles were sent to re-conquer British Somaliland after it had been invaded by the Italians. The War Office didn't want to deploy the unit against the Germans in North Africa in case some of the regiment were taken prisoner. Being Jewish, it was felt that they mightn't be treated as POWs by the Nazis. The Somali campaign was a side-show to the main event in Libya, and only about five thousand British troops were involved. But it was a brilliant campaign, and resulted in the collapse of Mussolini's East African empire, including Abyssinia, and the surrender of over 120,000 Italian troops. Many of our officers wore decorations such as the DSO and MC, and Staff Sergeant Major Moses had won the DCM.

At OCTU we enjoyed some of the privileges reserved for officers. We had sheets and pillowslips on our beds with mattresses instead of palliasses, and at our canteen we could buy wine and spirits, instead of just beer. But training was rigorous, although there was sense in all of it. Nobody bellowed at us, not even the NCOs. If we performed some task badly, an officer would drawl, 'I think you made rather a hash of that, don't you Cadet McRobbie? Would you like to have another go?' But I rarely made a hash of anything. I had been an under officer in the cadet corps and had experience in handling and motivating men.

Some of my fellow cadets were senior NCOs who were trying to become commissioned officers. Until I started at OCTU men such as these—who included two sergeant-majors—had been the terror of privates or lance corporals like me, and if they'd spoken to me I'd have jumped to attention. Now, as officer cadets, we were all equal and on first name terms. My fellow cadets included two titled men who had never been in the ranks. At eighteen they had gone from public school into a special potential officer unit where they were given six months basic training before passing on to pre-OCTU. They were wealthy young men who had their own MG sports cars, which they were allowed to keep in the camp. Before World War II, the British army drew its officer corps almost exclusively from the upper classes—huntin', shootin' and fishin' types. These men rarely went through the ranks so had no real idea of how the common soldiers lived, although this changed dramatically during the war. Our two titled cadets were a throwback to the old system, and their cars were regarded as the modern equivalent of an officer's horse.

I got along well with Cadet the Lord Lichenham (Larry) and Cadet Sir Ronald Bakerfield (Ronnie). They mucked in like the rest of us, displaying no 'side', and only their very la-de-da accents marked them out as almost caricatures of the upper class British officer. My mother was highly impressed when I wrote and told her I was sharing a hut with a lord and a baronet.

It was Larry and Ronnie who backed me when I proposed that we put on a show during our final week at Alton Towers. Over several nights I wrote the script for a variety show entitled

'The Ghost of Alton Towers', and when I took the script and proposal to Major Gershwin the old trouper was delighted by the idea. 'I'd be happy to do a turn for you, but don't let me upstage you. This is an excellent script! You must be the producer. No one must outrank you on stage!'

At OCTU, I had much more talent at my disposal than I'd had at Cameron Barracks. A former dance band pianist organised a seven piece band, and two excellent singers were unearthed, as well as a good juggler and an acrobat. The rest of the show was made up of comedy skits.

Costumes were no problem. The CO readily made money available from the amenities fund, and Larry drove me to Birmingham in his MG where we visited a theatrical dealer and hired the costumes. Another cadet, whose father owned a printing works in London, arranged for proper programmes to be printed at no cost. From Birmingham, I managed to get an attractive girl singer and a tap dancing duo to give the show some glamour, and altogether 'The Ghost of Alton Towers' was a slick, professional show.

The week before the show was presented, we moved out of Alton Towers and bivouacked in a camp near Prestatyn in Wales. The camp was in rugged mountainous country which had been taken over by the army for battle training, and during our stay there we fired live ammunition continually and had it fired over our heads by marksmen. We threw hand grenades under battle conditions—not from the safety of a grenade range, but from any depression in the ground that gave protection from flying shrapnel. We drove Bren carriers, armoured cars, fired anti-tank guns and slept on the ground in our greatcoats, living on iron rations while we skirmished all over the mountains. It was very primitive living and as near as possible to spending a week in action.

During this week we were closely observed by our syndicate officers: our performance under stress would decide our final markings for the course. At each of my monthly assessments, I'd maintained an AAA grading, and Major Gershwin had told me that I was in the running to receive the Sword of Honour, presented to the cadet with the best record at our passing out parade,.

When the week was over we moved into a hutted camp for one night before being trucked back to Alton Towers the next morning. It was nice to sleep indoors on a bed again, and we were told we could have the night off and visit the nearby village, as long as we were back in camp by midnight. This was terrific—at last we could taste beer again.

After he'd announced that we had been granted a pass for the night, Sergeant Major Moses barked, 'Except for you Cadet McRobbie. You will be guard commander for the night—and make sure that everybody signs in and out.'

I was annoyed. What had I done to deserve this? But after he'd dismissed the parade, Sergeant Major Moses beckoned to me, and as I stood to attention before him he said, 'Somebody had to be guard commander and stay in the camp as all the officers and NCOs are going into town too. So you'll have the camp to yourself.'

He grinned then added, 'We felt that the cadet who's in the running for the Sword of Honour should be given this honour too. Dismiss!' He laughed like a drain as he strode off.

At five o'clock I settled at the desk in the guard hut at the camp entrance. I had an exercise book to write each cadet's time of departure and return in, and I'd been instructed that nobody, except the staff, could leave before six pm. I was to report anyone who returned after midnight.

Long before five thirty all the officers and NCOs had cleared out, taking our trucks with them, and my fellow cadets, about ninety of them, were champing at the bit to get out of camp and start the half-hour walk into town. The men surrounded the guard hut and tried to persuade me to let them sign out

270

before six. I could see no reason why they couldn't go earlier; it would be six or after when they reached the village and started their night's leave, and as the pubs closed at nine, leaving early would give them some more drinking time. So I said they could begin signing out. But I marked their departure time as beginning at 1800 hours, and I warned them that I would show no lenience if they returned after 23.59 hours. I'd put offenders on report. They rushed off, marching smartly, some even trotting to get into town as quickly as possible and get at the beer—and hopefully the Welsh girls too.

It was boring sitting alone in the remote camp, but I passed the time reading until the cadets began returning at about ten. They were very drunk—but not as drunk as the later arrivals who had found an illegal source of potent Welsh wood cider after the pubs closed. But by midnight they had all returned, some of them carried into the camp by those who could still stand, and many of them vomiting. Within a week or so these men would all be officers and gentlemen in the British army!

The next day I came close to being returned to my unit in disgrace. Back at Alton Towers, I sensed that I was in trouble when Sergeant Major Moses strode into the mess hall where I was finishing lunch and barked, 'Cadet McRobbie! You're on CO's orders. NOW!'

I was quick-marched from the mess hall to the CO's office where the Colonel and all the OCTU's officers were assembled. They looked very grave, including Major Gershwin, who avoided my eye.

The CO said, 'As guard commander last night, did you allow any cadets to leave camp before 1800 hours?'

I glanced down, and under his desk blotter I saw the bottom of the guardroom exercise book sticking out. I knew I'd been found out. Some cadets must have been spotted in town shortly after six, so they'd obviously been released from camp well before then. I knew that if I lied, I would be finished, so I squared my shoulders and said, 'Yes, sir.'

'How many?'

'Quite a few, sir.'

He grunted. 'As many as ninety?'

'Probably, sir.'

He grunted again. 'Why did you disobey your orders?'

'I couldn't see any harm in letting them go earlier. I used my initiative, sir' I added quickly.

He frowned. 'There are times when it is proper to use your initiative and there are other times when it is essential that you follow your orders. Last night was such a time.'

I nodded. There was nothing I could say.

The CO went on to tell me that Major Gershwin thought very highly of me, and that I had been an outstanding cadet who was in the running for the Sword of Honour. I was also producing the show which would be staged next week, and which everyone was looking forward to. To return me to my unit would result in disappointment for many people. He stressed that my future as an officer could be over before it began, and then dismissed me, saying that his decision, and that of all the officers, would be conveyed to me by Major Gershwin.

I was marched out by the Sergeant Major who looked at me and asked gruffly, 'Where are you going now?'

I said I thought I'd go for a walk in the woods surrounding the camp. I didn't want to go to my hut where my fellow cadets would want to know what had happened.

I was upset, and walked blindly through the bushes. At first I'd had no great desire to be an officer, but after six months of hard slogging it would be crushing to miss out on a commission at the last minute. For one thing, as second lieutenant, my pay would increase five fold. I tried to put on a brave face, but it was a struggle. But all of a sudden there was a crashing in the bushes and Major Gershwin appeared. He smiled and gripped my hand, saying 'It's all right, Alex. You'll be formally reprimanded by the CO, but you won't be RTU'd. However, you've lost your chance of getting the Sword of Honour.' He smiled again, and added 'I thought that was a fair compromise.'

I could barely speak but choked out, 'Thank you, sir.'

He laughed. 'Don't thank me. I think the decider was next week's show. I told the CO that it was absolutely excellent, but that it would suffer irreparably if you weren't there to produce it.'

I mumbled another 'Thank you, sir.'

He pressed my hand then said, 'Personally, I rather admired your—initiative. I think I might have done the same when faced with an order like that.'

I choked out some more thanks and saluted, before dashing off into the woods. It was a long time before I was able to return to my hut and face my fellow cadets who knew I had almost been RTU'd. They said they were sorry for having pressured me into letting them leave the camp early, but I told them that that hadn't been a factor. I'd taken it upon my eighteen year old shoulders to amend an order that I felt was senseless, and I had to face the consequences.

After passing out from OCTU I was posted to Fort George, the Seaforth Highlanders' regimental depot, from where I still hoped to be sent to join our 1st Battalion in Burma. But the atomic bomb dropped on Nagasaki and Hiroshima in August 1945 brought a sudden end to the war, and when I finally received an overseas posting I expected there would be little work for an infantry battalion. This forecast proved to be wrong.

While I'd been training to become an officer, I was still on a private soldier's pay of twenty-one shillings a week, and during this time I alloted about a third of my pay to my mother. When I became an officer there was no allotment system whereby money could be deducted from our pay. An officer had to open a bank account into which his pay was credited monthly, and at this time the allotment to my mother ceased.

It was a novelty for me to have a cheque book and bank account. For some reason of tradition, Lloyds Cox and Kings' branch in London was specified for all army officers. At OCTU we had been given a stern lecture on handling a cheque account. Our commanding officer told us, 'As an officer you may get away with unbecoming conduct, such as vomiting on the mess table, ill-treating a horse or impregnating the colonel's daughter. But write a cheque that is dishonoured and you will disappear from your regiment faster than a fart in a thunderstorm!'

In spite of my new bank account, I soon found that I wasn't much better off as a junior officer than I'd been as a ranker, although my pay as a second lieutenant rose to about twelve pounds a month. The dread of most subalterns without a private income was the monthly mess bill. This included a proportion of the cost of entertaining guests (usually officers from other regiments), and such a levy often comprised about half of my mess bill. A series of hard-drinking guest officers (or civic dignitaries) kept the host regiment's junior officers very poor.

I had intended to pay something to my mother every week, but I found that I could only do this occasionally. When I did send her money, it was always by postal order. My parents never had a bank account, not even a Post Office savings one, and whatever money came into the household was spent immediately. There was never any spare cash to 'put away for a rainy day'. Like most of Scotland's working class, we lived from week to week.

Apart from meeting mess bills, another reason I had little money to send home was because I had discovered girls. Taking a girl out cost more than it had done when I'd been in the ranks as she expected to go to the best places. Officers didn't go into public bars and have a cheap counter snack, but took their girls to the more expensive places, eating in hotel dining rooms.

My remittances home became very rare, but I salved my conscience with the knowledge that Bill and Jean were now working and earning money too. Along with my father's wages, and the housekeeping money she received from Uncles Tom and Alex, I knew that my mother was getting more money each week than she'd ever had before. I felt I had done my bit for the family finances. Home in Ayr now belonged to the past, and I had no qualms about enjoying the social life of a young officer.

At Fort George I had my own spacious quarters in the old barracks and was assigned a batman, or officer's personal servant. He was a born and bred Glaswegian, Private Joe Weir. It was Joe's duty to look after me, wash my clothes, polish my footwear, press my uniforms, and stand by and help me dress when ceremonial gear was called for. It was quite heady having a valet, although I was the despair of mine.

I intensely disliked spit and polish and longed to get away from the depot and its traditions. Veteran officers assured me that things were quite different in the field where there was the minimum bullshit and brass polishing. I was happiest in my battledress and didn't like dressing in my kilt and tunic and Sam Browne belt for formal mess dinners and ceremonial occasions. Most of all I disliked having to learn Highland dancing. Junior officers, from Captains down, had to attend Highland dancing classes at dawn every weekday morning as it was considered that an officer should be accomplished in the social graces. The classes were conducted by the pipe major, and on freezing winter mornings it was no fun to dance on the battlements clad only in plimsolls, a vest and a kilt.

We wore nothing under our kilts. In fact, it was a regimental offence to wear underpants while in the kilt, and the only time we were permitted to wear brief tartan trews underneath was when doing Highland dances while ladies were present. A kilted soldier found wearing underpants was put on a charge and usually got seven days confined to barracks. When inspecting a squad of men, one of an officer's duties was to use his swagger stick to occasionally raise a man's kilt from the rear and check that he was 'properly dressed', i.e.—bare-assed.

I didn't like Highland dancing, preferring modern dancing instead, although I was never very good at it. When I was still seventeen and went home to Ayr on my first week's leave, I decided I should learn to dance, to get closer to girls. There was a dancing academy in Ayr run by a gentleman called A Jamieson Munro. His adverts read 'I will teach you to dance in six easy lessons for only 17/6d', and although this was a lot of money for a private soldier, I felt it would be a worthwhile investment. I signed up with Mr Munro and paid my fee. In six lessons I would learn the quickstep, foxtrot, slow foxtrot, modern waltz, old time waltz and the rhumba.

Wearing my battledress and army boots I prepared to have my quickstep lesson. Music came from a gramophone, and I expected I would have a female partner to instruct me. To my horror, I got A Jamieson Munro himself. He was a small man, with sleek black hair and a greasy complexion, and after he had showed me how to hold him in my arms he began one-two-threeing, tugging me onto the slippery floor. I was mortified. I couldn't even think about what my feet were supposed to be doing, and I blurted out, 'Couldn't I have a girl to teach me?'

He shook his head. 'No, you want the crash course. You're only on leave for a week. I'm the only instructor who can get you through the course in that time.'

Red with embarrassment I managed to stumble through the quickstep half hour while other students took the floor, all being taught by females. I was certain they were looking at me and my two left feet, as I tried to hold this effete little man as far away from me as possible.

After the lesson I fled, promising to be back the next day for the foxtrot. I never returned, not even to try and get a refund on my tuition fee. Later I found I could dance passably well, at least under night-club conditions. I danced best with tall girls, all of whom assured me I was very good. I think they were so pleased to have a partner taller than themselves that they cheerfully put up with poor technique.

During the six months I spent at Fort George, I organised and compered regular weekly dance nights at a local church hall. I soon found that being an officer—even a lowly second lieutenant—definitely helped to get girls, and at last I experienced the joy of being able to pick and choose from a variety of willing candidates. For many girls there was a certain cachet in being an officer's girlfriend, and with any luck, an officer's wife, although I had no intention of going steady and being tied to one girl. At nineteen, all my desire was focused on going overseas—and as soon as possible.

But my time at Fort George wasn't devoted entirely to recreational pursuits. Among other duties I was appointed Weapons Training Officer, following a two week course of specialised instruction at a small arms and explosives school near Edinburgh. There I learned the skills of demolition—or blowing things up, and as WTO I controlled the arsenal with its stock of ammunition and explosives.

The range where we taught recruits how to fire rifles and throw hand grenades was alongside a long stretch of sandy beach. This had been sealed off from the beginning of the war and reserved as a firing area for the armed forces, and from 1940 until 1945 this isolated but lovely stretch of beach had been pounded by shells from naval vessels. The RAF had used it to practice low level strafing with cannon and rockets, and the army bombarded it with mortar bombs and anti-tank shells until its concrete 'targets' were reduced to rubble. After the Allied invasion of France, the range ceased to be used and was to be handed back to the civilian local authority. However, first it had to be cleared of the many missiles which had failed to explode and lay buried in the sand.

My CO asked if I would do a survey of the beach and estimate the likely number of unexploded bombs and shells that would need to be dealt with by the engineers. Using a battery-powered metal detector I scanned the beach from the waterline to the dunes. I estimated that there were less than fifty unexploded shells and bombs which had buried themselves in the sand. In addition to these, there were hundreds of unexploded missiles either lying on or partly buried in the sand, whose locations were obvious.

I reported to the CO that I could explode all of them and render the beach safe within two months, but that I couldn't be responsible for missiles which had landed under the water. He said that the navy accepted responsibility for clearing these—the shore was an army job.

It was summer when I began the task of blowing up the leftovers from years of practice firing. In the North of Scotland it was still daylight at eleven pm, so nearly every evening, after dinner, I would load a motorbike with slabs of gun cotton, detonators, instantaneous and slow fuses and Bengal matches, a sort which would stay alight in a hurricane. I wore plimsolls, carried a small wooden spade, and had nothing metallic with me, not even any keys in my pocket. These were elementary precautions. Although I wouldn't be clearing land mines, certain explosive devices could react to carelessly handled metal, such as a shovel. Many of the bombs had lain in the sand for years and were badly corroded. Some oozed sticky yellow explosive from holes in their casings—they were very touchy.

I must say that I enjoyed the two months I spent clearing that beach. Most of the devices were simple to detonate. Ten pound mortar bombs needed only an ounce of gun cotton with a detonator pressed into it, plus a length of slow fuse crimped to the detonator. After lighting the fuse I would walk to a depression in the sand and lie down, waiting with my hands over my ears until the bomb went off. The rule on such occasions was always to walk, not run away from the bomb, to avoid possibly tripping up. But there was never any need to run. I allowed enough fuse to give me plenty of time to take cover.

Some of the larger missiles, like two hundred and fifty pound aerial bombs, needed several slabs of gun cotton to trigger them. I attached the pads of cotton to the bomb with lengths of instantaneous fuse which was then spliced onto a long length of slow fuse. I used plenty of slow fuse because with these bombs I had a fair way to walk to lie down in a safe position.

The missiles which had buried themselves under the sand, mostly naval shells, took more time to explode because I had to dig around them with my wooden spade first. This made space for me to pack in the detonating explosive. I must have done a thorough job on that stretch of shore. After the navy cleared under water, the beach was handed back to the local authority. It's almost fifty years since I made the area safe and I haven't heard a report of anyone using it being blown up by a UXB.

Bomb clearing kept me occupied while I waited to be sent overseas, and it was a great day when my long-standing request to be posted to our 1st Battalion in North Malaya was approved. My orders were to take command of a platoon of thirty Seaforths and proceed by train to Liverpool en route to Singapore. One captain who'd just returned from Malaya told me that things were 'rather hairy' in the battalion's area. 'Lots of bandit chasing and that kind of stuff. You'll certainly get blooded, old chap!'

He'd certainly been blooded. He'd had his left foot blown off by a jungle booby trap.

GOING NATIVE

My platoon and I sailed from Liverpool on a grey rainy November day on board the troopship, SS *Staffordshire*. The war was over, so ships no longer sailed in convoys and without the threat of being torpedoed it was almost like a holiday cruise. There were even some women on board—nurses and a detachment of ATS and WAAFs who were being posted to SEAC headquarters in Singapore. They were outnumbered ten to one by soldiers and airmen, which made them very much in demand.

My first sight of the East came when we docked at Port Said, Egypt, and it lived up to all my expectations. We'd slipped through Gibraltar in darkness and arrived at our first port of call, Port Said, the next day, although it was only a refuelling stop and we weren't allowed off the ship. I was dazzled by the bright tropical sun and the exotic sights, sounds and smells of the East. Our ship was surrounded by bum boats from which Egyptian traders offered everything from rugs to the aphrodisiac, Spanish Fly. A 'gilly gilly' man came on board and did amazing conjuring tricks with day old chickens. It was all very exotic, and I knew I was going to like the tropics.

At Port Said we changed into our tropical uniforms of khaki shorts and shirts, and I felt a lightness of spirit I'd never known in Britain. My yearning to get away was over, and having achieved my heart's desire, I wasn't disappointed by what I found. At our next port of call, Colombo, we were allowed off the ship for a few hours. For the first time, I set foot on foreign soil. Colombo's heat didn't bother me—it was heaven to get away from a cold climate.

Singapore was as exotic as the other ports we'd seen and in 1946 the Lion City was still the steamy tropical colonial outpost which Somerset Maugham wrote about. Today it just looks like any other big Western city. We disembarked, joining a train for Ipoh in North Malaya, a journey which took about twenty four hours in carriages with open-slatted window screens, and no glass. The mosquitoes had a feast on our white skins. But it was a fascinating trip through dense jungle, rubber plantations and barren-looking tin mining areas.

At Ipoh we were met by a truck from our battalion, and a cheerful lieutenant, Bernie Brown, who was dressed in jungle greens and carried a Sten gun as well as his revolver. He had a jeep in which he drove me and my gear to Tanjong Rambutan where our battalion was based.

'Glad to see you, Alex', he said. 'We're a bit short of officers. All the old sweats have gone home to be demobbed, so replacements are welcome. We're down to about seventeen in the mess so we're spread pretty thin.'

An infantry battalion at full strength has about eight hundred men, including thirty two officers. Bernie told me that there were less than four hundred men in the battalion, plus the thirty I'd brought out from Britain. He waved a hand at the surrounding jungle and said, 'We've got a big area to cover. From here to the Siamese border. So we're kept on the go now that our Indian Army friends have gone home.'

The division to which our battalion nominally belonged was the 23rd Indian Division, which had fought throughout the Burma campaign. When India received its independence in 1946, the Indian army units all went home, leaving just three under-strength British battalions, totalling less than two thousand men, to carry out the role of a division of about ten thousand.

281

I asked Bernie if the battalion saw much action in the region. 'A bit,' he said, 'patrols mostly. Chasing bandits.' He grinned. 'You've heard about our bandits?' I said I had. He laughed, 'We're not allowed to call them Communists. You know, it might offend Joe Stalin and our former Russian allies. But they wear red stars on their caps. Anyway, the Adjutant will brief you.' He added, 'There's no risk during daylight. They only operate after dark.'

'What do they do?'

'Collect food from the Chinese villagers. All the bandits are Chinese too. Villagers who don't co-operate often have their throats slit. The bandits don't waste bullets. They get most of their ammo from raiding our depots. Guarding the depots uses up a lot of our men.'

He lit a cigarette and I followed suit. It was a rule that while driving military vehicles smoking was prohibited, and in Britain the regulation was strictly policed. But under field service conditions the rule was ignored and I was happy to find that it was one of many regulations that were relaxed when a unit was in the field.

Bernie said, 'Now to important things. Do you play football?'

'Yes, but I'm better at hockey.'

'Good! We play both. We play against some Indian civilian teams and the Manchesters who are in our division.'

Before we reached Tanjong Rambutan, Bernie told me the buildings the battalion occupied had been a lunatic asylum before and during the war. 'The poor blighters got short shrift from the Japs during the occupation. Those that were left were trucked off to Kuala Lumpar for hospital treatment. We took over the asylum.'

He grimaced. 'We still haven't got it really clean, but we're working on it.'

Helping to convert a filthy neglected asylum into a clean and tidy British Army camp was one of the first tasks given to me and my thirty new arrivals. We got stuck into it, and to set an example, I worked with my men clad, like them, only in jungle green shorts. We literally shovelled shit left behind by the poor crazed Malay, Indian and Chinese inmates, hosing down building after building then slapping whitewash on the walls until the quarters were fit for human habitation. Until the long thatch-roofed huts were ready we slept, like most of the battalion, in tents. It was a great day when we all had a roof over our heads.

Working Saturday and Sunday, my platoon finished the task in seven days. It reminded me of how I used to clean our home in Glasgow when my parents went out to the cinema. The CO was very impressed. 'New broom, sweeps clean, eh? Anyway, good show Alex. So, what else can you do to brighten our dull lives here in the jungle?'

After accepting a large Haig's, I asked if there was anything he especially wanted done? He said he'd like to see some kind of battalion publication produced, adding 'I see from your civvie record that you ran a paper in Scotland. Perhaps you could get one going here. It would be good for the Jocks' morale. Something light and funny. No heavy army stuff or anything about the bandits.'

It was almost like hearing Mr Binnie talking back in Prestwick, and I said I'd see what I could do, although I would need the use of a jeep to travel to and from a civilian print shop in Ipoh. 'I think we can find you one', he said. 'We've got no chaplain at the moment so his should be spare.'

In an army battalion, jeeps were keenly sought by officers. The CO and the four company commanders were each allotted one, plus a driver. The chaplain and medical officer also got one as did the motor transport officer, but other officers were driven in fifteen hundredweight Dodge trucks. It was a memorable day when I got my own jeep, and I managed to stick to one during most of my overseas service.

I settled down to produce a battalion magazine which I called 'The Antler' after the stag's head on our cap badge. Unlike other publications I'd produced, I was determined this one was going to be printed instead of duplicated, and in Ipoh I found an Indian printer who could do the job. The CO said that no army funds were available to produce the magazine, so I'd have to 'use my initiative' to raise the money myself. I financed the project by selling advertising space to Chinese and Indian traders in Ipoh, who owned a number of amusement parks with names like 'Happy World'. In the 'Worlds' there were dance halls where Chinese girl partners were available for ten cents a dance, and the proprietors were happy to advertise in the magazine because many of their patrons were off-duty soldiers.

Ipoh was off the beaten track compared with major cities such as Kuala Lumpar and Singapore, and many of the traders to whom I sold advertising space were far from fluent in English. One of the first things I did on arrival in Singapore was to buy a book on the Malay language, which was spoken by many Chinese and Indians as well as Malays. I studied the book and from speaking with villagers, I soon learned enough of the language to make myself understood. My knowledge of Malay was very useful when patrolling in the jungle, and it surprised me that few British soldiers ever bothered trying to learn at least some.

At that time, Ipoh's cinemas and amusement parks were controlled by two Chinese brothers, Run Run Shaw and Run Me Shaw. Later these gentlemen became multi-millionaires, developing business interests in Hong Kong where they dominated the colony's film industry and pioneered the Kung Fu movies. In 1947, the Shaw Brothers had a smallish office in Ipoh, but they were big advertisers in my magazine. When I visited their office I would clump up the stairs, Sten gun over my shoulder, to collect their copy—and their payment for their adverts. Run Run always paid cash from a thick wad of dollars he kept in his shirt pocket. As I wrote him out a receipt I'm sure the rows of Chinese clerks working industriously at their abacuses thought I was extorting money from the boss, as the occupying Japanese had done. But Run Run and Run Me advertised willingly. They were intensely loyal to Britain and were later knighted by Queen Elizabeth.

Having a healthy advertising revenue, I printed over 1,000 copies of the first issue of *The Antler* because many of the men wanted to send a copy home. The sports-mad CO was even more pleased when, on his urging, I produced a weekly *Sports Special* covering divisional sporting activities, and altogether, my literary work kept me busy in my off duty hours. I still had to carry out the regular duties of a regimental officer, taking my turn as orderly officer and leading my platoon on patrols.

Later, the CO asked if I'd like to take on the job of Entertainment Officer, saying 'It's pretty boring out here in the wilds. Not much for the Jocks to do. They can't afford to go into Ipoh every night, so maybe you could think up something to amuse them. A show or something, eh?'

I decided that a weekly show was the way to go. A dance was out of the question because there weren't any European women in the area, not even ATS girls, and Chinese girls weren't allowed in the camp as they could have been in league with the bandits. And the Muslim Malay girls were too modest to dream of dancing in public. But a weekly variety show was possible, although all the talent would have to come from within the battalion.

I staged the show in the canteen every Thursday night, the night before pay day when the Jocks were broke (that brought back memories of Glasgow!) I managed to assemble the essential band from among our pipers and located some singers and an impressionist, compering the show myself and distributing hastily typed scripts from which we worked up mainly ad-libbed comedy sketches. There was never any time for rehearsals. The shows were always packed and usually ended with an hour's community singing—the bawdy barracks room ballads which soldiers never seem to tire of.

Hogmanay, or New Year's Eve, is always a big night in a Scottish regiment, and on Hogmanay in 1946 the jungle around our camp echoed to the skirl of the bagpipes and sounds of drunken revelry. Discipline was relaxed, indeed it was almost non-existent as the Jocks caroused around the camp. In my role as entertainment officer I secured enough cases of Canadian Club whisky to provide a bottle per two men. It wasn't Scotch, but they didn't mind. Normally the other ranks only got an issue of beer for Christmas or New Year, but with plenty of beer and whisky, the Seaforths indulged in a real Celtic Bacchanalia on Hogmanay.

On the stroke of midnight the jungle was illuminated by dozens of flares and coloured tracer bullets from our Bren guns. Curious Chinese and Malay villagers gathered on the outskirts of the camp to watch the crazy Scottish soldiers celebrating. Fortunately, none of the onlookers were shot. The bullets were all fired into the night sky.

At about two in the morning a cry went up from the villagers, 'Rimau! Rimau!' I knew that this meant they'd spotted a tiger. At the time, tigers were numerous in Malaya. Before the war they had been a favourite target of white big game hunters, but during the three and a half years of Japanese occupation they hadn't been hunted, so the splendid beasts had thrived.

The word went round the Jocks that there was a tiger prowling the camp perimeter, and my inebriated Sergeant said, 'We'd better shoot it, sir, or it could take one of the natives!'

Incidents of a tiger mauling villagers, or eating their livestock, were quite common so I organised a tiger shoot. All the drunken soldiers wanted to be part of it and moved to arm themselves. But drunk as I was (and I was very drunk), I could see the danger in permitting a platoon of armed men to plunge into the jungle and start shooting in all directions. I said we would go in one jeep with a driver, two NCOs and myself, each armed with Sten guns. The headlights would provide illumination in the darkened jungle.

The jeep forced its way through the undergrowth, while we kept our eyes peeled for a pair of glowing cat's eyes. A crowd of village men followed us, and to my surprise they called to us not to shoot the tiger. I thought they'd have been glad to have it killed. My Malay wasn't good enough to understand what the village headman was saying, but it sounded like they wanted the tiger alive, for some reason of their own.

I ignored them, and the jeep slithered and slid its way into the dense undergrowth until my Sergeant, standing up in the seat behind me, fired off a volley into the darkness. 'It's over there, sir!' he bellowed. The Corporal beside him loosed off a burst of automatic fire. I thought I saw something straight ahead so I peppered the area with half a magazine of 9mm bullets. Needless to say, we didn't shoot the tiger, and it occurred to me later that any sane animal would have put miles between us and itself once we opened fire.

The next day I got a message from the headman, who knew me, that the tiger had been trapped and was being held by the villagers. Could I bring a camera and take some photos? With my Box Brownie I drove to the kampong where the villagers were very excited. The tiger had fallen into a pit trap they'd dug and they had covered the snarling animal with rattan netting and hauled it out. For the photo they had strung the poor beast upside down on two bamboo poles. It was a magnificent specimen, although it was looking very dejected with its mouth and razor sharp teeth covered by a rattan muzzle, and later the villagers sold it to a Chinese merchant. He kept it caged until he sold it for a good price to an animal dealer in Singapore.

Just after the war, hunters who supplied wild animals to zoos and circuses began re-visiting countries which had previously been their source of livestock. During the war there had been little such hunting, and there was a big demand for beasts like the Malay and Bengal tiger. A famous American hunter of the time was Frank 'Bring 'Em Back Alive' Buck, and several movie shorts were made of his exploits. While I was in North Malaya, Buck led a safari into our area and we provided an escort for him as the region was still not stable. He caught many animals but he let it be known that it was tigers he wanted most, and he offered the villagers the huge sum of a thousand Malayan dollars for any tiger caught alive. At that time, twenty dollars a month was a good income for a villager.

Frank Buck left our area with his government permitted quota of six fine specimens, and the villagers were very rich after his departure. I think Buck was even richer. He sold the tigers for thousands of US dollars or British pounds, and one of his customers was a private Scottish zoo.

After I had been in Malaya for several months, I seldom thought about my home in Scotland. I was kept in touch with what was happening to my family through my mother, who was the family letter writer, maintaining contact with her sea-faring brothers, her sister in Canada, and various aunts as far back as I can remember. In fact, my mother acted as a kind of central clearing house for family information. Everybody wrote to her and she passed on items of interest to other family members. She was a good letter writer, and after I joined the army she added me to her list of correspondents and I dutifully wrote back fairly regularly, although naturally I never told her anything which would have worried her.

My life with the regiment in North Malaya wasn't all socialising, booze-ups and fun and frolic. For several periods I was on detachment with my platoon about seventy miles north of Ipoh in an area where bandit activity was high. I loved going on detachment because it took me away from the battalion, where discipline wasn't irksome, but there was some spit and polish nevertheless. On detachment we roughed it, doing the kind of soldiering I had trained for. During a ten day assignment we lived outside a little village, sleeping in huts, or 'bashas', and sending out night patrols to search for bandits. We were in what was called a counter-insurgency role, but essentially it was a flag-showing exercise. It proved to the villagers that even in isolated areas, there was a British presence to protect them. Just as importantly, it showed that the British Army was not afraid of the bandits, and instead of remaining in the safety of our battalion barracks we posted small units in the thick of their territory to meet them on their own ground.

The immediate post-war political situation in Malaya was relatively simple to grasp. Traditionally, Britain regarded the Malays as the race which would take over when Britain left the colony, and nineteenth century treaties with the Malay Sultans guaranteed this. But since the treaties had been signed, the number of Chinese in Malaya had risen to almost equal the Malay population. The Chinese, initially brought to Malaya as coolies, or labourers, regarded the country as their home, and much of the country's commerce was in the hands of Chinese merchants. The Malays rarely became involved in commerce, nor did they like working as labourers, which is why the Chinese were imported. They were often described by the British as 'the Englishmen of the Far East'. The inference was that they were gentlemen and their word was their bond.

When Britain announced its intention to eventually hand over power to the Malays, many Chinese felt they would be in for a thin time. It was mostly Malays who were admitted into the civil service, and the country's indigenous military force, the British-officered Malay Regiment, had no Chinese members. The police force, also commanded by British officers, was almost entirely Malay, with a few Chinese detectives. Consequently many Chinese activists, heavily Communist-orientated, decided that they would need to fight for what they regarded as their rights. They felt that the insurrection should begin before the British left to show them that the Chinese population was a force to be reckoned with.

The Communists' main bases were in Southern Siam (later Thailand), from where they could move at will into Northern Malaya. When forced to retreat, they could skip back across the border where the British were not permitted to pursue them and it was against this background that our under-strength infantry battalion played its part in controlling insurgency and terrorism. Later, when it became clear that the attempt to take over Malaya and Singapore was part of a world-wide Communist plan, Britain poured troops into the Malay peninsula and declared a state of emergency. It was 1953 before the Communists were defeated and Malaya became an independent nation.

As an officer representing what I suppose could be called the occupying power, it was heartening to find that the British had the full support of the Malay people. Many Chinese were also far from being anti-British—they had prospered under British colonial rule and faced an uncertain future should the Communists seize power. But the Malay Chinese were under intense pressure to support their own people who claimed they were fighting to 'liberate' them. Long after the emergency was over I visited the National Mosque in Kuala Lumpur. I was pleased to find the Seaforth Highlanders' regimental insignia in a memorial area dedicated to the British forces who had made the emergence of the new state of Malaysia possible, and I would have been very unhappy to have been regarded as an oppressor during my service in Malaya.

When stationed on detachment near the Siamese border, I could slop around all day, stripped to the waist like my men and displaying no badges of rank. There was no saluting for the very good reason that it would have identified me as being in command. Any bandits observing us, which they did, would have marked me out as a target to concentrate on. For the same reason, when on patrol I wore no officer's insignia and carried the same weapon as my men did.

Some officers didn't like going on detachment, but I loved it because I was in complete command. I had my own hut where I slept which the men called the officers mess. Actually, it stored all our ammunition and rations as well as a table where I ate and wrote out reports. It also housed our long range wireless set which was supposed to keep us in touch with our base. But the radio was practically useless because the country was mountainous. To use it, the heavy outfit had to be carried to the top of the nearest hill. That was the task of my batman, who on active service became my radio operator and runner. In those days there were no lightweight transistor radios—it was all delicate valves and heavy batteries.

In spite of being a long way from the safety of the battalion, and living a Spartan life far from the dance halls and cinemas of Ipoh, my men liked being on detachment. I was never a 'bash on' type of officer, the kind the Americans call gung ho. I regarded my main task as being to keep my men alive, and the replacements I had brought from Britain became my platoon. After five weeks on board the troopship and some months in Malaya, we knew one another very well. Almost all of the men were young conscripts, aged nineteen or twenty. Our Burma veterans had gone home to be demobilised, and except for the CO, few officers or NCOs had any experience of jungle warfare, or more accurately, jungle guerrilla warfare.

Some of the lessons I learned during my childhood in Glasgow were useful in the Malayan jungle. These included resourcefulness, improvisation and cunning. I instructed my men never to walk along the myriad paths that criss-crossed the jungle, as the bandits often placed tripwire booby traps across these paths. So we walked to one side of a path, which often meant stumbling through thick undergrowth—and disturbing clouds of mosquitoes. It was uncomfortable, but better than having a leg blown off.

Most of the patrols I led were uneventful, although it was always nerve-wracking waiting for the next bang and whine of a bullet. We often heard the bandits and were shot at, although by the time we'd reached the spot where the shots came from, the bandits had melted away into the jungle. This was easy to do at night which was when we mainly patrolled.

Close to Alor Star, on the Siamese border, we did locate a bandit base, although it was deserted. We burned the huts and rice stock but discovered no ammunition or weapons. My only shoot-it-out encounter with bandits occurred as we lay in wait for an expected raid on a supply dump near Ipoh. When we surprised the raiders, a brisk skirmish took place with hundreds of shots being exchanged. After a long chase through secondary jungle on a moonless night I caught and disarmed one of the bandits. I could justifiably have shot him dead, but after a closer look at his face I saw he was old enough to be my father. So I kicked his behind instead. In Malay he babbled, 'Thank you, tuan, bad men made me do this.' I felt that that was a likely story.

But far away from the eagle eye of the Adjutant—the terror of junior officers—we lived a fairly leisurely life, at least during the day when we weren't patrolling. We swapped some of our rations with the villagers and in return received such delicacies as chickens, eggs and fresh fish they caught in a nearby lagoon. The Jocks tried swimming in the lagoon until they discovered that blood-sucking leeches made a beeline for their white skins, which the Malays found very amusing. For some reason the leeches didn't cling to them.

The horny young soldiers even managed some romantic dalliance with some Chinese girls from a village quite close to our camp. The Malay girls were out of bounds. As Muslims they were kept in a kind of purdah, although they didn't wear veils, but the Chinese ones were quite forthcoming. The Jocks wooed them with tins of English cigarettes which were scarce and expensive on the civilian market. Being in an active service situation, troops got an ample free issue of cigarettes, and the Chinese girls sold them for a good price on the black market.

Being away from the battalion, I permitted Chinese girls to enter our camp after quizzing them to ascertain if their loyalties lay with the Communists or with us. The girls all assured me that they loved King George and hated the bandits, as did their mothers, fathers, brothers, sisters and uncles. I wondered how the bandits were able to secure their daily rice from such Empire-loving loyalists. They said bad men made them give them rice and food, and I later found that they also made them give them cigarettes—our cigarettes.

In their colourful cheong sams, and their clinging dresses with provocative slits up one side, the Chinese girls were very decorative. I had a regular girl, Mary Tan, who occasionally shared my charpoy, or bed, after dining with me in the officers mess. The 'mess', as I have mentioned, was also our store hut and apart from our ammunition it contained odds and ends like spare tyres for our jeep. I had a man on guard outside the hut day and night.

While on detachment we received very few visitors. But one day I got a radio message from HQ to say that one of our lieutenants would be bringing two newly-arrived officers from the Manchester Regiment to stay with us for a night and sample life on detachment. When their jeep clawed its way through the mud to our camp I greeted the two young officers and my fellow Seaforth lieutenant. During the day I showed them what we did, displayed some captured bandit weapons, and generally familiarised them with detachment work. Warm tropical rain was lashing down so I told them we wouldn't be sending out a patrol that night. During heavy rain the bandits stayed in their camps and we were happy to do likewise. We might be fighting

293

a guerrilla war, but neither side saw any sense in conducting it in any more discomfort than was necessary.

The two young English officers, Nigel and Philip, were very pukkha chaps who had come straight from Britain to their regiment and were still adjusting to the East. To show them how we observed mess rituals, even on detachment, I arranged a special dinner. My batman did an excellent job and extended my table with some planks, finding three packing cases as seats for our guests. From the villagers he scrounged some batik material to make a tablecloth which he laid with the crockery and cutlery that he had somehow managed to produce. Our main course was an excellent Malay chicken curry which our cook prepared on a large platter. My fellow Seaforth officer, Colin, brought two bottles of Scotch and some wine, so we were able to drink a series of toasts—to the King, our regiments, absent friends and so on. Colin had even brought some Dutch cigars, so altogether it was a very civilised dinner despite the primitive jungle setting.

After we'd eaten and were finishing off with cigars and claret, Nigel lolled against the hut wall then cried, 'Now it's time to bring on the dancing girls, Alexander!'

Phillip said, 'I think that would be asking rather much, old chap. Alex has done us proud.'

'Of course there will be some entertainment,' I replied, winking at Colin who was seated alongside me, facing our two guests. I'd already told him what I'd planned and warned him to to show no surprise when the 'entertainment' began. Then I signalled to my batman, who was acting as mess steward and he slipped out of the hut. He'd dressed for the occasion, which meant he'd put on his jungle green shirt. Within a minute Mary Tan appeared and began to do a sensuous dance, singing some kind of ditty in Cantonese as she undulated before us. My guests' eyes popped as Mary slipped out of her cheong sam, standing naked except for her brief white panties. They were even more surprised when she slid the panties off and moved to the end of the hut where my batman had suspended a jeep tyre from a rafter.

Naked, she began to swing gracefully on the tyre, concluding her performance by wriggling through it and taking a bow. Nigel and Phillip applauded wildly but Colin and I adopted nonchalant expressions as if this was an after-dinner diversion we saw every night.

When she'd finished her act, Mary sashayed to my side and bowed, lifting my dinner plate to remove a Malayan ten dollar note from under it. 'Thank you sir,' she said demurely. 'Same time tomorrow?'

'Of course,' I said.

Nigel and Phillip were tremendously impressed. Nigel said, 'Gad, you Seaforths know how to look after yourselves! Is it always like this on detachment?'

'Always,' Colin and I assured him. Colin said loftily, 'We don't abandon civilised amenities just because we're in the jungle, you know.'

'Exactly,' I said. 'It's important that we avoid going native when we're in the colonies.'

I added, 'My pater taught me that.'

SINGAPORE MOONLIGHT

When our battalion moved to Singapore it was back to spit and polish. Our new home, Gilman Barracks, had been purpose built in peacetime and things were almost as regimental as they had been at Fort George. We mounted ceremonial guards at the Governor's residence and were obliged to entertain senior officers from GHQ and visiting journalists from overseas. Generally we had to be on our best behaviour. I'd been happier roughing it in the jungle.

A notable visitor who we entertained at our mess was my Uncle Alec, who was still at sea and still a Chief Engineer. After his glamorous wartime days in the Merchant Navy he had begun to serve on ships of steadily decreasing size and impressiveness. Smarter ships had few openings for a permanently drunken engineer, so Alec was reduced to sailing on tramp steamers where quite often the Captain was also four sheets to the wind. I often wondered how such rusting old tubs found their way from port to port. I suppose they must have had some officers who could navigate and keep the engines running, and I suspect it was the Second Officer and Second Engineer.

Through a letter from my mother, I learned that Uncle Alec's boat (she always called ships boats) the SS *Trader*, would be in Singapore for a few days. I kept an eye on the shipping arrivals and when I heard that the *Trader* had docked I drove to the quay where it was tied up. It was a typical pre-war tramp steamer of about eight thousand tons. Had it not been for the wartime need for ships of any kind, I'm sure it would have gone to the scrapyard long before. But its owners were determined to squeeze a few more profitable voyages from the hulk before it foundered or lost its seaworthiness certificate.

When I strode up the rickety gangway, it was obvious that the *Trader* had brought a cargo of coal to Singapore. This was being unloaded manually, and clouds of black dust hung in the humid air. To touch the railings resulted in black palms, and after being on board for two minutes a thin film of coal dust settled on my epaulettes. I found Uncle Alec in his cabin wearing a grimy singlet and underpants. He had his porthole closed to keep out the dust, so the cabin was stinking hot, while a fan the size of a small soup plate stirred the air. My unshaven uncle had a cigarette hanging from the corner of his mouth and there was a half empty bottle of whisky on his bedside table. A half full glass stood beside it. It was ten o'clock in the morning.

Alec didn't look particularly hot, nor did he display any surprise at my appearance, saying blearily, 'So you're in the army. Your mother told me you were out here.'

I said I had been in the army for three years.

'Would you like a dram?' he asked. I declined, and he looked disappointed. In spite of the closed porthole, a film of coal dust covered everything in the cabin. There were even flecks of dust in his eyebrows.

'Aye,' he sighed. 'It's a dirty cargo. When it's unloaded we'll be loading tin ingots. They're a lot cleaner.'

I discovered that Alec's ship would be in Singapore for three days, and said he must let me show him the sights. He grumbled that he wasn't interested in sightseeing and didn't plan to leave the ship, although the crew were eager to have some shore leave. Alec also told me that the *Trader* had a football team and the men hoped they might be able to play a game somewhere on shore, so I offered to arrange a match between his ship and one of our teams. We even had our own soccer field at the barracks. I made arrangements to send a truck the next day at ten to collect him and the ship's team.

'We'll look after them,' I assured him. 'They can have some practice in the morning before we start a match.'

The next morning I sent a truck to bring the seafaring footballers to our barracks. Uncle Alec had shaved and spruced himself up, and looked quite presentable in his officer's tropical whites, although he'd obviously been at the whisky bottle since breakfast time. But the crew members were a motley bunch dressed in a variety of civilian gear. There were about twenty of them, including supporters.

Our battalion team captain, Sergeant McKechnie, led the *Trader*'s team to the dressing rooms from where they emerged in football boots, black shorts and yellow shirts. We left them alone while they had an hour's practice, and they hadn't been booting the ball for long before it became obvious that they weren't very good. 'They're bloody terrible!' Sergeant McKechnie muttered to me. 'Our blokes will *murder* them!'

Our battalion team was very good and included a former Scottish International player. The Seaforths were regularly at the top of the army soccer league in Malaya.

'Will you ask our fellows to take it easy? We don't want it to be a massacre,' I said. 'These sailors don't get much chance to practise.'

McKechnie sighed. 'I'll do my best, sir.'

When the match began there were about two hundred spectators. Many of our men had been given time off to watch the match, and I stood with my uncle and the small group of *Trader* supporters, hoping for the best. I must say the Jocks were very sporting. Word had got round that the sailors' team were from my uncle's ship, and that they were badly out of practice, so the Seaforths cheered each time one of the *Trader* team did something worth cheering, which wasn't very often. On the field, Sergeant McKechnie kept his men well reined in. But in spite of their best (or worst) efforts, they couldn't help scoring. By half time it was eight nil to the Seaforths.

During the second half our full back 'accidentally' kicked the ball into his own goal. When the sailors managed to get into a scoring situation, our goalkeeper dived the wrong way and the ball went into the net. Two players retired hurt, faking ankle injuries. But even playing two men short couldn't stop the Seaforths scoring, and it was 10-3 to us when one of Singapore's daily tropical downpours lashed the field. Sergeant McKechnie yelled out, 'Game abandoned! Three cheers for the Traders! Hip hip hooray!'

After the dripping sailors had been led from the field and got changed, they were taken to the sergeants mess for a lunch accompanied by all the grog they could drink. I drove my uncle to the officers mess where the CO had said he would be very welcome to dine with us.

By the time we reached the mess, Alec's hands had begun shaking—he hadn't had a drink for nearly three hours. But a double whisky from a mess steward settled his nerves and he responded amiably as I introduced him to the CO and our officers in the ante-room. During lunch at the long mess table he was seated on the Colonel's right while I sat next to him. The old sea dog refused wine or beer during lunch, in fact he hardly ate any of our curry tiffin. However, the mess Sergeant kept his glass half full of neat whisky and Alec became very expansive after he'd adjusted to the formality of our very traditional mess.

During dessert he became particularly loquacious. 'Aye,' he told the Colonel, 'my nephew here and his brothers used to play some terrible tricks on me when I was home. Did he ever tell you about the time they put a piece of bloody liver on my pillow so I'd think I'd spewed my guts up?'

The Colonel said I'd never told that story, so Uncle Alec proceeded to relate it, going on to tell how my brother Bill had once put Condes Crystals in his teeth glass while he slept. Alec plucked his top plate from his mouth and held it out to the Colonel. 'See,' he said, 'you can still see the stain on the plate.'

Our easy-going CO took all this quite well although he quickly changed the subject. Fortunately, Alec soon reached a semi-comatose state, speaking little and almost nodding off. But every now and then his hand reached for his whisky glass and he would drain it in one gulp. The mess Sergeant later told me admiringly that he had never seen a mess guest consume so much whisky in such a short time.

After lunch I managed to get Uncle Alec into my jeep without incident. I drove to the sergeants' mess and rounded up the *Trader*'s sailors who were loaded into one of our trucks. After the hospitality of the mess, the inebriated seamen could hardly stand upright. We drove them back to their ship where Uncle Alec thanked me profusely, promising to tell my mother all about it when he got home. 'And I'll tell her you look very braw in your kilt.'

The regiment had taken to wearing the kilt again, and in the tropics, it wasn't my favourite form of dress. In the intense humidity the heavy kilt was uncomfortable and it chafed round my middle, causing prickly heat which developed into a bad case of tropical dermatitis. I felt disgusted with myself. The dermatitis became so bad I was sent to the military hospital where I spent three weeks. But the infection became resistant to penicillin, and I was dispatched to the Cameron Highlands in Central Malaya where the climate was similar to England's. Eventually my dermatitis healed.

On returning to Singapore I found that our easy-going Commanding Officer had been ordered back to the UK, and his replacement was something of a martinet. I applied for a transfer to Ceylon where the army was recruiting a new unit to be brought to Singapore, where it would assist with post-war reconstruction work. I was promoted to Captain and received a welcome pay rise.

I spent six weeks in Colombo, before returning to Singapore with a battalion of a thousand mixed Sinhalese and Tamil soldiers. The British had recruited ten battalions of Ceylonese, and all of them were stationed in Singapore quite close to one another in tented camps, virtually in jungle country. I liked the cheerful Sinhalese and coal black Tamils. At the time, the enmity between the two races was not apparent, at least not while they were members of the British army. I learned a little of their language, enough to exchange jokes with them.

In Singapore we needed a sense of humour as conditions were primitive and often uncomfortable. Just after the war, there was a widespread shortage of rice throughout the Far East as the output of major rice-producing countries like Burma and Siam had been affected by war and the Japanese occupation. Consequently, rice was imported from Northern Australia to help feed Southeast Asia's multitudes. This was known as 'pullit' rice—a disparaging term—and using normal cooking methods our Ceylonese cooks couldn't make it fit to eat. Instead the rice ended up as a tasteless, sticky, glutinous mess, rather like rice pudding.

I was well aware of the importance of rice to Asians. The Ceylonese ate it for breakfast, lunch and dinner, usually with a hot curry. But the curry liquid didn't soak into pullit rice, it just slid off the sticky pile. All of the ten Ceylonese battalions in Singapore were having the same problem, and in some camps the men were close to mutiny, although they were all volunteers. None had been impressed into the British army, but had joined instead for what was relatively good pay—and three square meals a day.

At that time I was regularly eating curries. I'd developed a liking for hot spicy food and ate the same food as my men, and didn't need convincing that there was something wrong with the rice. I discussed the problem at length with my Sinhalese batman, Private Joseph Fernando, a convent-educated man who spoke excellent English and had worked in restaurants in Colombo. Joseph had a theory that the rice could be made acceptable, but that it would require special cooking and treatment, so I accompanied him to the cookhouse where he demonstrated how it could be done. His method involved lightly cooking the rice then shovelling it on to fine wire mesh screens and shaking it vigorously to remove the water, then lightly re-cooking it in the minimum water, after which it broke up into individual grains. The end result wasn't as good as No.1 Siamese brown rice, or Burmese white, but it was much improved.

While it was relatively easy to cook and treat one pot of rice as Joseph had done, cooking food for a thousand men required big vats. The new process would need many large mesh screens and lots of muscle to shake them, so I ordered the screens to be made, then promoted Fernando to sergeant and placed him in charge of the cookhouse. The regular cook sergeant was lukewarm about the new method because it would involve him and his cooks in considerable extra work, so I drafted twenty additional men to cookhouse duties. The next evening we had our first meal of rice cooked by the new method. It was well received by the men, and after they'd eaten their dinner they assembled around me and began a long chant in my honour, although I told them that Sergeant Fernando deserved the credit.

Our rice problem was solved, but it was a labour intensive business preparing it properly, and the sweating cooks had hardly finished one meal when they had to start on the next. Nobody liked pushing heavy trays of soggy rice, but it was the only way to make it reasonably edible.

The rations we drew from army stores were more suited to the tastes of European troops than Asians, and the basic 'fresh' meat was frozen mutton from Australia. But a steady diet of mutton curry became monotonous, and I applied myself to putting some variety into the men's meals. We had abundant supplies of canned evaporated milk which my men hardly used. Ceylonese are great tea drinkers, but they don't put milk in their tea, and my men didn't eat desserts made with milk either. However, on the civilian market in Singapore and Malaya, canned milk was scarce, and it commanded a good price on the black market.

Once a week I had a three ton truck loaded with hundreds of cartons of canned milk, and with two men to do the unloading I drove across the long causeway which connects Singapore island with Johore in Malaya. We went around the villages where I bartered our milk for chickens, eggs, fish and vegetables. It was completely illegal, a British officer trading army rations on the black market, but I wasn't doing it for profit, and that would be my defence if I was caught and court martialed.

When we returned to camp we had enough fresh food to make about six curry meals for the battalion. The chicken, fish and vegetable curries made a nice change from mutton, but I met some opposition when I suggested that we made one with eggs. Indeed, the cook sergeant said the men wouldn't eat it. I thought this might be for religious reasons, but after consulting Joseph Fernando, he assured me they probably would. Joseph cooked a trial dish which we thought was very tasty. So for breakfast one morning my men had their first egg curry. They only received the equivalent of one sliced boiled egg per man, and Malayan chicken eggs were very small, but with some vegetables it made an appetising curry.

I always ate with my men, waiting until they had been served before presenting my mess tin for my ration, and like them I was quite happy with the variety in our diet. The soldiers ate from their mess tins with their fingers. How they did this without burning themselves was beyond me, although I didn't try to emulate them, eating my hot curry with a fork instead. After each meal Sergeant Fernando made the traditional orderly sergeant's call, 'Any complaints?' There were never any after we fixed the rice problem.

Unfortunately, the other nine battalions of Ceylonese didn't adopt our rice cooking method, although I told their British officers how we did it. Dissatisfaction with their food led one night to what the civilian newspapers called the Great Ceylonese Mutiny. During this carnage, nine of the battalions ran riot, burning some of their tents and looting stores after chasing their British officers and NCOs from the camps. My battalion didn't mutiny. Indeed I used my men to quell the mutineers in the camp adjoining ours.

When the British army finally arrived in force the mutineers were placed under armed guard and the ringleaders trucked off to Changi jail. My battalion continued its work as usual, and after a lengthy Court of Enquiry I was commended for maintaining control of the situation. Within a few months all nine battalions were sent back to Ceylon and disbanded. The men of my unit received honourable discharges.

After the Ceylonese Corps was sent home, I was assigned to command a Japanese prisoner of war camp in the centre of Singapore island. There were several thousand POWs at the camp and each day they drove into Singapore in their own trucks where they worked at reconstruction sites. There were no armed British guards or barbed wire around the tented camp, and the only British presence was myself and my Sergeant Major. We slept in marquees in the middle of the camp, but we were in no danger. The Japanese wished only to be sent home, which they would be after they'd repaired war damage in Singapore. Many Malay and Chinese civilians, who had endured three and a half years of an often brutal occupation, gave the toiling POWs a hard time.

Our POW camp included several generals, admirals, air marshals and other high ranking Japanese officers. Under the Geneva Convention officers could not be forced to work, but I did insist that they paraded each morning while their NCOs and men were assigned their tasks for the day. Before jobs were assigned, all the POWs, led by their officers, bowed to me and the Union Jack which my Sergeant Major raised on its pole. Under the British flag he then raised the Rising Sun flag. The Japanese always winced at this loss of face.

The Japanese officers were a scruffy-looking bunch. They weren't allowed batmen so had to look after themselves, and after the surrender their treasured swords had been taken from them, although they were ordered to wear the empty scabbards as evidence of their defeat.

Being the twenty-year-old commandant of the POW camp was relatively uneventful. The only break in the routine of camp life was when the Military Police called with an officer from the War Crimes Tribunal and took some officers away for trial. None of the senior Japanese officers returned to the camp. Many were found guilty of wartime atrocities against Allied POWs and civilians, and were hanged in Changi jail.

I remained at the camp until August 1947 when I became due for demobilisation, and opted to take my discharge in Singapore rather than return to the UK. While in the army I had been writing for the *Malaya Tribune* and also wrote some documentary film scripts for the Malaya Film Unit. I planned to live in Singapore as a civilian, at least for a year. To gain more income than could be earned from writing, I opened a private security agency in partnership with a Chinese lawyer. The main function of the Security and Investigations Bureau was to provide bodyguards for wealthy Chinese merchants, known as towkays, as there was considerable lawlessness in Singapore and Malaya in the immediate post-war period. Wealthy merchants were the target of bandits who kidnapped them and held them for large ransoms. The bandits were the same types as we had fought in North Malaya, and ransom money gave them a source of funds.

Quite a number of British soldiers were opting to be discharged in Singapore and enter civilian life, and it was my intention to recruit them as reliable bodyguards for the Chinese merchants. But after interviewing a number of discharged servicemen, I decided that they were likely to be unreliable. They were mostly soldier of fortune types who hoped to make a quick killing as mercenaries, and I saw no place for them in civilian life in post-war Singapore. I wanted solid, law-abiding men, not a bunch of cowboys. Consequently we didn't supply many bodyguards, and I did most such work myself.

I also carried out some general investigation work, and was retained by a large mining company to try and track down a group which was stealing refined tin ingots and smuggling them to Hong Kong. Post war there was a world-wide shortage of tin, and metal from Malaya, the world's largest producer, had been unobtainable during the Japanese occupation. Now there was a big pent up demand for it and on the Hong Kong black market, one ingot sold for $750, Malayan currency.

A large tin smelting plant was situated on a small island off the coast of Singapore, and refined ingots were being stolen from its stockpile, before being whisked away by motorised sampans. It was suspected that the thieves had inside assistance, or that the smelter's guards were being bribed to look the other way.

I spent several nights prowling around on the island, after being dropped off by sampan. During these visits I carried a revolver, for which I had no permit. It was my army Smith and Wesson, which I had 'forgotten' to hand in when I took my discharge. The job was moderately dangerous because in the island's centre there was a huge smelter—a vat of molten tin which was kept at white heat, its surface bubbling like lava in a volcano. Anyone thrown into that would have vanished without trace.

There were about a hundred workers, mostly Chinese, who

306

lived in a hutted encampment on the island. There were also a dozen or so Sikhs who were the guards, or nightwatchmen. They were unarmed but carried long sticks called *lathis*. On my third night on the island I discovered how the tin ingots were being stolen. About ten o'clock I saw a squad of Malay police led by a white officer arrive on the island, at which time the turbanned Sikhs were withdrawn from their desultory patrol duties and the police took over. But I saw no police at my end of the island. They stayed away from the ingot stockpile.

Around midnight, a large motorised sampan pulled in to the jetty and a number of Chinese jumped ashore. They brought several rubber-tyred wheelbarrows with them which they pushed to the stockpile of ingots and loaded up with metal before returning to their sampan where they stowed the cargo on board. There was nothing furtive about their behaviour. They talked and laughed, slung a lamp above the sampan and generally behaved as if they were legally loading the vessel. They showed no fear of being discovered. Obviously the police had been paid off.

I could have come out of my place of concealment and attempted to arrest them, but that would have been foolhardy, and I had no power of arrest anyway. I wasn't a soldier on duty any more, merely a civilian illegally carrying a pistol, and I didn't know what weapons the raiders carried on their sampan. At the time there was a large trade in stolen military firearms, many of which were smuggled to Java where the Indonesians were fighting their Dutch colonial masters. Other weapons went to French Indo-China where the Vietnamese Communists were preparing to oust the French, and some went to our old adversaries in Malaya. South East Asia was in turmoil as the indigenous peoples prepared to throw off the colonial yoke.

Lying in a dirty set of jungle greens, watching tin ingots being stolen, I knew this was not the time for heroics. Instead, I watched the loaded sampan chug away into the night then made myself as comfortable as possible among the hungry mosquitoes until the police contingent left the island.

The next day I discreetly asked a British police officer who I knew quite well, and who I trusted, about what I had seen on the island. But my trust was misplaced. Within twenty four hours my very agitated Chinese partner told me he'd received a tip that the police were out to close our agency down. Their target was me, and they reckoned they could take me in for illegally carrying a firearm. In Singapore at that time, this was a serious offence, punishable by the death penalty, and I promptly dumped my revolver and ammunition in the harbour.

Later, a friendly Scottish police officer told me that I would be wise to leave Singapore very soon. He indicated that the man I'd confided in was corrupt, saying 'You know what it's like. If we set out to get somebody then we'll get them eventually—on some kind of charge. Some officers wouldn't be above planting a gun among your gear.'

He strongly advised me to leave Singapore before the weekend. I could have got aboard a ship for the UK. My demobilisation leave still had a few weeks before it expired, and until then I was technically still in the army, so was entitled to a free passage home.

But I had no desire to go back to Britain. My long term plan was to get across the Pacific to Canada, stay for a while and maybe even settle there. However, the only ship sailing that weekend was the SS *Gorgon*, bound for Fremantle, Western Australia. So I re-donned my captain's uniform, visited an officer friend at army headquarters, and he supplied me with a free first class warrant to Fremantle. I left Singapore carrying all I possessed in one suitcase.

I boarded the ship in the middle of the night, keeping a weather eye out for a squad of police led by a certain officer, and was relieved when the *Gorgon* finally sailed. A few years' rigorous imprisonment on a trumped-up charge was not a pleasant prospect. Years later I read with interest that the crooked cop's corruption had been exposed and he spent a long time in prison.

In Australia, I only knew two people. One was a private soldier from Melbourne, Tom Lockwood, who I'd met in London while he was there with the Australian contingent at the Victory Parade. I was on leave in Britain at the time as a second lieutenant, and we went around boozing together for a few days. Tom took a shine to me because his regiment in Australia had Scottish affiliations. He kept pressing me to come to Australia and settle after I'd completed my military service, but I said I wouldn't know anyone there except him.

'No worries,' he said. 'I know a nice girl. I'll get her to write to you. Then you'll know two people in Melbourne.'

The girl did write to me and we corresponded all the time I was overseas. When I reached Melbourne I finally met her, and soon afterwards, we got married. But first, after reaching Fremantle, I decided to walk across Australia from the west coast to the east, a distance of 2,240 miles. That delayed me from reaching Melbourne for nearly six months!

WALKING ACROSS AUSTRALIA

Walking across Australia is a feat which could classify one with eccentrics—the types who row across the Pacific or drift over the Atlantic by balloon for the sheer challenge of it. But I had sound reasons for undertaking my trip. I wanted to see the outback, and learn as much as I could about Australia.

It wasn't a foolhardy venture. I had a Shell road map so knew how far I had to travel. I was aware that about eight hundred miles of the route lay across the barren and sparsely inhabited Nullarbor Plain, called the Great Australian Desert. And I knew that wartime petrol rationing was still in force in Australia, so there was little traffic on the west-east Eyre Highway—a gravelled sand track made during the war by Italian POWs.

Anyway, I had just completed three and a half years as an infantryman, and was used to long marches carrying heavy equipment in tropical conditions. I was young and fighting fit, and just as important, I was resourceful and confident that I could cope with any challenge. Having survived an impoverished Glasgow upbringing, I was sure I would survive the Great Australian Desert. My Glasgow had been dirty and full of people, so I relished the prospect of the vast empty desert.

However, some things hadn't changed since my childhood, and when I began the trek I had very little money. After buying a .22 rifle, camping gear and some supplies, I had about fifteen pounds left, ten of which would have paid my fare for the four day train trip across the continent. I planned to write articles during my trip, stopping to work for a while when I needed money.

I looked forward to the journey. For the first time in my life I would be responsible for no-one but myself. In Glasgow and Ayr I'd had to worry about my younger siblings, and in the army I'd been in charge of up to a thousand men at a time. I revelled in the prospect of experiencing the first truly carefree days of my life. I'd turned twenty one when I reached Australia in December 1947, and this trip seemed a fitting beginning to my adulthood.

Although I'd already been in the army for three and a half years, I wasn't legally an adult until my 21st birthday. Until I turned twenty one, I couldn't do such things as sign a hire purchase contract without an adult guarantor, nor could I have bought a rifle before then; ironic, as I had been firing all kinds of weapons since my childhood.

While I was at Perth's suburban Karakatta Police Station getting a firearms licence, the police sergeant asked why I wanted the rifle. I told him I needed it to shoot game while I walked across Australia. In the magistrate's court next day, the sergeant told a Perth *Daily News* reporter about the mad Scotsman who was going to walk to Melbourne. The reporter later sought me out, and during an interview he asked why I intended to walk over two thousand miles in the middle of the blistering Australian summer?

Flippantly, I said that the train fare was 'too dear'. The reporter was English so I knew he would appreciate this admission by a 'thrifty Scot', and indeed my statement was manna to newspaper sub-editors all over the world. Headlines read, SCOT TOO MEAN TO PAY TRAIN FARE. WILL WALK ACROSS AUSTRALIA INSTEAD!

I became a celebrity overnight, and was dubbed 'The Walking Scot', a notoriety I was unprepared for. Instead of a leisurely amble across the country, I was met at most towns by reporters and radio station correspondents. I even appeared in a newsreel, there being no TV in those days. Details of my progress were broadcast regularly on national radio and I sometimes felt like speeding up to keep faith with my 'public'. But I set my own pace of thirty miles a day.

The 2,240 mile trek took about five months. This included time out to work down a gold mine, on a cattle station in the Nullarbor, with a gang of railway fettlers on the Eyre Peninsula and even row a dinghy down the Murray River for a change of pace.

During the trek I carried everything I needed on my back. I shot, bought, scrounged and cooked my own food, carried no tent and slept on the ground. In the more arid areas, water was a major problem. With a heavy rucksack, two quart water bottles were as much as I could carry.

By the time I reached Norseman on the edge of the Nullarbor Plain, I knew I would need more water than I could carry. The journey from there to Eucla was about four hundred miles and there were only four cattle stations in that distance, unfortunately not very evenly spaced. Between the stations, there was no habitation of any kind.

I left Perth in December and it was February when I tackled the Nullarbor, the hottest month of summer. I estimated I'd need a gallon of water a day. The longest stretch between stations was a hundred and seventy five miles, so that meant I should carry eight gallons for safety. Relying on passing cars for water was risky as days could elapse between vehicles making the crossing. There were some wells and rock catchments marked on my Shell road map, but there had been a severe drought for three years prior to 1947 and I learned that many of the wells were dry. Anyway, I reckoned that a four gallon drum of water plus a water bottle and a two gallon waterbag would see me through, and I'd be unlucky not to meet at least one vehicle making the crossing.

To carry the water drum, plus some extra food and other essentials, I acquired a small cart—just a wooden packing case on two bicycle wheels, with a handle for pulling or pushing, depending on how sandy the terrain was. It was similar to the 'barrow' which I'd used to collect horse manure for our garden in Ayr.

Thus equipped, I strode off from Norseman to the cheers of the miners I'd worked with for a fortnight. It was early February and by ten am it was one hundred and four degrees in the shade—a typical Nullarbor summer's day, but not as hot as it could, and did, become. Before I left, the Norseman police sergeant told me, 'If you get in real trouble, cut the phone line and we'll come out and get you.'

The trans-continental phone line across the Nullarbor was a couple of strands of wire which more or less followed the route of the track. The wire was sometimes strung from poles, but was often hooked onto an occasional tree. If the link was cut—deliberately by a desperate traveller, or by accident—a PMG gang came out to repair it. That was the desert emergency service in those days.

I carried basic hard rations—tea, sugar, condensed milk, processed cheese, boiled sweets, biscuits and flour to make damper (flat bread). I shot everything else—mainly rabbits and small wallabies (for their tails only) and an occasional scrub turkey. In settled areas, I bought food.

Usually I walked thirty miles per day. I walked for fifty minutes then rested for ten, rolling a smoke and having a drink. My pace was the infantry soldier's traditional three miles in the hour. With an hour for lunch, ten hours marching notched up about thirty miles daily, and left an hour or so of daylight to prepare dinner and write up my notes.

The longest distance I covered in one day was forty three miles. The temperature had been over one hundred and ten degrees for days and after twenty four hours without water I arrived at a well to find it dry. I'd done twenty miles to get to the well, but it was essential to press on during the cool of the night for another twenty three miles to reach a rock catchment where there was supposed to be water. But the catchment was dry. Instead of containing water, it was covered to the top with hundreds of dead rabbits. By moving layers of rabbit corpses away, I reached a sludge of greenish liquid at the bottom. I filled a billy with this then boiled it for a while, adding two water purification tablets. Then I strained the boiled mixture through my muslin fly veil and ended with a pint or so of green liquid, free of rabbit remains. I couldn't face drinking this so added a handful of tea and boiled it up again. With condensed milk and sugar it was bearable, and kept me going until I reached a station.

The reason I got into such a predicament was simple. At the gold mine where I'd worked I'd had a four gallon petrol drum steam-cleaned so I could use it to carry my main water supply. Unfortunately, the cleaning hadn't been properly done. Traces of petrol contaminated the water, although I didn't find this out until I began drinking it after being on the track for two days and having used the other water from my waterbag and water bottle.

The petrol-tainted water made me sick, causing fever and delirium, hence the urgency of reaching a well quickly. After I drank some of it I must have gone round in circles. During that day I only progressed two miles along the track. In my darker moments I reflected on the fate of my Uncle Bertie who had gone to Australia after World War 1. He died of black-water fever somewhere in Western Australia, and I hoped history wouldn't repeat itself.

Later, at a cattle station, I got a clean water drum which I carried until my barrow broke down in the middle of the Nullarbor and I had to abandon it. This posed problems. I could carry about a gallon of water without bursting myself, but this

314

wasn't enough to survive on. Instead, I learned how to get water from the roots of a certain tree and by digging deep into the bottom of dried up watercourses then waiting for water to seep into the hole.

Apart from running out of water, my most hazardous experience involved almost being shot. This happened on the Nullarbor when I heard an engine noise then finally saw a vehicle approaching me. I kept walking towards it, when it suddenly stopped about four hundred yards away. Next came the crack of a rifle shot over my head. I took cover and fired off a shot in return.

The vehicle started up and as it approached there was a man standing on the running board (which cars had in those days) while his mate drove. The standing man carried a .303 rifle. As I rose to meet him he jumped off then cried, 'Jesus, mate! I thought you were a flamin' roo!'

In the shimmering heat haze, his error was understandable. Many of the big kangaroos I saw were as tall as a man. Over some warm but welcome beer the motorists carried, I asked the man how he felt when I returned his fire. 'I got the shock of me life!' he said. 'First time a flamin' roo ever shot back at me!' Kangaroos are normally not dangerous or savage animals, although it is unwise to get too close to a female when she is carrying a joey in her pouch.

In the desert, snakes were plentiful but not aggressive. They usually slid away as I approached, although they would sometimes curl up outside my sleeping bag during a cold night. Dingos were an unknown quantity. Often one or two would follow me all day, keeping parallel with me, but just out of range of my single shot Mossberg .22 rifle. At nights I usually kept a big fire burning and in the mornings I often found dingo droppings quite close to my camp, although none ever bothered me.

The most dangerous wildlife I encountered were creatures

called sergeant ants. They were only an inch long but were very aggressive, and forced me to hurriedly abandon several camps. Old bushmen told me these ants had been known to kill a man by getting inside his sleeping bag and stinging him to death. I was bitten once and a very painful swelling took days to go down. They are one of the few Australian bush creatures that attack without provocation.

Flies were a constant nuisance and to keep them off I had a muslin veil attached to my slouch hat which I tucked into my collar. Without this I think they could have driven me crazy.

However, my worst experience wasn't heat or thirst—but rain. I'd been months on the track and it hadn't rained once. In fact, I hadn't seen rain since arriving in Australia, and I'd abandoned all normal protection against it—even throwing away my waterproof groundsheet to lighten the load after my barrow broke down. But after years of drought, torrential rains suddenly brought floods to South and Western Australia, stopping trans-continental road movement for weeks. It rained behind me and it rained hundreds of miles ahead of me, but it didn't rain on the arid Nullarbor. At least, not for some weeks. But the rain was the reason I walked for ten days and never saw a human being.

When rain finally fell on the Nullarbor I awoke in my sleeping bag to find I was lying in a pool of very cold water in a scooped out depression in the ground. Everything I had was soaked, and my fire had gone out. I spent a miserable night stomping around to keep warm.

At dawn it was still raining but it was essential to get a fire going to dry my clothes and sleeping bag. My matches were a sodden pulp and my lighter had stopped working days ago. There was no sun, so no chance of starting a flame by using a magnifying glass, not that I had one anyway. Rubbing two wet sticks together would have been pointless.

I had a dry handkerchief and I scooped shavings of dry bark

from the underside of a tree into this. I added some sheets of rice paper from my notebook then the cotton wool from my lighter. I made a ball of these combustibles inside the hankie then fired my rifle through it, pressing the muzzle against the cloth so that the blast burned it.

After many tries I got a little smouldering ring around one of the bullet holes and by breathing gently I coaxed a tiny flame from the cotton wool until the ball began burning. I transferred this to a prepared pile of wood shavings and dry bark and eventually got a fire going. This took several hours—but I wasn't in a hurry.

Having crossed the Nullarbor Plain, I reached more settled areas where water ceased to be a problem. In the parts of South Australia where coach tours travelled I became a tourist attraction, and the Pioneer buses would stop so that the passengers could get out and photograph me.

Near Mount Gambier I met Laurence Olivier and Vivien Leigh who were then touring Australia. They insisted on having their photo taken with me, but sadly never sent me a copy. Perhaps the address I gave them—Walking Scotsman, c/o East-West Highway, Australia—was insufficient, although I received a lot of mail addressed that way, including several marriage proposals.

After four and a half months on the track, I got a great welcome when I arrived in Adelaide, with a pipe band and other manifestations of Scottish pride waiting for me. It was very strange to be a celebrity and have people ask for my autograph.

I was never lonely during my trek. As I walked, I observed and framed notes for articles and stories, which I jotted down at each hourly stop. Walking promotes thought, and it's also a great way to really see wildlife and be at one with nature. Animals aren't scared off by a walking human as they are by vehicles. In fact, they often didn't even run away when I approached, regarding me with curiosity, but as a natural part of the bush, which is something that I'll always remember.

In spite of occasional discomfort, I felt the trek was worthwhile. I saw parts of Australia many Australians hadn't seen and quickly gained a feel for the country. Today, when I visualise Australia I don't think only of the urban areas I have mostly lived in, but of the outback as well, and the people there I lived and worked with. I gained an understanding of bush life, and an appreciation of 'bushies' that has never left me.

During the trek I wrote something every day—in longhand. When I reached a town I borrowed a typewriter and typed up my stories, then sent them to publications in the East and back to Perth. I did quite well, with articles on the outback way of life and its characters. When I reached Melbourne I had little trouble getting a staff job and joined the Melbourne *Argus*.

My transition from boy to adulthood found me in a new country a long way from Scotland. But my trip had been avidly followed by my parents and siblings back in Ayr. My trek was covered widely in the British press so my mother more or less managed to keep abreast of what I was doing. I did write to her while I was on the track, but they were the kind of letters soldiers send home, the kind which avoid mention of hardship or hazard.

I think my mother had hopes that once I reached Melbourne I might start heading back to Britain. I'd told her that my long term plan was to try to work my passage on a ship from Australia to Canada, then spend some time there before returning to the UK. Instead, I met the Australian girl in Melbourne who had been a pen friend for a couple of years. When we decided to get married I wrote and told my mother the news.

My mother probably realised that her oldest son would settle in Australia, and she took the news quite well. At the end of her letter she had only one query: 'Don't think it matters to us. We're just curious. The girl you're going to marry—is she white?'